MISSING

Also by Mary Stanley

Retreat

MISSING

Mary Stanley

review

First published in 2002
by REVIEW
An imprint of Headline Book Publishing

10 9 8 7 6 5 4 3 2

Cataloguing in Publication Data is available from the British Library

ISBN 0 7472 6936 X (hardback)
ISBN 0 7553 0308 3 (trade paperback)

Typeset in Minion by Palimpsest Book Production Limited,
Polmont, Stirlingshire
Printed and bound in Great Britain by
Clays Ltd, St Ives plc

HEADLINE BOOK PUBLISHING
A division of Hodder Headline
338 Euston Road
London NW1 3BH

www.headline.co.uk
www.hodderheadline.com

for Lucy
who has held my hand through life

Prologue

The room filled with chatter and laughter. Fur coats hung in the hall. The girls circulated with trays of food. The buzz in the room increased.

'Like some more champagne, Mr Robinson?' said Baby to the Australian attaché.

'Yes, yes,' he said, eyeing the ravishing eldest Dunville daughter, who topped up his glass.

'Here's to you, Mr Robinson,' she said to him, raising the bottle slightly.

'And to you,' he replied.

'Recovered from the bash in your car?' asked Baby, looking him straight in the eye.

'What's that?' he asked, straining to hear in the crowded room.

'Oh, there's Mrs Robinson,' Baby said, looking over towards the door, where her mother was chatting to Magda Robinson.

'While the cat's away,' he chuckled to Baby.

'The mouse can pay,' Baby replied.

'Play,' said Mr Robinson.

'No, I said "pay",' Baby repeated. 'You forgot to pay my sister Becky for babysitting.'

'Did I?' He seemed surprised. 'Crikey . . . er . . . will you give it to her?'

He reached into his pocket and pulled out a wad of notes. Peeling off a one-pound note, he handed it to Baby.

'That doesn't cover a kiss,' Baby said, looking at the note.

'Oh, do I get a kiss?' Mr Robinson smiled at her, looking at her very pink lips.

'I meant the kiss you gave Becky,' Baby said. Her mouth seemed to smile at him, but her eyes did not.

'Oh,' he said. 'Er . . . that . . .'

'Or does Mrs Robinson think that that's part of the job?' Baby asked. 'I must ask her.'

Mr Robinson surreptitiously peeled off two five-pound notes and handed them to Baby.

'I'm sure that will cover everything,' he said hurriedly, and turned away.

'Yes,' said Baby, looking at the money in her hand. 'I think it will.'

Chapter One

The doors of the assembly hall opened, and the sixth-form girls of St Martin's led the way out into the corridor. Baby Dunville, with her limpid blue eyes and her long blonde curly hair tied back, was the first through. Her dark green school tunic over her white blouse and green tie could not hide the curve of her hips and the swell of her breasts, and her walk accentuated her suppleness.

'Merry Christmas, Reverend Mother,' she said, lowering her eyelashes as she passed the head nun. There might have been the slightest tinge of irony in her voice.

'In single file, girls,' responded Mother Immaculata in the sternest of voices. Dressed in long black flowing robes, with high white regalia on her head, she was standing just inside the door and watching the departing girls. The other nuns, similarly attired, watched from the stage.

As soon as she was through the doorway, Baby Dunville pulled off the rubber band which tied back her hair and let it fall on her shoulders. She ran a hand through her curls to loosen their flow. The single file broke up straight outside the door and her closest friend, Anne Marie O'Mahony, pushed past their classmates to join her. They glanced at each other and raised their eyes to heaven.

'Praise be to the Christmas season, booze and fags,' murmured Anne Marie.

'And to the male anatomy,' replied Baby in a quiet intonation, barely moving her lips.

'Six more months, and we will be liberated,' Anne Marie said.

'Thus spake the Lord,' said Baby, the scathing irony now clear in her voice.

Both girls stood slightly taller than their peers as they headed for the cloakroom to get their coats. It was the end of their last day of term and the start of the Christmas holidays.

In the tiny mirror, which Baby had stuck on the inside of her

3

locker door, she checked her face, running one finger over her perfect cheekbones, and around the curve of her jaw. Looking good, she thought. She undid her tie and, rolling it up, put it in her pocket. Baby Dunville's skin was peaches and cream, smooth and clear, and with her blue eyes, blonde curls and cupid's bow mouth, she mostly chose to look angelic.

'Want a lift?' Anne Marie asked her. Her legs were as long as Baby Dunville's, but overall she lacked the curvaceousness of her friend's body.

'Adam coming to get you?'

'Yes. I asked him this morning.' Adam was the O'Mahonys' chauffeur.

'Great. It'll save the trek to the bus stop,' Baby said. 'Why walk and sweat with the plebs when we can sit in comfort?' which summed up her general approach to life.

They sat on a bench in the cloakroom, killing time until the doorway cleared so they would not have to push through the main mass of girls from all the different classes. Baby Dunville crossed her long legs and sat very still, with a slight smirk on her face, surveying the bedlam going on around them.

'You better not let Mack see you with your hair loose and your tie off,' Anne Marie said. The Reverend Mother was traditionally known by a different name to each of the classes in the school. To the sixth form, she was Mack or Mack the Knife.

'Last day of term ... what can she do?' Baby replied. At almost eighteen years of age, she had very little interest in the school rules. Both Reverend Mother and her sidekick, Sister Rodriguez, would have said she never had sufficient interest in them other than as a means of avoiding trouble.

Anne Marie shrugged.

As soon as the first lot of girls pushed through the door, the two of them got up and followed.

In the hallway, they passed Mother Immaculata, who had just pulled Baby's youngest sister Brona aside.

'Brona Dunville,' they heard her voice as they skirted behind her back, 'is that chewing gum you are consuming?'

Brona Dunville, aged fourteen, with one sock down and one up, the top button of her blouse missing, and her tie at half-mast, looking like a smaller, younger and more unfilled version of Baby, shuffled from one foot to the other, trying unsuccessfully to swallow the offending

4

gum. Her long curly hair was darker than Baby's, and although her eyes were just as blue, her face was slightly easier to read. It smacked of naughtiness rather than superiority.

Mother Immaculata produced a piece of paper from her pocket and held it in front of Brona's mouth. Reluctantly Brona pushed the offending piece of gum with her tongue into the piece of paper.

'Stand against the wall and wait until every last girl has left the school,' said Mother Immaculata as she wrapped the gum in the paper. 'And contemplate on the disgusting nature of your crime.'

'Yes, Reverend Mother,' Brona said, scowling.

Baby Dunville glanced at her, pretending not to recognise her sister as she tossed her blonde hair around her shoulders and headed out the door and down the steps.

'Any idea who that child was?' she asked Anne Marie, who laughed by way of response.

Descending the steps which led from the main building of the four interconnecting Georgian houses which made up St Martin's, Dublin's finest girls' school, both sauntered down the road as dozens of girls swarmed past.

Meanwhile, Becky, the middle Dunville sister, smaller, tidier and with tiny bones compared to her siblings, was heading, alone as usual, for the back gardens behind the school. At fifteen she looked like a different species to both Baby and Brona. Her dark, neatly brushed straight hair was cut into a bob just above shoulder length. It curved inwards around her oval face. Her skin was sallow, her tie still neatly knotted and in place. Her socks were pulled up and her coat buttoned and belted. She slipped out into the gardens and endeavoured to give the impression of someone looking for something. The four gardens behind the school buildings were connected by arched gateways. She walked down the path to the archway which separated the first garden from the second.

'Oh, hello,' she said, as if surprised to see Simon Carter, the junior gardener, who was crouched in front of the statue of St Martin.

'Hello,' he said. He was wearing a navy woollen sweater over scruffy grey corduroy trousers. 'Are you looking for something?'

'I've mislaid my gloves,' said Becky Dunville carefully. She was afraid that she sounded prim, but she found it difficult to express herself differently. 'I wonder, did you see them? I think I may have left them out here at break.'

She knew exactly where she had left them, but she searched around vaguely.

'I'll help you look,' Simon Carter said. He had a freckled open face and red hair.

'Are you sure?' Becky asked politely.

'It'll give me a break from this.' He gestured towards the statue, whose pedestal he had been scrubbing to clear it of the moss which had built up on it in the damp weather.

Becky was surprised at how easily he spoke to her. Normally he said nothing, but then again, he was usually being overseen by the head gardener, and talking to the girls was not on his list of duties.

'I was in the furthest garden, I think,' Becky said, trying to sound worried. 'I do hope my gloves are there because they don't look like they're here.' They walked through the archways until they came to the last one, and there on the garden seat lay her black gloves.

'Oh, thank you so much,' Becky said, as if Simon Carter had personally retrieved them. She looked shyly up at him from under her dark lashes, and couldn't think of anything else to say.

'I better go,' she said as she slipped her freezing hands into the equally freezing wool.

'Do you want me to let you out through the back gate?' he asked her. 'It would save you having to go all the way back through the school, miss.'

She didn't really like the way he said 'miss'; he made it sound like he wasn't relating to her as an equal, and that was not what she wanted. She also was not too keen on the way he didn't pronounce the 'th' in words – he made *through* sound like *true*, and *the* was *de*. But Becky was in a pragmatic frame of mind, and reassured herself that when he found out her name and whispered it lovingly to her, at least there would be no 'th' in it for him to mispronounce. With that thought in mind, she tried frantically to think of something interesting to say to him to prolong the brief interaction between them, but words failed her.

'Thank you,' she said again, as he unlocked the wooden gate and she went out on to the lane, which was out of bounds. It was very unlike her to do something contrary to school rules, but she had felt it would be churlish to refuse his offer.

'Have a happy Christmas, miss,' he said, smiling at her.

And then he closed the door and she was alone in the laneway. She felt reasonably pleased, reassuring herself that the next time she saw him she would have more to say, and that he might feel less inclined to address her as 'miss'. Checking her watch to see if she would make the bus before it left, she realised she just had enough time if she hurried, and so she hastened down the lane and out on to the street and off in the direction of the bus stop.

Baby Dunville, first to arrive home, courtesy of Adam, the O'Mahonys' chauffeur, let herself into their large house on Lansdowne Road. She replaced the key under the terracotta pot in the porch, and stood in the hall, listening to confirm that she was alone. The hall was a large square room, with the first flight of stairs curving up one side, and doors leading off in various directions, all of which were closed. An unusual antique clock stood on a table, covered by a glass dome. The mahogany hall-stand boasted a mirror, two umbrellas and nothing else. They kept their coats in the small room under the staircase, and the hall-stand was kept free for visitors. Against one wall a telephone sat on a small low table, beside which was a straight-backed chair. Baby stood beside the brass table on the thick red carpet in the centre of the hall. Above her head the glass chandelier with its two hundred pieces of hanging crystal, which had recently been taken down and washed for Christmas, glistened and shimmered as the light glowed and refracted. An olde-worlde gentility presided, with black-and-white photographs of the girls adorning the staircase, with its gleaming polished banisters. After a moment's silence, during which she listened intently, Baby called, 'Hello, anyone there?' The house was still.

She picked up the post from the floor inside the hall door, sorted through it quickly, and then went to the kitchen, where she steamed open the envelope which contained the Dunville girls' reports. She perused the pages before replacing them in the envelope and putting it back in the hall where she had found it. After which she ascended the first flight of stairs and glanced cursorily around the landing before heading up to her bedroom on the top floor of the house. There, with her customary care, she started to undress. She took off her school uniform and hung her tunic in her wardrobe on a wooden hanger. Her tie, which she removed from her coat pocket, was neatly re-rolled and placed on a shelf. Blouse, knickers and tights went into her laundry basket, and she dressed in jeans and a white sweater. Stretching out on her bed she contemplated the holidays. After a few minutes she got up again and went to her desk. From the top drawer she took out a block of writing paper, and from her school bag she extracted a pen.

Dear H, she wrote.

Was I ever glad that the holidays are here, except of course that I'll miss you. Last night was great. The plants are doing fine. By the time you get this you'll be back from England.

She sucked the top of the pen. She couldn't think of anything else to say. Putting the block back into the drawer, she covered it with a Latin book, and leaned back on two legs of the chair.

Now what? she thought.

Going back to the bed, she lifted her pillow and looked at the various items under it. Picking up an envelope, which she opened, she removed the sheet of paper from it. She smiled as she read it.

Hmmm, she thought. Naughty. Naughty and costly.

She went downstairs and pulled out the ironing board in the breakfast room, and plugged in the iron. In the kitchen she got a clean tea towel and wet it thoroughly under the tap. Squeezing it out, she wondered where everyone else was. Back in the breakfast room, she laid the right side of her long curly blonde hair on the ironing board, and covered it carefully with the damp towel. Then she placed the iron on the tea towel, close to her ear, and listened to the scorching sound of the heat hitting the wetness.

When she had finished, and her hair was straight, she cleared away and went to the phone in the hall.

'Anne Marie?' she said when the phone was answered. 'It's me. Are we okay for tonight?'

She listened, both to the voice at the other end, and for any noises in the house.

'No, I haven't said anything yet. There's no one here. Anyway, I thought I'd wait to hear if it was all right your end . . . No, there won't be a problem. There are no surprises in my report. I steamed it open when I got in, and it's fine. I'm sure they will let me over to your place for the evening, but I'll have to wait until they get back.'

In her bedroom, with the door ajar, Becky Dunville listened to her older sister talking on the phone in the hall. Baby must have been in her room when I got in, she thought. The conversation was not completely clear, as the hall below was quite some distance away, with walls and corridors and staircases muffling the sounds to a certain extent. But she nonetheless got the definite feeling that Baby thought she was alone in the house, and that Baby was planning on going out for the evening.

She lay perfectly still, looking at the ceiling, and wondered if their father would bring the tree home that evening. He had said he would, if he could.

She did hope so.

The tree would then stand overnight in the porch, and the following day it would be positioned in the drawing room for the girls to decorate. She quite liked that. She looked forward to the smell of it, and Christmas music playing in the background, and maybe Scrabble in the evening after dinner. She wondered if he'd bring the holly home too at the same time, and mistletoe.

No, she thought. He mightn't be able to get the mistletoe in the same place as he gets the tree.

She smiled as she thought how the tree would look with the white lights on it, plugged in, and the main light in the room turned off.

Magical.

She rolled over on to her stomach and started to pick idly at the candlewick on her bedspread. She thought about Baby. It was difficult to know what if anything Baby might be up to, but Becky always had the feeling that there was something simmering under the surface.

She heard the hall door bursting open and banging off the hall-stand behind it.

Guess who that is, she thought.

Brona Dunville, her hair tied in two untidy bunches, stood in the hall, her clothes dishevelled, the toes of her shoes scuffed, one sock still around her ankle, glowering at Baby, who was still on the phone.

'I missed the bus,' she said.

'My fault?' Baby asked icily, putting her hand over the mouthpiece while she spoke.

'Oh, shut up,' Brona said, dumping her school bag in the hall. Heading for the stairs, she took them two at a time.

'I missed the goddamn bus,' she shouted at Becky's half-open door. 'And I know you saw me running for it. You could have asked him to wait.'

She slammed her own bedroom door behind her and, stripping off her uniform, kicked her shoes, tunic, blouse, tie and socks into the corner behind the door before throwing herself on to her bed on her back. Shifting her weight up her spine, she rolled upwards so that she was on her neck and shoulders, and brought her legs over her head until her feet rested on the wall behind her bedhead. Her bare feet were hot from the walk home, and they marked the wall so that the damp imprint was clearly outlined on it.

'Cow,' she said out loud, referring to her sister, even though she knew she wasn't being fair; as if the bus driver in question would ever have held the bus for a girl running. 'But Becky didn't even bother to ask him, did she?' she said to her knees.

'N,' she said to one knee. 'O,' she said to the other. 'No, no, no.'

A while later the gong in the hall rang for dinner.

Baby, her long blonde hair now ironed out straight, descended slowly and silently from the top floor of the house, preceded by Brona, who was now dressed in green jeans, a red sweater and slippers. Becky was already in the breakfast room, where the table was laid for three. She was still dressed neatly in her school uniform.

'*Christmas is coming, Becky's getting fat, Please put a penny in the Dunvilles' hat* . . .' Brona sang as she came into the room.

'What did you say?' Becky said furiously.

'Nothing. I was *singing*, not saying. And anyway, I wasn't singing about you. I sang *Baby's getting fat*,' Brona replied with a grin.

'What did you say?' Baby snarled, appearing in the door behind Brona and taking her by her hair.

Brona screamed as she was dragged backwards.

'Mummy, Mummy, help!' she yelled.

Their mother, Elizabeth, tall and elegant, with slender bones and a gentle, slightly vague look on her face, appeared in the doorway from the kitchen.

'Now, now, darlings,' she said lightly. 'Come and help me bring dinner in.'

'That smells horrible,' Brona said, rubbing her head as she was quickly released by Baby.

'The dinner?' her mother said, surprised.

'No,' Brona answered. 'Baby's armpits.'

'I'll kill you,' Baby hissed as Elizabeth disappeared back into the kitchen.

Brona scooted out to the kitchen after their mother and assiduously helped bring in the plates.

'Mmmmm, smells divine,' she said, smiling at Baby, who said nothing, just bided her time.

*   *   *

'Mum, Dad, what was my report like?' Baby asked her parents in the drawing room after dinner. The girls had eaten by themselves in the breakfast room; as it was a week night, their parents would eat later in the dining room. The house was run as in a bygone era, with Mrs O'Doody, the housekeeper, doing the cleaning and much of the cooking, and John and Elizabeth Dunville dining alone, except at the weekends, when the girls, suitably attired for the occasion, would join them in the dining room.

John Dunville, dressed in a suit with a white shirt and blue silk tie, smiled at her. 'A clean bill of health,' he said.

'It's such a tough year,' Baby said, working on their sympathy. 'I'm so relieved that it's good. I was bothered about Latin and History,' she said, trying to sound worried, as she knew that they were the two subjects in which she had done best.

'Don't worry, Baby,' her mother said. 'Your father says he's pleased with the report, and he feels you're on the right track.'

Elizabeth Dunville left such matters to her husband, relying on his observations completely. She sipped her drink and brushed a speck of dust off her straight dark skirt. Her slender ankles were crossed, and despite the fact that she was clearly there, sitting across from her husband, she gave an impression of distance and etherealness which was difficult to define. A portrait of her above the fireplace showed a more youthful Elizabeth, with her fair hair pinned up, dressed in an evening gown of some dark silk or taffeta, lace around the slightly cut-away throat, and a soft look on her face as though she were dreaming. She still had that look on her face, but while it was peaceful in the picture, in reality she sometimes looked haunted.

'That's very reassuring,' Baby said, her voice concerned and serious. She was careful to address her remarks to both parents, even though she knew that the last word always came from John. Her father, almost ten years older than her mother, demanded and received complete courtesy towards both himself and Elizabeth from the three girls.

'Is there anything I should be worried about in it? Anything I can learn from for next term?' She sounded both dutiful and sincere.

'A little extra work in mathematics,' her father replied in his plummy English voice.

Baby nodded as if she were noting his words carefully.

'I'll put in an hour a day over the holidays,' she said. 'On maths, I mean. Of course I'll be working systematically on all my subjects.'

11

'All work . . .' Elizabeth said vaguely, looking at her gin and tonic and not completing the proverb.

'I know,' Baby said, as if it had suddenly occurred to her that maybe she should take a little time out. 'Actually, Mum, I'm thinking of going over to Anne Marie's for a bit. She said I could stay the night. That okay?'

'Not for the night,' her father interjected, looking at her over the top of his glasses. 'You can go over for a bit, but be home by ten thirty.'

'Aw, Dad,' Baby said, but then changed her tone quickly. 'I was really hoping to stay the night there, but if I've to come home, please make it a bit later.'

'How much later?' he asked.

'Well, how about twelve thirty?' she asked hopefully.

'Eleven,' he said.

'Aw, twelve?' she tried.

'Eleven thirty – and no arguing.'

They both smiled. It was a regular game – a routine to be gone through – and the final call was always halfway.

'Fifteen minutes' leeway?' she asked hopefully.

'Fifteen minutes' leeway,' he said. 'Shall I come and collect you?'

'Oh no,' said Baby, looking lovingly at him. 'Adam – you know, the O'Mahonys' chauffeur – he'll drop me home.'

'All right, Baby,' he said. 'Now give me a kiss and then skedaddle.'

John and Elizabeth Dunville looked at each other and smiled.

Baby gave them each a kiss before slipping out the door, leaving them sitting comfortably in the armchairs on either side of the coal fire.

As Baby exited from the drawing room, Brona was on the phone in the hall, sitting cross-legged on the floor.

'Hold on, Rhona,' she said to the mouthpiece. 'Big sister is lurking.'

'If that's your pal Rhona,' Baby said, 'ask her if the rumours about her are true.'

'What rumours?' Brona asked.

'That she's about to be expelled,' Baby said, taking the stairs two at a time.

'Tell that effing sister of yours that I'm not about to be expelled. That it's just wishful thinking on her part,' Rhona yelled into Brona's other ear.

'She's not being expelled,' Brona shouted up the stairs after the disappearing Baby.

'Well, she will be yet,' Baby called down the stairwell.

'Tell her I can hear everything she's saying,' Rhona said on the other end of the line. 'And I know she's only trying to annoy me. Actually, don't say that to her. I'm going to make a New Year's resolution to keep out of trouble.'

'You're not!' said Brona with interest.

'Well, no, you're right. I'm not. But The Brush with Death told me to.'

The Brush with Death was Brona and Rhona's private name for Mother Immaculata.

'She told me to make a special Confession, and to follow it up with a resolution to steer clear of trouble. No, I think she said a resolution not to start trouble. And I never start trouble, do I, Bro?' Rhona said.

'Well . . .' Brona hesitated, not wishing to offend. 'It's not so much that you start trouble, as that somehow it seems to sort of lurk around you.'

'Not my fault. But according to The Brush with Death, it's *mea culpa, mea culpa, mea maxima culpa* all the way. Life's a bitch, isn't it, Bro?'

'But holly-wollies now,' replied Brona happily. 'So what'll we do?'

'Cinema tomorrow,' Rhona replied.

'It'll have to be very early afternoon as we're doing the tree, I think. And I can't miss that.' Brona didn't add that she didn't want to miss that. 'I'll ask Mum if you can come over to dinner, 'cos I'll never be back from town in time if we go to the cinema. Can I come over in the morning instead? I have a brilliant idea.'

'Yes,' replied Rhona. 'What is the brilliant idea?'

'Can't tell you over the phone. You know, the walls have ears here.'

'Ears?' asked Rhona in surprise.

'It's just an expression,' Brona explained patiently, because she was used to Rhona's rather literal attitude to her comments.

In her bedroom on the first floor, Becky, at her desk, was making a list of people she still had to get Christmas presents for. She glanced at her watch. She was babysitting at eight.

Better go, she thought. Maybe they'll be extra generous because it's Christmas – maybe fifteen shillings.'

Brushing her hair quickly, so that it sat smooth and shiny, she tucked the front bits behind her ears, put her list away in her desk drawer, and ran lightly down the stairs.

'I'm off, Mum and Dad,' she said, putting her head around the drawing-room door.

'What time will you be back?' both parents asked simultaneously.

13

'It'll be late – it's Mr Robinson's Christmas party. Most likely one or so. But they'll drop me back.'

'How are you getting there?' asked her father.

'I'm walking. It's not far,' she replied reassuringly.

'Be sure to let us know when you're home,' her father said.

'Oh, did our reports arrive?'

'Yes, Becky,' he said.

'Is mine all right?' she asked.

'It's just as it always is,' her mother replied.

'You can see it in the morning,' her father said.

She rather wished that someone had said 'Well done', because she knew she was top of the class again, but they did not say anything. Once she had asked about their lack of congratulations on her achievements, and was told quite firmly that as long as each of them worked according to their abilities, it would be unfair to give extra praise to one just because she had greater academic abilities. That had seemed fair enough, but she still felt a little approval would not have hurt.

She took her school gabardine from the cupboard in the hall, and around her neck she wrapped the striped woolly scarf she'd knitted in first year.

In the porch she touched the Christmas tree which was propped against the wall. Already the smell of damp pine filled the small area.

Down the path she went, thinking how much she liked this time of year. The night was freezing, with a clear sky. Millions of stars twinkled above her. She paused outside the Botanic Gardens on Lansdowne Road and peered in through the railings at the little house among the gnarled trees. Behind the house, in the clear moonlight, she could see the ivy-covered wall surrounding the gardens. The house reminded her of the cottages in fairy stories.

Hansel and Gretel, she thought, as she so often did. Small spangled windows made of sugar, and a witch waiting behind the door.

She let her mind wander as she walked quickly on up the road. She often wondered if that was the same story as 'Babes in the Wood'.

A variation on it, probably, she thought. So many stories with such similar themes. Bad people, witches, careless parents . . . children not being properly cared for, or being abandoned, or getting lost.

She wondered if Baby was being driven up the road to Anne Marie's house. Trying very hard to distract herself from that thought, and some of the emotions which it evoked, she reassured herself that she preferred to walk up to the Robinsons'.

14

The Robinsons were ready to leave when she arrived.

'The kiddies are asleep,' said Mr Robinson with his Australian twang. 'We've left our number. With any luck the little beggars won't waken.'

The little beggars did not waken, and Becky sat in a squishy armchair and read for a while. In due course she turned on the television – a rare treat, as the Dunville household had not yet acquired one. Becky, who had no close friends, enjoyed the companionship which the television offered her, and wondered if her father would ever get one. He had strong views on entertainment and distraction, she thought, just as he had strong views on everything. Maybe he was right, she continued the thought, but then abandoned the process as she settled down to watch.

Baby was driven by her father to Anne Marie's house. Leaning over in the car, she lightly kissed his cheek before getting out.

'See you later, Daddy,' she said.

'You too, Baby,' he replied.

'You go on, Daddy, now,' said Baby, her limpid blue eyes smiling at him. 'Just see I get up the steps all right, and then feel free to go. You know how long the O'Mahonys take to answer the door. And your dinner will be on the table for you when you get back. Don't keep Mum waiting.'

He laughed, and said, 'You're right. Off you go.'

At the top of the steps, she turned and waved to him and put her finger on the bell, which she did not press.

He waved, and drove off. Baby waited until the sound of the car was gone, and then she hastened back down the steps and around the side of them and down to the basement, where she opened the window which Anne Marie had left slightly ajar. Into the basement she climbed, sure-footed in the dark, and sat on a chair.

A few minutes later, Anne Marie put her head around the door.

'You there?' she called into the darkness.

'I'm here,' said Baby. 'You ready?'

'All set. I just have to say goodbye to the parents. Here, I've brought you down some of your clothes from my room.'

Anne Marie passed several items to Baby.

'What time do we have until?'

'I've to be home by eleven forty-five,' Baby replied.

'Let yourself out again, and I'll meet you at the corner,' Anne Marie said. 'I just have to tell them that I'm off to your house. Then everyone is happy.'

Becky, abandoning the squishy armchair, curled up on the sofa and watched the news. She always found it interesting how different it seemed to listening to the news on the radio. There were pictures of Lieutenant Calley, arrested for the massacre of five hundred and sixty-seven people in My Lai two years earlier. 'He was only following orders' was the defence.

Is that sufficient? she wondered. If Mother Immaculata orders me to massacre a couple of the littler children, and I am supposed to be obedient to her, do I do it? Perhaps the analogy is bad. If Mother Immaculata orders Sister Rodriguez, who has taken a vow of obedience, to do something she intrinsically knows is wrong, and Rodriguez does it, who is responsible? But then Rodriguez isn't trained to kill . . .

She gazed at the fire, watching the flames leaping up the chimney.

I must never get myself into a position where I am not responsible for my own actions. *Neither a soldier nor a nun will I be, Becky Dunville is me.*

She hummed this thought, then, getting up, she went up the stairs to check on the Robinson children, who were sound asleep.

From the doorway of their room, she could hear their even breathing, and the light from the landing shone through on to their beds, where their chubby faces with closed eyes were just apparent to her.

Back in the Dunville home, John and Elizabeth were finishing their main course when Brona came and joined them.

'Mind if I play some music?' she asked.

'Mind if we talk about your report?' her father responded.

'Was it good?' she asked with feigned excitement. 'Oh, please, please tell me it was good. I tried so hard.'

'Some of it was good.' He nodded. 'It's in the drawing room on the little table. Bring it in to me.'

'It could wait until we're finished,' Elizabeth said gently to him.

'Let's get it over with,' he said, taking it from Brona when she came back into the room.

'There are several comments about being easily distracted, and not having the same concentration as your sister.'

'It's not fair that I should always be compared with Baby and Becky,'

Brona frowned. 'People are always saying, "You're not as clever as Becky," or "You're not as pretty as Baby." It's not fair,' she pouted.

'Of course that isn't fair,' her father replied. 'I think the point is that you should concentrate more.'

'But if I don't have the same concentration as Becky, that's not my fault,' Brona whined.

'Look,' he said, handing her the report. 'Read it, and then we'll discuss it.'

'I'm just a loser, as Baby says,' Brona whinged. 'The third is never wanted. That's what Baby says.'

'Nonsense,' Elizabeth replied too quickly. 'It's the middle one who's never wanted. I mean,' she corrected herself quickly, 'it's the middle one who feels they're never wanted. Now, don't go listening to Baby. Your father and I don't compare you with the others. You're all individuals, and that's the way we like it.'

'But the nuns want us to be the same. Just like they are. The same as each other, I mean,' Brona complained.

'Don't complain about the good sisters,' John said. Don't get me started, he thought to himself, but did not utter the words aloud.

'The nuns are wonderful,' Elizabeth said. 'In my day, I know, in no other institution would I have received such care and such education. And it's still like that.'

'I'd like to go to a mixed school,' Brona said. 'With boys, and sport and—'

'Back to that report,' her father interjected. 'Read it, and then we'll talk about it.'

Brona sighed.

Baby and Anne Marie took the bus to town. There were a few whistles from the back of the bus as they reached the top of the stairs and headed for a seat. Both girls ignored the whistling and sat coolly gazing ahead.

'Has Hugo gone home for the holidays?' Anne Marie asked, referring to Baby's boyfriend.

'Yes,' Baby replied. 'They took the ferry this morning. He was mouthing about having to spend two weeks with his parents, but that was just for my benefit. It'll be a round of parties.'

'Wish we lived in London,' Anne Marie said. 'It's so dull here at Christmas.'

Baby grunted in agreement and looked out the window.

'Wonder what the nuns are up to.' Anne Marie tried again to get Baby's attention.

'Praying for your soul, no doubt,' Baby replied. 'What was your report like?'

'Don't know. I didn't see it. Maybe it didn't arrive in the post today.'

'Ours did, as I told you. One envelope for the three of us. The nuns saving money on the postage, no doubt, even though we don't get the fees three for the price of one. Becky's report would make you sick, it was so perfect.'

'And Brona's?'

'I didn't bother to look. But I suspect she's going to be in trouble. Mummy said Daddy was going to "have a word with that young madam" when he got home.'

Anne Marie laughed.

'Whose report would you say was the worst?'

'In the whole school? Probably Rhona Brophy.' Baby smiled. 'She should be locked up, and the key thrown away.'

'I think she's quite funny,' Anne Marie said.

'Well, you wouldn't if she were your sister's best friend and was always on the phone or dropping in.'

Becky got up and changed channels. There didn't appear to be much on. She settled for what looked like a film, and went back to the sofa, where, kicking off her shoes, she curled up on her side.

A milkman in a milk cart appeared to be driving down a road.

She closed her eyes.

Hours to go before they come home, she thought.

She dozed on and off, and when she next opened her eyes the milkman was standing in a hallway in front of a woman, and holding a bottle of milk in one hand. His other hand was pulling open the laces on a garment the like of which Becky had not seen before. It appeared to be made of soft plastic. She thought it might be a corset, laced down the front, with bulging white breasts popping out of the top of it.

Becky's eyes opened in amazement. The milkman ran the bottom of the milk bottle over the top of the breasts.

'Chilly?' he asked.

'I'm very hot,' the corseted women replied. 'It'll cool me down.'

The milkman leered at her.

Becky got up and turned the television off. She was about to sit

18

down again when she suddenly changed her mind, and turned it back on.

I might learn something, she reassured herself. Broaden my horizons.

Settling back on the sofa, she watched in interest as the milkman slowly unlaced the corset, and then, taking the woman into the kitchen, where the floor appeared covered with lino, he opened the milk bottle and flicked the foil lid towards the sink. The woman looked at him through half-closed eyes. He poured the milk over both of her now partially exposed breasts, his tongue flicking down into her cleavage. The man's back was now blocking a clear view of what was happening, as the camera shifted to a different perspective so that the woman's bared breasts could not be seen, but Becky could imagine him licking and sucking her nipples.

Geeny, she thought. Wow.

It never failed to surprise her what adults got up to.

An ardent reader, she had ploughed her way through thousands of sagas, both modern and historical, and had acquired bits of information which she had tried to piece together to come up with some kind of an explanation of the often-alluded-to 'facts of life'.

She suspected that Brona knew more than she did.

Probably that's down to Rhona, she thought. Brona's best friend certainly gave the impression of knowing things that others didn't.

Pity I can't ask Baby, Becky then thought, vaguely realising that there was probably nothing that Baby didn't know.

The milkman was now sucking away happily.

Becky frowned. It was exciting to watch, but she was puzzled. She knew that babies suckled. She knew that their mothers produced milk. Now she wondered if she had got that right.

Is there any chance that I've misunderstood? she thought. Could it be that some mothers pour milk into baby bottles for their babies to drink, and other mothers want to hold their babies closer, and so they pour the milk on to their nipples? It didn't make sense.

But then, a lot of things didn't make sense. But it was exciting. She could feel the thrill of excitement rush through her body.

Baby and Anne Marie sat in a pub off Grafton Street, long booted legs crossed, a fair amount of thigh showing, cigarettes lit.

'Mind if I join you?' a man asked them.

'We're waiting for friends,' Baby said, eyeing him with interest.

He was tall and dark, and probably mid thirties if not more.

'Okay,' he said. 'May I buy you a drink while you're waiting for your friends? I have to be off soon anyway.'

'Great,' said Baby. 'Mine's a Guinness. My friend Anne Marie likes Dubonnet. By the way, I'm Barbara.'

Becky's film over, with more questions unanswered than answered, she turned the light off and settled on the sofa again to watch the late-night news, and before she knew it she was asleep.

She woke much later to the sound of the hall door closing and footsteps moving across the plush hall carpet, accompanied by the low murmuring of voices. The fire had died out, and the only light in the room was coming from the fuzzy picture on the television screen.

The lights in the hall were turned off. Hearing the footsteps on the stairs ascending to the next floor, she froze.

If it were the Robinsons, she thought, they'd come in here. God, what will I do?

Her heart was pounding. The hairs on the back of her neck seemed to shift, and she felt very cold. For a frozen moment she wondered if she were capable of moving at all, but then the thought of the sleeping children upstairs galvanised her into some sort of action. Silently she swung her legs off the sofa, and found her shoes. At the fireplace she picked up the poker. Her antennae seemed on full alert, as if she were more highly aware of where things were positioned than she would normally be. Part of her brain was aware of this magnified alertness, and she found it interesting, but knew there was no time now to contemplate the significance of that.

In the hall she listened carefully. There was a light on the landing above.

She was unsure whether to head for the hall door and the street, where she could call for help, or to go up the stairs. Having no idea of the time, but instinctively knowing it was very late, she reasoned, correctly, that there might be no one outside.

And then what will I do? she asked herself.

On silent feet, she headed for the stairs, heart pounding, focused only on the sleeping children.

On the landing, Mr Robinson suddenly appeared out of the bathroom.

'Flying Jesus,' he articulated in a rather slurred way. 'Are you still here?'

Becky stood at the top of the stairs. Her initial shock at seeing him was replaced with complete relief that it was Mr Robinson and not some intruder, which was what all the signs had seemed to show.

'Of course,' she said. 'I'm babysitting . . . you know . . . until you come home.'

Her voice trailed off. She felt like she wanted to sit down and cry.

'We forgot,' said Mr Robinson. 'Magda drank a little too much, and she's in bed . . . I forgot you were here.'

At this point he seemed aware that his trousers were open, and he reached down and zipped them up.

'Better get you home then,' he said.

As Becky trailed down the stairs, he took in the fact that she was carrying a poker.

'You planning on hipping me on the bed with that? I mean, bipping me on the head?' he asked, taking it from her. His words were garbled and she could smell the drink on his breath.

She shook her head.

'I thought you were an intruder. I thought the children . . .'

Again her voice trailed away as the shock of what she'd feared might happen shook her.

'Afraid someone would kidnap the little beggars?' he asked jokingly, too drunk to take in the state Becky was in. He pronounced afraid as 'afry-d'.

'Come on, get your coat on and I'll drive you home,' he said.

In the car Becky wanted to cry, but there were further shocks in store for her when it transpired that Mr Robinson could hardly see the road. They swerved around the corner, narrowly missing a parked car, whereupon he mounted the pavement and touched a lamppost, then, with amazing panache, regained the road and headed on towards her home.

Becky was flung from side to side, unable to grab hold of anything to give herself support. At one point she banged her head on the dashboard; at another she wondered should she grab the wheel.

'Mr Robinson,' she said, 'you can drop me here. Honestly, here is just fine.'

Her voice reached a peak as Mr Robinson once again mounted the pavement, only this time he embedded the car in a garden wall. Becky was now trapped against the wall, shaken, shocked but unhurt. This was a night that she would not forget for a while.

At that point, Mr Robinson leaned across and said, 'God, you're more

21

beautiful than Magda,' and planted his slobbering drunken mouth on her small pink lips.

Becky struggled.

Mr Robinson was a big man, and it was with a great deal of difficulty that Becky managed to push him off her, and then to struggle over the seat into the back of the car, and then out the door on to the road.

She ran as fast as she could in the twinkling starlight under the bright winter moon, down the road, and up her own driveway.

At her hall door she fumbled in the porch, looking for the key to let herself in. At first she could not find the pot under which the key was kept safely hidden. At last she let herself into the house and closed the door behind her.

Her watch showed that it was after three.

She sat on the stairs, the key clutched tightly in her hands, and felt tears well up in her eyes. She was shaking and a wave of nausea overwhelmed her, and she rushed to the downstairs bathroom, where she retched and retched.

She was too distressed to work out what to do, and so she abandoned her coat and the key on the bathroom floor, and when she got the energy together, she climbed the stairs and went to bed.

In bed she thought of going up to Baby – but not to her parents.

What would I say to them? And they're friends of the Robinsons. She shuddered as she thought of Mr Robinson's mouth descending on hers.

My first kiss, she thought. Oh God.

She nearly got out of bed to go up to Baby because she was desperate for kindness and sympathy, and even Baby was better than no one.

But the thought of going up the top flight of stairs in the dark scared her, and she didn't want to waken her parents, and anyway, she thought, Baby would not be too receptive at any time, let alone in the middle of the night.

She wondered how Brona would have reacted had such a thing happened to her.

As it happened, such a thing had already happened to Brona. Not with Mr Robinson, but with Mr O'Brady, father of the children Brona called the O'Brady Bunch, and for whom she occasionally babysat.

On that occasion, Mr O'Brady had said to her, 'How old are you now, Brona?'

'I'm fifteen,' lied the fourteen-year-old, to whom truth had never come easily.

'Sweet fifteen and never been kissed,' said Mr O'Brady, moving in and planting a kiss on her pouting lips.

She gave him an almighty push, and said, 'Yuck, you stink of booze, and anyway, it's sweet sixteen and never been kissed.'

When she told Rhona about it, Rhona said, 'Great. And then what happened?' with considerable enthusiasm.

'Oh, I pushed him so hard,' Brona laughed, 'that he fell backwards on to a chair. He said something like "Oh, fair enough. I'll try again next year."'

'And then what?' Rhona asked.

'And then, nothing,' Brona replied. 'We both laughed, and I asked for my money and home I went.'

But back in the Dunville house that night, Becky lay shivering in bed.

And I didn't even get paid, she thought sadly.

John and Elizabeth Dunville slept deeply, unaware of the distress of their middle daughter. Elizabeth turned in the bed and the flickerings of a nightmare, which kept reoccurring, hovered on the edge of her mind.

Her subconscious struggled to hold it away, as images from long ago, when she was a young girl and went to stay in London with her brother, James Fitzgerald, and his wife Nancy, came and went.

She had gone there at the age of eighteen, a gentle girl straight out of the confines of the convent where she had been educated. In her dream she could hear the priest reading on the altar: '*Consider the lilies of the fields, they sow not, neither do they reap . . .*' and she was again eighteen years old, head bowed, kneeling in front of the wooden pew. The lilies are blighted by their own beauty, she'd thought back then. That's what the nuns said. We are born with original sin. We are flawed.

She remembered a day long ago in the convent, and one of the nuns, an intelligent woman with a serene face, saying to her something about her youth and her beauty, and how she must not let that distract her from God's plan.

She wondered then what the nun had meant.

Was it God's plan for me to do wrong? Did I have a real choice? Do any of us have a real choice? In her dream her hand reached out to open a door, but John rolled over in the bed and put his arm around her, and the dream changed and her level of consciousness shifted and she slept easily again.

Chapter Two

Elizabeth Fitzgerald, as a demure and middle-class Dublin girl, went to visit her brother James and his wife Nancy in London in 1950. At a dinner in their house on the first night, she met John. An amusing and witty man recently seconded into civil aviation, with two years of the war followed by the Berlin Airlift under his belt, he looked across the table and he winked at her, as her brother pontificated about everything imaginable.

John Delaware had had, as they said, a good war.

'And what do you think?' John asked her, and as she opened her mouth to reply, her brother cut across her with an observation about the weather.

Elizabeth blushed slightly. She had not managed one sentence all evening. There had been no opportunity for her to say anything. She lowered her head quickly, hoping that the flush would not be as apparent as it felt.

And after dinner, when they went through to the drawing room for coffee, John sought her out.

'Let's try again,' he said, looking down at her long ivory neck and the smooth fair skin, and sitting beside her on the two-seater sofa where she seemed so uncomfortably perched. Her blonde hair was pinned back off her face, and with one slim hand she reached up and touched it in a gesture that might have been one of confidence except for the shyness which she clearly portrayed.

She smiled what she hoped was a winning smile, praying that she was projecting herself as a woman of the world, used to dinner parties, which of course she was not.

'What do I think?' she asked, wondering what he was specifically referring to.

'Yes, what do you think?'

'Oh dear,' she said. 'I'm not sure what we're talking about.'

He laughed.

'Neither am I,' he replied. 'I just wanted to know what your voice sounded like.'

'What are you saying to my little sister?' asked James Fitzgerald as he came over to them.

'We're talking about the fuel shortage and the stamps, and how you managed this dinner, in fact,' John said to James with a laugh.

'Oh, Elizabeth brought half of this with her from Ireland,' James joked. 'That's why we invited her to stay. It's ridiculous when you think that Bonn is talking about ending food rationing in Germany, and I still have to get my mother in Dublin to send me butter rolled out thinly in sheets of greaseproof paper in a newspaper.'

'You what?' John said in amazement.

'And ham,' Elizabeth said, pleased to be able to contribute to the conversation. 'That's how we send ham to James and Nancy.'

'What a racket,' John laughed. 'You'll have to send me some too.'

She smiled, delighted.

'Have you been here before?' John seemed to focus on her alone.

'It's my first visit,' she replied.

'She's only just out of school,' James said, and she cringed, believing that it made her seem a baby in their midst. '*Convent* school,' he added, making Elizabeth feel that she had the word *virgin* written across her forehead.

'Five months out,' she said, wishing her brother would leave her alone.

'So this is quite exciting for you?' John tried again.

And she nodded shyly, looking up at him with her blue eyes and thick dark lashes. It *was* exciting. The war – or the Emergency as they had called it in Ireland – was ended. Eisenhower had become Europe's Supreme Allied Commander. Other wars had taken over. North Korea had invaded South Korea, and now British troops had gone to Korea to join the West's offensive. She knew from James and Nancy what was happening in the real world. Life and death occurred at the flick of someone's fingers. Life was for living. And Elizabeth Fitzgerald wanted to live it.

John took her out. John wined and dined her, held her hand when they went to the zoo, sent her flowers, and wooed her.

She went home briefly to Ireland, but missed him so terribly that six weeks later she returned.

She took a job in London and stayed with her brother and sister-in-law.

James and Nancy Fitzgerald seemed happy to have her back with them, and Elizabeth and Nancy, who really had very little in common, spent time together. They seemed to have different values and different views, but Elizabeth was younger and had little enough self-confidence and was content to watch and learn from her elders.

'I love him,' she confided to her sister-in-law.

Nancy, five years older, smiled at her.

'He's in love with you,' she reassured Elizabeth.

'But how do you know?' Elizabeth asked.

'It's obvious,' was the reply. 'And he's such a catch. All that saving-the-world stuff ... mmm. Night flights in and out of Berlin. Don't you love it?'

Some weekends John was not around, and Elizabeth did the rounds of parties with James and Nancy and waited for him to return to town. And he invariably did return.

'Sleep with me,' he said to Elizabeth, now approaching nineteen.

'I can't,' she said. 'I'm a Catholic. I can't ... you know. I can't.'

A week later they bumped into him at a dinner and he had a girl called June on his arm. He looked at Elizabeth across the room, and he smiled his bedroom smile, and butterflies flapped frantically inside her and she tightened her lips.

'Oh, Nancy,' she said, 'Nancy. What'll I do?'

Nancy, fiddling with flowers in the drawing room, said, 'What do you mean?'

Elizabeth blushed.

'Nothing,' she said, 'It's nothing.'

'No, go on. What do you mean?'

'He ... you know ... he wants ... well ...' The words wouldn't come, but Nancy knew. Nancy had been there, and knew what she was hinting at.

'If he loves you,' she said, 'if he truly loves you, he'll respect you and he'll wait.'

'Did James ... you know ... did you and James ... well, wait?'

'Yes,' Nancy said firmly.

In due course he announced his engagement to June and the Fitzgerald trio were shocked.

'But I love him,' Elizabeth said miserably to Nancy. 'I wanted to spend the rest of my life with him. He made me feel so happy.'

'He may have made her feel happy,' James said to Nancy in the privacy of their bedroom that night, 'but now he's made her totally miserable.'

'What does that mean?' Nancy asked.

'Well, if he's able to make her that miserable, then he's surely not the one for her,' James said.

Nancy, her dark hair tied back, peering in the mirror as she removed her make-up, wondered at the logic of the observation.

'I don't quite follow,' she said, tentatively.

'If you love someone, you don't make them miserable,' James said. 'He's made her miserable, ergo, he doesn't love her, ergo, he's not the one for her.'

Men are so clear-cut in their thinking, Nancy thought, and planned a dinner to distract the stricken Elizabeth.

Elizabeth, in her nightgown, ran her hand across the bare flesh above her breasts and thought how John had opened a button on her blouse and run a finger down . . . down . . .

Oh God, she thought. How can I bear to be without him?

John Delaware, smooth, clean-cut, elegant, married within just a few weeks, and six months later June had a baby.

Elizabeth, sitting with Nancy, said, 'Was it early? I mean . . . was it born . . . you know . . . too early?'

Nancy shook her head.

'No, it was full term.' She swallowed and stretched her mouth uneasily. 'I think perhaps he wasn't all one would have wanted him to be.'

And Elizabeth counted the months on her fingers and knew that he must have been doing things with June round about the time he was trying to do things to her. It hurt.

If I'd gone all the way? she wondered. Then would he have married me? But then, how would I have felt later?

She lay in bed. She had thought in terms of marriage, and making love, of gentleness and kindness and hope, and now there was sadness.

Nancy threw her dinner party, and at that dinner Elizabeth Fitzgerald met John Dunville.

Same name to murmur in my mind, she thought when John Dunville took her to the cinema and kissed her when he brought her home.

27

Same name, dark hair, kindly . . . but I love someone else.

But the other John was married, and John Dunville kept pursuing her. She would come home from work and there would be a message . . .

'Yes,' she said. 'I will,' when he asked her to marry him.

Why not? she thought. He's decent. He's kind. I don't think he's lying. I don't think there is anyone else in his life. Why not?

'Nancy, Nancy,' she said to her sister-in-law. 'What do you think?'

'I think he's lovely,' Nancy said. 'I think he's handsome and kind. He's intelligent and supportive, he's a doctor and he'll be a good provider.'

What more do I want? the nineteen-year-old Elizabeth asked herself. My heart almost pounds when he kisses me. I like the way he is always there to open a door. And he doesn't push me to sleep with him.

And John Dunville, running a finger up and down her cheek, and his hand through her hair, whispered to her, 'I can hardly wait.'

But wait he did. And she was glad.

They married in Dublin later that year. Bells rang in the church and the organ played and Elizabeth counted her blessings. John Dunville was kind, if a little remote and austere. He took over from James, her brother, in caring for her, and they returned to London. They socialised, and as bad luck would have it, John and June Delaware moved in the same circles.

At dinners and parties, John Delaware would try to isolate Elizabeth so that he could talk to her, but she studiously avoided him, or called on her husband or James and Nancy to join them.

'I wish he wouldn't do that,' she confided to Nancy.

'He's a bounder,' Nancy pronounced. 'He's no right to do that to you. Shall I get James to say something to him?'

'Oh, no, don't,' Elizabeth replied. 'No. Because then he'll think I still carry a candle for him and that I've a reason to avoid him. And I just want him to leave me alone.'

'Well, don't worry,' Nancy said. 'As long as we're there, I'll make sure he doesn't corner you again. And by the way, I think the expression is "to carry a torch for someone".'

Nancy smiled affectionately at her sister-in-law.

Baby Dunville was born in London in 1953. Secretly, both her parents had wanted a boy, but Baby, lying in her tiny cot with her little hand pulled up to her mouth, and her cherubic face, wiped such wishes from everyone's minds.

She gurgled and snuffled, hunting for a breast to suck, and slept so peacefully when full that her mother couldn't sleep for joy as she held this baby bundle in her arms. Her father, tall, serious and austere, melted when her tiny hand grasped one of his fingers and wouldn't let go.

Baby Dunville had truly arrived. Her parents sat in awe beside her cot and gazed in wonder at their baby.

In the hospital Elizabeth was unable to sleep. She just wanted to hold Baby, and could not wait for her to be brought up in the mornings from the nursery.

She, John and Baby Dunville sat together. The feeling of family, of being family, of being part of her own special unit made Elizabeth feel like her heart would burst with happiness.

I have it all, she thought.

'God, you're so lucky,' Nancy said. 'We've tried and tried, and I can't get pregnant.'

'I want one of those,' Nancy said to James in their marital bed. 'I need one of those.'

'We'll have one,' he said to her. 'It'll just take time.'

And he was right. It would take time, another four years in fact, before Eleanor Fitzgerald was born to James and Nancy.

James and Nancy moved back to Dublin, leaving John and Elizabeth to their life in London.

'Are you happy, my darling girl?' John Dunville asked Elizabeth one night in London after a party. They had just checked on Baby asleep in her cot with her blonde curls lying on the sheet. She was one year and three months old. She smelt of sleeping baby and talcum powder, and even in her sleep, her little hands opened and closed as she moved busily through her dreamland.

'Yes,' Elizabeth sighed contentedly, as she got ready for bed. 'I am happy.'

It was the last night that she would be happy.

The following morning John Dunville went to work, and left Elizabeth tidying the kitchen with Baby busy on the floor.

'See you tonight, my darling girls,' he called from the door. And he was gone.

Elizabeth and Baby moved through the morning. They did the shopping, they dusted and cleaned, played games, read a book, and then at about two o'clock Baby yawned, ready for her afternoon nap. A precocious child who had stood up at nine months old and was walking at ten, she was formulating phrases at a year and three months.

'Uppity-up,' she said, and clambered into her mother's waiting arms. 'Uppity-up,' she said again, as Elizabeth Dunville carried her up the stairs to her tiny cot. She had long outgrown it, but refused steadfastly to get into the small child's bed in her room.

'Downedy-down,' she said to Elizabeth as she was lowered into her bedding and the covers were pulled over her shoulders.

'Sleepy-pie,' she said as she yawned again.

Elizabeth left her to sleep and went back downstairs hoping for a doze in the drawing room on the sofa, as she had had a late night.

She thought about the previous evening and wished Nancy had been there.

Really, it's too bad, she thought. What does June think of her husband behaving like that? Fawning all over me. It isn't flattering. It's awful. And I once . . . I still . . .

She found it difficult to finish the thought. She knew that her heart still pounded when John Delaware put a hand on her shoulder, and she wished that she did not feel that way.

Thinking about it, she sighed, and just as she was settling herself on the sofa there was a knock on the door.

She thought momentarily about not answering it, but then she stood up and slipped her feet back into her shoes and went to open it.

It was John Delaware.

'Hello,' he said.

'What do you want?' she asked in total surprise.

'I need to talk to you,' he said. 'Please let me in for a few minutes.'

They went into the drawing room.

'We could have had a room like this together,' he said, looking around.

'You have a room just like this with June,' she said firmly. 'Your wife,' she added as if to remind him.

'But June's not you. Our room doesn't have your touch to it,' he said.

Elizabeth Dunville didn't answer. She stood there awkwardly in the middle of the room, watching him.

He leaned an elbow on the mantelpiece and lit a cigarette.

'What do you want?' Elizabeth asked him again, nervous, tentative.

'I want to spend some time with you,' he said. 'It's torture meeting you at these parties all the time, and you have no time to talk to me, always with other people around you. And I want to talk to you.'

'What do you want to say?' she said briskly. 'Say whatever it is and please go. John will be home soon. And what about June? What would she say if she knew you were here?'

'Don't talk to me about June,' he said, dismissively. 'And John – he won't be home for hours.'

'Come on, John,' Elizabeth said, moving towards the door. 'Please go now.'

He threw the rest of his cigarette into the fire.

'Not until you kiss me,' he said, reaching her just as she put her hand on the door handle.

He spun her around to face him, and losing her footing she found herself wrapped in his arms, and his mouth descending on hers.

'No, no,' she said, gasping for breath, trying to push him away. 'No, don't . . . don't do this . . .'

Upstairs Baby woke and gave an irate yell.

She twisted this story a thousand times in her mind to find a version she could live with. She tried this one for a while.

'Please go . . . please.' Elizabeth beat at him with her hands.

'Don't do that,' he said angrily, pinning her arms to her sides.

She struggled, and as she tried to release herself from his grasp the door opened behind her. At the same moment she lost her footing completely and the opening door handle hit her head as she fell. Outside the door a furious Baby yelled, 'Oped dat door.'

Time seemed to stand still. There had been a lull of some sort, a silence in which all she could feel was the throbbing in her head, and then John Delaware was on top of her. His kisses varied between being both tender and angry. His fingers unbuttoned tiny pearl buttons as he sought his way through the delicate layers of her undergarments, and then with raw brutality her skirt was lifted and her clothing torn and he entered her ruthlessly.

Her feeble struggles were weakened by the blow to her head, but still she protested. She could hear her voice repeating the word 'no' over and over.

And then it was over and he was gone. She heard the front door slam and silence settle momentarily on the house.

She lay on the drawing-room floor, trying to pull the pieces of thin silk back around her. Dazed, frightened, hurting, cut and bruised, she listened to the silence in the house and then she could hear the echo of Baby's voice shouting somewhere in the distance. This was one of many twists to the real version which Elizabeth ran in her mind in an effort to live with herself.

By the age of two, before the arrival of the next Dunville girl, Baby ruled their home. Grandparents came and were smitten. In dungarees, with blonde curls and blue eyes, and her legs just a tiny bit too long, Baby scuttled busily from room to room, ran in the park kicking the fallen autumn leaves and chuckled when a chestnut falling from its tree landed on her head.

Her first words had been 'Give me,' rolled perfectly into one. 'Gimme,' she said happily, pointing to her mother's pearls. 'Gimme,' she ordered, pointing to her father's lips, and they did. She wore the pearls when she wanted, and she was kissed on demand.

Rebecca was born when Baby was two. A small, sallow-skinned child, with dark hair and brown eyes, quiet and undemanding, Becky Dunville watched and observed the pecking order in her home.

By the time they moved back to Ireland for both the conception and the birth of their third child, John, Elizabeth and Baby were a close threesome.

'Leave her,' Baby would say to Elizabeth Dunville when Rebecca, the second baby, cried for attention.

'Play with me,' she'd order John on his return from work.

'Put Becker down,' she'd insist when Rebecca sat on the lap of the parent Baby wanted to control.

As parents they did their best.

'You mustn't let her get away with quite so much,' Elizabeth's mother and mother-in-law would say, as Baby sat Becky behind the sofa in the drawing room.

'But she's so determined,' Elizabeth would reply.

And both mother and mother-in-law would look at Elizabeth in mild surprise. Elizabeth did not seem to have the strength and determination she once had, and it puzzled them both. There was an uncertainty about her, a frailty that neither had been aware of before. Where she had once shown simply a lack of self-belief, but with the ability to mature into a confident woman, she now displayed weakness, fragility and distraction.

Meanwhile Baby knew that her sibling was there to stay, but she didn't have to look at her when she didn't want to. 'Out of sight is out of mind' was her motto.

Elizabeth tried her best to balance the roles of wife and mother, but something had gone out of her – perhaps her innocence – or maybe it was that something had entered her that could not be got rid of. Guilt ate into her heart because there was a truer version of what had happened that afternoon in London. And it was the truth she could not handle. Lust was a sin, and she had sinned. She pushed that truth away – holding it as far at bay as she could – while it tormented and teased her, always on the outskirts of her mind, and eating into her sleep.

Back in Dublin Brona was born to complete the trio of girls. 'My darling girls,' as John said, with Baby sitting on his knee, Brona feeding at her mother's breast, and Becky sitting quietly on the floor watching. Brona was a demanding child, but Baby held her ground and her parents' attention and love. She pushed her way consistently to the fore, sang songs and danced to keep their eyes on her. People were drawn to her – attracted by her beauty and her confidence. Becky's self-containment kept her intact and she was drawn to books and fantasy, a private world in which she thrived silently and discreetly. By comparison Brona, who looked like a smaller version of Baby but with light brown hair, held her own both by being the youngest and by having a strong spirit. The three girls clashed constantly but Baby always came out on top.

'What do you want me to bring you for Christmas?' Santa asked her in his grotto in Pims, a large department store south of the river.

'No more babies,' she said seriously, her blonde curls bobbing, her little pink hands tugging at his beard. 'And all the toys in the shop,' she added, as if she reckoned that a lack of further babies might leave space to be filled in their home.

'And are they your sisters?' he asked the five-year-old, whose precocity surprised him.

She looked back at her mother at the top of the queue, just out of earshot, holding Becky and Brona, aged three and two.

'No,' she said firmly.

*   *   *

'But Sister,' Baby said to the nun at religious class, aged seven and a bit, 'what do you say in Confession if you haven't committed any sins?'

Sister George looked at the little upturned face and was momentarily silenced. This was a question she had never to date been asked.

'There is always something, Barbara Dunville,' she addressed the child. 'Every single person commits sin. We were born with original sin marking our souls, and because of that, we sin, and so we go to confess and to get forgiveness.'

'But Sister,' said Baby, wide-blue-eyed innocence, 'if I've done nothing – nothing, nothing, nothing – and I go in and confess, that's a sin, isn't it?'

Sister George said, 'You squabble with your sisters. Every child does. That's a sin. That must be confessed.'

'But Sister,' said Baby Dunville, 'I don't squabble with them.'

'You mean there are no arguments between you three Dunville girls?' said Sister George, surprised.

'Oh, there are rows, Sister,' replied Baby Dunville firmly. 'They squabble with me. Not me with them. I was there first.'

Sister George sighed.

'Well, whether you like it or not, that is a sin, Barbara Dunville,' she snapped. 'And anything naughty that you do – that is a sin too.'

Baby Dunville sat there looking at Sister George and felt a sense of self-righteous determination.

'Examine your conscience,' said Sister George to the seven-year-old. This was a term all the girls were well used to.

So Baby examined her conscience.

'Daddy,' she said that evening, sitting on his lap in front of the fire, 'I can't think of any sins to say in my First Confession.'

John Dunville looked at his eldest daughter.

'What are the other girls going to say?' he asked, curiously.

'Well, we're not allowed to say in class what we're going to say, because it's between us and God, but Mary Jones hit her sister and bit her dog, and Carla MacAntee never does what her mother says. And Anne Marie O'Mahony is always late for school, and Sister George says that's a sin, even though they have a chauffeur, but he has to drive her dad into his office first and it makes her late.'

'I see,' said John Dunville, wondering whether he should tell her that he wasn't a Catholic.

Elizabeth had been adamant that the girls need not know. 'It's not

34

important for them,' she said. 'But it is important for me,' he replied. 'But we're bringing them up as Catholics,' she argued. 'They don't need to know that you're not of the true faith.'

He said nothing at first, and then brought it up again. 'They'll find out at some time or another. They'll know I go to another church.'

'But you come to church with us – they need not know.'

'They'll find out,' he said. 'They'll ask questions sooner or later. Why doesn't Daddy take Communion, for example. Better that they are told early so that it is not an issue.'

'But it is an issue,' she said.

'Elizabeth, I am not a Catholic. I'm doing everything you want to have the girls brought up in your faith, but you have to understand that I'm not ashamed of not being Catholic. My religion is as important to me as yours is to you. Don't you see that?'

Eventually she agreed.

'Well, when the time comes, I'm not going to lie about it,' he said. 'You wouldn't want me to do that, now would you?'

And so they agreed that if and when the time arose he would tell it as a matter of fact to the girls. 'Then they'll just absorb it into their lives. It changes nothing for them, whereas the lie would when it eventually came out. Lies always come out in the end.'

And Elizabeth had shivered.

'Baby,' he said tentatively now to the seven-year-old, who was watching him carefully, 'I'm not a Catholic, and that's why I'm not so good at working out what is and isn't a sin.'

'You're not a Catholic?' said Baby, her little face lighting up. She knew from the nuns that not being a Catholic was as bad as could be. 'Oh, good.'

'Bless me Father for I have sinned,' said Baby Dunville at her First Confession. 'My father is not a Catholic. For this sin, I am truly sorry.'

The priest glanced sideways and saw the perfect upturned face, and the large blue eyes, which seemed to shine in the darkness of the confessional. He waited for the usual litany of sins, but there were no more forthcoming.

'It's not your fault your father is not a Catholic,' he said. 'What I'm going to suggest is that you try and convert him.' I imagine he would do anything for you, he thought to himself. I would.

'Yes, Father,' said Baby Dunville, thinking about her new white bag, which matched her First Communion dress, and how she would look walking up the aisle.

'A Bride of Christ,' Sister had said. 'You will be married to God.'

'Say one Hail Mary, my child,' the priest said to Baby Dunville. 'Now say the Act of Contrition.'

Baby recited the Act and then left the confessional, as the little door separating her from the priest slid closed.

Outside she knelt with the other girls and said the Hail Mary as she had been instructed. Convert Dad, she thought. She almost smiled. You converted black heathens in jungle places and made sure their babies were brought up to be Catholics and that they didn't run around naked. But not people like her father. He was his own self and she knew that. She knew from watching him that being a Catholic was not important to him, but that being a doctor was, and being a father, and having Mummy as his wife and Baby as his daughter. She was secure in her world, and converting her father was not of any interest to either her or him. The priest just said to *try* to convert him, she thought.

'Daddy,' she said that night, 'did you ever think about being a Catholic like Mummy and me?'

'No,' he replied. 'We're brought up in a religion, and if it suits us, if we are comfortable with it, and live a good life, why change it?'

That made sense to her. She knew he was both comfortable with and reliant on himself. These abilities she had learned from him. She also knew that the way he felt about himself was more solid, more complete than the way her mother felt, but she was too young to delve into that or to try to make any sense of it.

That's that, she thought. He's fine the way he is, why try to change him?

Becky, by comparison, examined her conscience, and the sins she found there were the ones detailed in school: fighting with her sisters, being angry with them, lusting after Baby's toys, which Baby guarded assiduously. She craved the attention she watched Baby getting, but she held her peace on that one, as she instinctively knew that there was nothing she could do about it.

Brona, kicking the furniture and tearing the last page out of the novel Baby was reading, spilling water on the picture Baby was painting, and pinching Becky any time she thought about it, approached her First Confession with a momentary commitment to avoiding such sins in the future. 'I'll try harder,' she said to the priest. 'I will be good, I will be good,' she said to herself in a mantra quickly forgotten.

'You,' said Baby Dunville to her sister Becky on the morning of Brona's First Communion, 'are the only Dunville girl not to have got a new Communion dress.'

Becky, who had in fact been aware of this, said nothing.

'How does that make you feel?' Baby asked.

Becky shrugged. She struggled to stay silent.

'I got a new dress,' said Baby, 'because I am the oldest.'

'And I got a new dress,' said Brona, 'because I am the youngest.'

Both sisters eyed Becky, wondering how long it would take them to get the desired response.

Becky bit her lip, willing herself not to react.

'Second-hand Becky,' said Baby.

The words were building up in Becky, her face changed and her eyes narrowed.

'It must be an awful feeling,' Baby continued, eyeing her sister with interest.

'I'm not second-hand,' Becky said. 'Not any more than Brona would be third-hand if she fitted into the dress.'

'But she doesn't fit into the dress, does she,' goaded Baby. 'Mummy had to cut my dress down to fit you because you are undersized, and that's why it doesn't fit Brona. So Brona got a new dress and you didn't.'

'It's just a dress,' Becky said, trying to keep her voice steady. 'And I'm not undersized – I'm just small.'

'Very small for your age,' Baby amended. 'That means undersized.'

Becky knew the way this scene would end. Like it always ended – in tears. So she swallowed the responses, bit back the tears, and tried to make her face impassive.

'But we don't mind you being undersized, do we, Brona?' Baby continued.

Brona shook her head, delighted to be safely on Baby's side in this particular scene. She knew from experience that Baby's side would be the winning side.

'Brona doesn't mind you being smaller than her at her First Communion, do you, Brona?'

'Not at all,' said Brona.

And later that day, Becky said to her mother and father that she did not want to go to Brona's First Communion, that there was school for the other classes anyway, and she could just go there instead.

'You can't do that,' Elizabeth said. 'It's Brona's big day. We all go as a family.'

'Do I have to?' Becky asked. 'I don't really want to miss school.'

'Stop being selfish, Becky,' John Dunville said. 'Your mother just pointed out that it's Brona's day, and we should be there to support her.'

'Brona doesn't even want me there,' Becky pouted.

'Stop whingeing,' her father said. 'If you're going to behave like that of course Brona doesn't want you there. Let her go to school, Elizabeth,' he said. 'It'll be more peaceful.'

Baby, sitting on the sofa with a book, smiled as she turned the page.

At twelve, Baby went to secondary school, and she ruled there too.

'I'll sit at the front during winter,' she said to her acolytes. 'Beside the fire. And in spring, I'll take a window seat.'

Her peers squabbled to sit beside her.

The nuns were fooled.

'You can always tell the industrious ones,' they said, 'by who wants to sit in the front row.'

They did not take into account that Baby liked warmth and comfort, and the front row was closest to the open fire. Baby was prepared to put up with the tag of industry in order to get what she wanted.

'Tie your hair back, Barbara Dunville,' said Sister Rodriguez to Baby Dunville on the day she started secondary in St Martin's.

'Yes, Sister,' replied Baby, with her large blue eyes and her long blonde curls, and, taking a length of bottle-green satin ribbon from her gymslip pocket, she tied her hair back off her shoulders.

Sister Rodriguez was taken by surprise. She had meant that the following day Baby should arrive in school with her hair neatly plaited or pony-tailed, but she felt she would diminish herself if she admonished such immediate obedience.

To her surprise, the following day, almost the whole class was wearing their hair tied with a ribbon in different colours of satin.

'Do I ignore this on the grounds that it may go away?' Sister Rodriguez asked Mother Immaculata in serious tones.

Mother Immaculata shook her head.

'Give them an inch, and there will be anarchy,' she pronounced.

'Girls of St Martin's,' she addressed the assembled forms the following morning. 'There will be no gaudiness of dress. Our rules for the uniform are clear. You *may* wear a green ribbon in your hair to match your tunic. No other colour will be permitted, and by the time you reach your classrooms this morning, no other colour will be visible.'

And no other colour was visible when first class commenced. And Baby Dunville, who had set the trend for ribbon in their hair, sat calmly in the front row of her class, with her long blonde curls loosely tied back with green satin, and looked as if butter wouldn't melt in her perfectly formed, pink-lipped mouth.

Becky, meantime, both in primary and later when she started in secondary school, had learned so well at home how to disappear, how to be silent, how to keep herself to herself for her own protection, that she now found she had no idea how to relate to her peers. She kept her head down, lived in her own private world, and protected herself as best she could.

At the age of fourteen and three-quarters, Baby sat on the floor at her father's feet in the drawing room.

'Daddy,' she said demurely, looking up at him.

'Yes, Baby,' he responded, lowering his newspaper so that he could see the golden head and the wide blue eyes.

'Daddy,' she continued, now that she had his full attention, 'I'll be fifteen in two months and twenty-seven days.'

'Indeed,' he said, smiling inwardly as he admired the angelic beauty before him. 'And what would my girl like for her birthday?' he asked.

'Well, Daddy, I don't want to put you to excessive expense,' said Baby carefully, smiling lovingly at him. 'So, what I'd really like is just to change my bedroom.'

'You mean have it decorated?' he asked.

'Well, no ... no, that's not what I meant,' she replied. 'You see, I keep thinking about those wasted rooms on the top floor of the house, and because I'm the eldest and I need more space and quiet than the little ones ...'

Needless to say, the 'little ones' weren't present during this conversation.

'I would like to have one of those rooms as my bedroom.'

'Wouldn't you be quite isolated up there?' he asked her.

'I would love it,' she said. 'The view, the peace to pursue my homework with extra diligence.'

'I'll talk to your mother,' he said.

And on her fifteenth birthday, Baby ascended to the top floor to her new bedroom under the roof. The two rooms up there stretched the depth of the house. Both had windows looking out in the direction of the coast. One now contained empty suitcases, boxes, bags of their baby toys and old unused furniture. The other was freshly decorated in shades of honey and white. A carpenter had fitted a sliding white wardrobe and dozens of shelves.

Baby smiled happily.

'And Mummy,' she said, 'Mrs O'Doody's not to be coming up here to clean. Those stairs would wear her out. I'll vacuum once a week, and do my own dusting.'

And so Baby acquired the isolation she wanted, and now ruled the house from the uppermost realms.

Baby's first school report commented on her evident leadership qualities. Her marks were good, but not startlingly so.

By the time she was fifteen, her report still commented on the leadership qualities, but stressed that the sisters would like to see her directing those qualities in a positive way.

'She's not quite wholesome,' said Sister Rodriguez to Mother Immaculata. 'There's something indefinable about her ... I'm never quite sure what she's thinking.'

'Her marks are holding, though,' said the Reverend Mother, as she signed the report.

'You never really know what she's thinking,' repeated Sister Rodriguez.

'She's popular. She gives no trouble. I've had few or no dealings with her,' said the head nun. 'Is there anything further that can be added to it?'

Sister Rodriguez shook her head.

She didn't like Baby Dunville, and as Baby grew up, she liked her even less.

*   *   *

Aged sixteen, Baby entered the Venetian Café in Ballsbridge one Saturday morning, as part of a personal improvement plan on which she was working. Her idea was to improve her confidence, which in fact needed little if any work on it.

She walked up to the counter and took coffee and a Kit-Kat, paying at the till, and while she surveyed the room, looking for a table, she slipped her change back into her bag.

There was only one table free, and so she went and sat with her back to the wall so that she could watch the activity in the place. Immediately afterwards, a man who had followed her in brought his coffee to her table.

'Is this chair free?' he asked her, gesturing to the chair opposite her.

She nodded coolly, and took a sip of her coffee.

He picked up the Kit-Kat, and tearing open the red paper, he broke the two-fingered biscuit in half, and ate one of the fingers.

Baby took this in with a certain amount of amazement.

Cheeky devil, she thought, as she reached for the other half, and slipping off the silver paper, she nibbled the finger slowly, looking up at him from under long thick eyelashes.

After a few minutes, he picked up his cup and left the table.

Baby shrugged, though she was surprised. I thought that was a new type of come-on, she thought, as she drank the rest of her coffee.

There wasn't much happening, and she was sorry she hadn't asked Anne Marie to meet her there, as it was quite boring, which was something she hadn't expected.

She pushed her cup into the middle of the table, and getting up to leave she observed that the man who had previously sat at her table was now sitting near the door. As she passed his table, she couldn't help noticing that he now had a cream doughnut in front of him.

Baby Dunville eyed the man. Then Baby Dunville eyed the doughnut.

This is part of my confidence therapy, she reassured herself, and she reached down and, taking the doughnut, took an enormous bite out of it before returning it to his plate.

Then she walked out the door.

She was still chewing and swallowing at the corner when she opened her bag to get money for a magazine, and to her surprise she saw that the Kit-Kat she had bought earlier was in her bag.

Oh my God, she thought. Oh my God. That must have been his biscuit on the table.

And Baby Dunville started to giggle as she moved as fast as she could away from the Venetian Café.

'What are you laughing at?' Becky asked her, catching up with her on the bridge.

'Go away, squirt,' said Baby Dunville, walking a little faster.

Becky dawdled to put distance between them, because Baby, in that mood, was not to be trifled with.

Baby Dunville had a best friend. She was spoilt for choice, as most of the girls in her year tried to woo her, but Baby chose carefully. She needed someone with adequate affluence and a relatively similar background. She needed them to enjoy each other's company. And she needed the other person to have little or no supervision at home. She was good at assessing her requirements and identifying both the weaknesses and strengths in other people. This ability was not something she had thought about, it just seemed to be part of her general make-up. And so she looked around at her adoring classmates and Anne Marie O'Mahony fitted the bill.

Anne Marie O'Mahony lived less than a half mile away, on Raglan Road, and her father had a chauffeur. Her mother was a big spender, of both time and money. Mr and Mrs O'Mahony spent a lot of time out of the country, and Anne Marie's two older brothers had little interest in Anne Marie, although they were supposed to keep an eye on her while their parents were abroad.

Anne Marie did her own thing. Tall and dark, she contrasted well with Baby Dunville, and they did girly things together in their early teens as they went through puberty, and shared what information they had gleaned as to what was happening to their rapidly changing bodies. They made plans for 'boys', both how to meet them, and what to do with them.

Sprawled on Anne Marie's bedroom floor on sheepskin rugs in the last winter of flat chests and hairless bodies, both girls laughed as they tried to pick each other's brains.

'We'll get periods,' Anne Marie said helpfully.

'Periodically,' replied Baby Dunville.

'And we'll be hormonal and horrible,' said Anne Marie O'Mahony. 'Like Kate O'Brien,' she continued pensively.

'She was horrible anyway,' Baby Dunville added. 'But we won't smell. We'll use deodorant.'

'And talc and perfume.'

'And we'll take baths.'

'In asses' milk.'

'Like Marie Antoinette.'

'Did she? In asses' milk?'

'I don't know.'

'And we'll put slices of cucumber on our eyes. And we'll use Tampax.'

'I don't think Catholics are allowed to use Tampax.'

'Why ever not?'

'Someone in class said that that was the same as losing your virginity.'

With hysterical giggling, they rolled on to their backs.

'Then let's go and buy some straight away.'

They both developed late, constantly asking the other if there was any sign of the long-awaited period. And then finally, the summer after they turned fourteen, within two weeks of each other they began to menstruate.

'Great,' said Baby Dunville. 'That's that.'

They were lying on the grass in the O'Mahonys' back garden.

'Now what?'

'Well, now we're ready.'

'Ready for what?'

'Oh, come on, Anne Marie. Ready for the next stage. Ready for life. Ready for dances and parties and dates and things,' said Baby confidently. 'Coffee and drinks and things like that.'

'They'll never allow you to go to a dance, will they?' Anne Marie asked.

'Hah,' sneered Baby Dunville. 'But they'll allow me to come to stay with you. They always have done. And off we'll go.'

Anne Marie had not seen it quite as clearly as that, and could see a few problems to be overcome.

'But if my parents are here, I'm not sure they'll allow me.'

'Oh, don't be so thick. First of all, your parents are never here. And secondly, if they are, we'll just say that you're coming to me for the evening. That way everyone will be happy,' said Baby, who planned carefully and well.

'And,' continued Baby, 'we're too grown up for this nonsense. So enjoy it. It'll be our last.'

She was referring to the long glass filled with ice cream and lemonade which they were sucking with straws as they lay, sprawled in the heat of the afternoon.

Anne Marie sighed, but nodded agreement, and sucked her straw a little slower in order to lengthen the pleasure.

'And,' continued Baby, now on a roll, 'we mustn't waste any opportunities. This is a time for learning and notching up experiences. So, instead of sucking that straw, lick it and kiss it, and then you can suck.'

'What?' asked Anne Marie, perplexed.

'It's called something like fleshio. It's what you do to a boy.'

'What?' repeated Anne Marie, now utterly bewildered.

'Honestly. Trust me. I heard about it in school. I overheard two girls in the gardens. They were talking about it. Two sixth years. It's what you do to a boy's thingy.'

'You are joking?' said Anne Marie in amazement.

'No. I'm not. That's what they said.'

Anne Marie looked at her straw and giggled.

They were playing 'Can't Take My Eyes off You' at the end of the last set at their first dance. Baby, leaning against a boy, with their arms wrapped around each other, shuffled slowly from foot to foot. Over his shoulder she caught Anne Marie's eye, Anne Marie being locked in a similar embrace, and Baby winked. It had been a successful evening.

It had started at seven thirty with Baby's arrival at the O'Mahonys', complete with a small overnight bag, and a lot of make-up, which her mother did not know she possessed.

'Your brothers gone yet?' she asked Anne Marie as they bounded up the stairs in Raglan Road.

'No, not yet. They'll be off any minute,' was the reply.

With that, Anne Marie's two brothers appeared, aged twenty and twenty-one.

'You two going to be okay?' asked Brian, the older one.

'Yes, we'll be grand,' was the simultaneous response.

'Don't get up to mischief,' he said.

'What time will you be back, Brian?' Baby asked, all blue-eyed innocence.

'We're going to be late. It'll be one or two in the morning,' he answered. 'You sure you'll be all right?' he asked, taking in the two girls properly, and thinking how Baby had grown, in her tiny miniskirt and tight sweater.

'We'll be great, Brian,' she reassured him. 'An evening of listening to music is the plan.'

And indeed that was the plan. But not in the O'Mahonys' house.

The brothers left and the two girls gave them twenty minutes to clear the area before they set off.

They were just outside the gate when Adam, their father's chauffeur, who lived in the mews behind the house, arrived back.

He pulled up in front of the house.

'Where are you off to?' he asked.

'Oh, we're just going out for a bit,' said Anne Marie nonchalantly.

He looked doubtful. He knew the rules, lax and all as they were. He knew her parents were away and that the brothers were going out.

'Tell you what,' he said. 'I'll give you both a lift.'

Anne Marie was about to object, when Baby said, 'Brilliant. Thank you.'

And she told him where they were going.

'And how are you getting home?' he asked.

'We were going to walk.'

'Do your parents know you're heading out?' he enquired of the pair in the back of the car.

There was silence for a minute. The silence told all.

'Look, don't answer,' he said. 'What time is the dance over at, and I'll be there to pick you up. Just down the street, so as not to embarrass you.'

'And you won't tell?' Anne Marie asked.

'Tell who?' he replied. 'Tell them what?'

He winked at them in the mirror.

'This is the life,' Baby Dunville said to Anne Marie as they headed out of the dance and down the driveway to where Adam was waiting in his long black car. And home they went, in comfort and style.

'But what if he tells?' Anne Marie said.

'He won't,' replied Baby. 'He can't. He brought us. It's his fault.'

Anne Marie did not quite follow the logic of this, but it all worked perfectly, and they were back in the house in bed by the time the brothers returned home.

'What did you do last night?' John Dunville asked his daughter the following evening.

'Nothing much,' she said. 'Listened to music and chatted. It was really nice.'

'We'll go back next week,' Baby said to Anne Marie. 'I saw someone I liked the look of. He had a foreign accent. Did you notice him?'

Anne Marie nodded.

'Wouldn't it be easier,' she asked, 'if we just asked our parents if we could go? I know mine would let me.'

'But mine wouldn't,' Baby said. 'Trust me. They're so fussy about us. I'm sure about this one. You know what they're like. In their little idyllic world . . .'

Anne Marie did not answer. Parents were a mystery to her, as was the concept of parenting.

And so the weeks went by, as did the terms, and Adam was easily coerced into giving the girls a lift again and again, and in due course Baby Dunville met Hugo Mombay Humphries.

'That's a bit of a mouthful,' she said, a month later.

And she was not referring to his name.

Chapter Three

The morning after the girls had begun their Christmas holidays, Elizabeth Dunville lay in bed looking at the curtained window.

'Did the girls wake you when they got in last night?' she asked. 'I never heard a thing.'

There was silence from John for a minute as he thought about this.

'No,' he said. 'No ... oh,' as the implication of this dawned on him.

They both jumped out of bed.

'Get back in and lie a little longer,' he said. 'I'll go and check.'

Becky's door was closed. He opened it quickly, and saw Becky's head sideways on her pillow, with her dark straight hair curved around her sleeping face.

He was about to close the door, thinking that she must have woken him when she got in, and that he simply couldn't remember. The end of a long week, he thought. And I was tired.

Becky sat up in the bed, startled.

'Oh, hello, Dad,' she said.

She felt jumpy, nervous and uncertain.

'Did you wake me when you got in?' he asked.

'I'm sorry, I didn't.' She hesitated, then went on truthfully, 'It was so late that I didn't want to disturb you and Mum.' She did not add that she was so sick and shocked and frightened that she just had not thought about it.

'You're supposed to wake me,' he said. 'That's the deal. And Baby, she didn't either. I better check on her.'

He headed for the top floor and Baby's rather off-putting door, with its sign that said ENTER AND DIE. He opened it gently so as not to waken her, and found to his dismay that the bed was made, and there was no sign of his eldest daughter.

'Becky's in bed, but Baby's not back, Elizabeth,' he said, going back to their bedroom. 'Will you phone the O'Mahonys and check that she is there?'

Becky got out of bed and looked at herself in the mirror. She was very pale, with shadows around her eyes. She had slept badly, and she felt shaken. She wondered if Mr Robinson was still embedded in the wall on Lansdowne Road.

What'll I do? she thought. They'll say I shouldn't have left him in the car. Maybe he's dead.

Baby would just have thought 'dead drunk', but Becky did not.

The O'Mahonys were immediately phoned. A disgruntled brother answered the call, then, going to check, said the girls were asleep in Anne Marie's bedroom.

'They're out for the count,' he told Elizabeth Dunville. 'Shall I let them sleep on, or do you want Baby home at once?'

Elizabeth hesitated.

'Just one moment,' she said to him, 'I need to consult my husband.'

'Baby's asleep at Anne Marie's,' she told John. 'Should I get them to waken her and send her home?'

'Oh, let them sleep on,' John said. 'Just be sure she's home by midday.'

'If she's home by lunch,' Elizabeth said into the phone, 'that'll be fine.'

She almost added, 'Did they go to bed very late?' But she did not, as she just assumed that Baby was tired after the long term.

'The O'Mahonys are useless,' John said to Elizabeth when he brought her up tea in bed. 'I mean, Baby just went over for the evening. She said they were going to drop her home.'

Elizabeth nodded.

'Well, at least she's safe. And she needs a good lie-in. They all do, now that term is over.'

Becky, meanwhile, was washing and dressing and trying to work out what to do. She kept thinking there was going to be a knock on the hall door and that somehow she was going to have to explain what had happened the previous evening. In the kitchen she poured herself a cup of tea from the teapot, which had now gone cold.

Should I go and see if Mr Robinson is still in the car? she wondered.

Her hands were shaking slightly, and she poured the cold tea down the drain.

Her father came into the kitchen.

'Don't you ever not waken me again,' he admonished her.

'Sorry,' she said. 'I . . . it was so late . . . I just thought you and Mum . . . I'm sorry.'

'Not acceptable,' he replied.

'I know,' she said. 'I'm really sorry.'

She made fresh tea and brought it into the breakfast room, and they ate toast in silence.

Becky kept looking up, trying to judge his mood. She could not bear it when he was brusque with her.

'Were you pleased with my report?' she asked hopefully.

'Yes,' he replied, looking up briefly from the newspaper. 'But you were down one per cent in maths.'

'Oh.' She did not say anything for a bit. 'Does that mean I got ninety-nine per cent?' she asked, trying to work out what he meant.

He nodded. He returned to the paper, and she thought about how he always seemed so hard on her. She doubted if either of the other two had got her marks but she knew not to make comparisons.

'May I see my report?' she tried again.

'Yes. It's on my desk. I'll give it to you later. But why did you only get ninety-nine per cent?'

'I don't know,' she said miserably.

It felt like she could not get anything right.

All she could think was that if she did not usually get one hundred per cent then he might have been pleased with the ninety-nine per cent. It did not seem fair, and yet she did not know how to explain this to him.

At eleven thirty she could not take it any more, and she went to get her coat, having decided to go out and look at the Robinsons' car, and to see if Mr Robinson was still in it. At first her coat was nowhere to be found, and then she suddenly remembered throwing up in the downstairs bathroom. Beside the coat on the floor she saw the key.

One more thing I did wrong, she thought. Good thing no one noticed.

Picking it up, she replaced it under the flowerpot on her way through the porch. She was so distressed that she did not even notice the smell of the Christmas tree leaning against the wall, which would normally have cheered her.

Going up Lansdowne Road, she felt puzzled, as she could not spot the car. Then she saw the wall where the car had ended up, and it was with disbelief, and also a sense of relief, that she realised that the car was gone. There was navy blue paint on the wall, and the brickwork was scratched and scraped.

On up the road she went, and around on to Northumberland Road, and to her surprise there was the car, badly damaged admittedly, but parked outside the Robinsons' house.

Did he manage to drive it home? she wondered. He must have. Or did I imagine the whole thing?

She hesitated, unsure what to do. Then she noticed that one wheel was on the kerb. That ties in with the way he was driving, she thought. He must be all right. At least that's something.

She turned and retraced her steps. On the corner of Lansdowne Road, she spotted Baby, dressed in jeans, sweater and a jacket, hurrying around the corner. She hovered, waiting for Baby to see her. Baby, moving in an unfocused and slightly disjointed way, with as much speed as she could muster, all but bumped into her.

'Hello Baby,' Becky said.

Baby looked at her in surprise.

'You okay?' Becky asked.

'I feel sick,' Baby said, too queasy to be her usual blasé self.

'Are the parents livid that I didn't come home last night?' Baby asked, as an afterthought.

'I don't know,' Becky replied miserably, as they moved on down the road. 'They're livid with me, though, because I didn't waken them when I got in.'

'I fell asleep at Anne Marie's,' Baby said by way of explanation. 'Tired. Just fell asleep, and didn't wake up until this morning. What about you? 'Are you only coming home now too?'

'Oh, no. I got home late last night. Dad was annoyed.'

'They'll be okay about it,' Baby said.

Becky shrugged and said nothing.

'By the way, where are you coming from now?' Baby then asked with momentary interest in what Becky might have been doing.

'You wouldn't believe me if I told you,' Becky said.

'Well, what were you doing last night?' Baby enquired.

'Babysitting . . . for the Robinsons,' came the answer.

50

'That kangaroo Charlie and simpering Magda? And you're just coming back now?'

'No. I told you. I got in last night but I didn't waken the parents, and they're cross with me.'

Baby suddenly appeared more interested, as it looked as if the parental anger might well be pointing in a different direction.

'So where *have* you been just now?' she continued.

'The most stupid thing happened,' Becky said. 'Doesn't matter.'

They were approaching their home at this stage.

'Well, tell me,' said Baby encouragingly, with a sideways glance at her sister.

'Mr Robinson was driving me home, and he was drunk as anything, and he crashed his car back there,' Becky said. 'Into the wall. And the only way I could get out of it was to climb into the back of the car and get out the back door. And I left him there.'

It was all coming out in a rush now in the need to share at least part of the trauma she'd been through.

'And I was afraid that he might have died of the cold or something in the car, because I just came home and went to bed. So I went back to see if he was still in the car, but it's parked outside their house.'

Baby smiled.

'You just left him in the car?' she asked, with interest. 'How bad was the crash?'

'Not bad,' Becky replied. 'I mean, he was driving very slowly, but he was veering all over the road. I don't know how he got home. He was awfully drunk. Like when he and Mrs Robinson got home, they'd forgotten I was there, and they just went to bed. And I'd been asleep, and I heard someone and I thought it was a burglar, and I took the poker upstairs because I was afraid . . .' Her words came out in a rush.

'You what?' Baby said, with a rare moment of admiration for her sister. 'God, I'd have run out of the place screaming.'

'I wish I had,' Becky said. 'It was awful. He slobbered all over me in the car,' she added.

'The bastard,' Baby said lightly.

'And he didn't even pay me,' Becky added.

'For slobbering on you?'

'No. For babysitting. And now they probably won't remember,' she went on. 'And I needed the money for Christmas presents.'

They were at the hall door now.

'I'll get it for you,' Baby said. 'If you can help me with the parents.'

'Oh, that's easy enough,' Becky told her as she took the key from under the pot. 'Just say you fell asleep at Anne Marie's, woke some time after three, because that's when I got home. Say you ran all the way home and the key wasn't under the pot. You see, I was so upset that I forgot to replace it, and you didn't want to waken everyone, so you went back to Anne Marie's.'

Becky's logic always impressed.

'Brilliant,' Baby said with real admiration. 'But will they believe that I did all that running?'

Becky thought about Baby's addiction to comfort and agreed that it was unlikely they would swallow the idea that she had walked from Raglan Road, let alone run.

'No,' said Baby. 'I'll say that their chauffeur brought me home and then took me back to the O'Mahonys', and I'll get Anne Marie to tell him in case I need a back-up story.'

'Will you really get the money for me?' Becky asked hopefully.

So in they went, Baby and Becky Dunville, in a rare moment of mutual agreement.

Becky was relieved to have told someone about what had happened, and added to that, Baby had said that she would get the money for her.

Baby, who had had the sensation that she might die as she came back from Anne Marie's, now had the feeling that the pressure was somewhat off her. She was grateful that Becky had not only given her a solution to her problem with her parents, but had also confided that she had had a pretty dreadful evening. For some reason this comforted Baby. She was unsure, and in fact didn't care, whether the comforting feeling came from the fact that Becky, who was normally so tight-lipped, had confided in her. Or if it was because of the fact that Becky was in trouble with the parents, which probably meant that she, Baby, would get off easier.

Because that was usually the case and she knew it.

Baby got away with murder, Brona got away with blue murder, and Becky got away with nothing. When Anne Marie had once commented on this to Baby, she had replied with a small smile, 'That's family for you.'

On different levels the three sisters were aware of this, and knew how to use it. Brona would howl, 'It isn't fair, just because I'm the youngest ...' and Elizabeth would say, 'Of course it isn't fair. Now let's find a way around it.'

Becky, when she was younger, used to try the same tack, 'It isn't fair, Dad,' to which the usual response was a rather short 'Life isn't fair, Becky. And the sooner you get used to that the better.' Baby was above the line 'It isn't fair.' She manipulated everything to suit herself so that it was fair for her if not for the others. The only place where she knew there was a problem was in straightforward disobedience, and so she always covered her tracks. But on this occasion she was worried, as she did not want her plans for the Christmas holidays thwarted by one evening having gone wrong.

'You're very pale, Baby,' her parents said simultaneously.

No wonder, thought Baby, with her limpid blue eyes, and her green face.

'I'm so sorry you were worried,' Baby said, wondering how quickly she could get through this and up to her room.

'Why didn't you come home?' they asked as one.

'Oh, Daddy, Mummy,' said Baby, tears almost coming to her eyes as she told them about falling asleep, and waking late.

'It was after three,' she said, 'and home I came of course. Adam drove me. You know, their chauffeur. But the key wasn't there. And I couldn't ... I wouldn't ... you know ... wake you. It was after three. So I went back. Adam ... their chauffeur ... had waited to see that I got in safely, thank goodness. Or I'd have died of the cold in the porch. And now, I'm so tired. I can't tell you how tired ...'

'My fault,' Becky interjected. 'I forgot to put the key back when I got in. I'm sorry.'

Baby had the grace to blush red over her green pallor as both parents turned as one, and took strips off the unfortunate Becky.

'How dare you,' they shouted.

'I'm sorry. I'm sorry,' wailed the distraught Becky, who suddenly felt she couldn't take any more. 'I'm so sorry. I didn't think.'

'You never do think,' they cried unfairly.

But I do think, Becky thought as she lay on her bed. I do. I always consider them. I hate them all. And I hate the Robinsons. I hate his big fat paunch and his leery, drooling mouth. And I hate his stupid wife. What kind of a way is that to behave when you have little ones in their beds, and they don't even remember they have a babysitter? And I hate that disgusting milkman with his bottle of milk, and his lewd suggestions. And I wish I belonged somewhere else. I wish . . .

Her thoughts trailed off. She wondered if Baby and Brona ever felt like this – really badly done by. She felt hurt by her family, hurt by their horrible friends for whom she had babysat, and on top of that, rejected despite her excellent report.

I do my best, she thought.

Down in Rhona Brophy's house in Sandymount, Brona and Rhona were sitting on the floor in Rhona's room. They were dressed in bell bottoms and tight knitted sweaters. Both girls had their long brown hair tied back. Rhona's bedroom was small, smaller than Brona's, but it was warm, with an electric fire plugged in, and a thick wall-to-wall carpet.

'Where did you get them?' Rhona asked, looking at the packet in her friend's hand.

'Dad brought them back from Holland or Germany or somewhere. He was over on the Continent giving a lecture,' said Brona, opening the first packet.

'They're very pretty,' Rhona said. 'What on earth are you going to do with them?'

Brona shook the packet of foil-wrapped chocolates out on to the floor.

'This is going to take a great deal of skill,' she informed Rhona. 'When we've finished, no one must know what we've done.'

'I don't get it,' Rhona said.

'Look,' said Brona. 'It's quite simple. We're going to eat the chocolate, and replace it with this.'

From her shoulder bag she took out a small box of nougat.

'You see, no one in our house likes nougat. This has been sitting at the back of a cupboard for simply ages. What we're going to do is cut the nougat into the right shapes – bells, Santas, whatever – and then refill the wrappers.'

'Wow,' Rhona said in amazement. 'Er . . . won't anyone notice?'

'They'll never guess,' Brona replied, confidently. 'As long as we do it carefully. We just have to make sure that we don't tear the foil, and that we put the little gold threads back in securely so that they can be hung on the tree this afternoon.'

'So that's why you wanted me to have a sharp knife and a board,' Rhona said, producing the aforementioned from under her bed.

'Dexterity is what's required,' said Brona with a laugh. 'That's the word, isn't it?'

'I've no idea,' said Rhona. 'I never heard of it.'

The two girls got started. They each carefully opened a foil-wrapped chocolate.

'Don't eat it yet,' Brona said, as Rhona was about to pop one into her mouth. 'Not until we're sure we can refill them properly.'

With the knife she carved a piece of nougat to roughly the same shape as the chocolate she had removed, then wrapped the nougat up in the foil.

'See?' she said, delighted with herself. 'Isn't that brilliant?'

'It certainly is,' said Rhona with admiration. 'How many chocolates are there?'

'Three packs of twelve,' grinned Brona. 'And loads of nougat to replace them with.'

Both girls got busy.

'Pity we can't do carpentry at St Martin's, Bro,' Rhona said. 'We'd be brilliant at it, wouldn't we?'

'We'd get full marks,' Brona replied, concentrating on the job in hand.

Meanwhile, Baby slept soundly in her bed, her ironed blonde hair lying limply on the pillow, her smooth clear skin losing its greenish pallor. Becky, too, dozed fitfully, trying to make up for the lost sleep from the previous night.

Will Baby really get me the money? she wondered as she tossed from one side to the other. She also wondered what state the Robinson parents were in.

I'm never babysitting for them again, she thought. Though they probably won't ask me anyway.

She glanced at the clock on her bedside table.

I've three hours until we put the tree up, she thought. I must sleep.

Becky counted slowly backwards from one hundred, but sleep did not come. It was as if she slipped in and out of semi-consciousness, where waking and sleeping images mingled, and she was unsure which state she was in.

In this dream Mr Robinson appeared on a milk float, and she, Becky, became the woman in the film, except she was no buxom blonde with breasts bulging from her bodice. Instead she was just Becky Dunville with her small pale face and her dark hair, and her slim, small-breasted figure, and Mr Robinson looked more like Simon Carter, the younger of the two gardeners at St Martin's. Like Simon he had red hair, but he had Mr Robinson's height and Australian accent.

'I fancy some milk,' he said to Becky as she stood in the Robinsons' kitchen.

He undid the laces on this garment which she was wearing, the like of which she had not seen before. Her breasts appeared as the laces came apart, and she looked down to see her nipples like small snouts, waking from their sleep, and standing to attention. She looked up at Mr Robinson, who, fortunately, because it enhanced the quality of the dream, now looked even more like Simon Carter. Mr Robinson/Simon Carter had already flicked the foil cap on the bottle towards the sink, and holding the bottle in one hand, he dipped the forefinger of the other hand into the creamy topping on the milk and ran it across Becky's now open lips.

She felt her tongue stretch out to touch his finger, but he shook his head, and then she woke again.

Her body was aroused, and she tried to bring herself back into the dream at the same point, conjuring up the silence in the kitchen, the intensity of Simon Carter's gaze as he looked into her eyes, the slow dripping of a tap, the black laces hanging open exposing secret parts of her, as yet unseen and untouched by another. He brought his finger back to the top of the bottle, and again he dipped it in. They both watched the cream drip back down his finger, before he reached out towards her left nipple.

'Becky, Becky.' Her mother's voice jolted her back to consciousness. 'It's three o'clock. Are you coming?'

Becky looked at her clock in amazement. Somehow it really was three o'clock. She could hardly believe that three hours had passed while she slipped in and out of sleep and such an exciting dream.

'Mumsy, Mumsy,' said Brona. 'Anything I can do to help?'

Brona was feeling a little uneasy as the boxes of Christmas decorations were brought down, and opened on the drawing-room floor. Elizabeth Dunville was sitting in front of the fire with a gin and tonic in hand and a relaxed look on her face.

'Don't ask me, Brona,' she said. 'This is something I just leave you all to do and I sit and watch you.'

'Oh, I was thinking about tomorrow,' said Brona chirpily, hoping to distract everyone, as the moment of truth was nearly at hand. She had brought back the foil-wrapped nougat and replaced it in the cupboard. The packaging was of course now unsealed and she was poised to race out and get them when the time came so that she could pretend to open them on her way back in. 'I meant your party and if anything needed doing.'

'Plenty needs doing,' her mother smiled. 'But they're mostly last-minute things – things to do tomorrow, like pricking the sausages and cutting the cheese and pineapple and the other bits to go on the cocktail sticks.'

'Oh good,' said Brona. 'I want to do that.'

'What's got into you?' Baby and Becky asked as one, and Brona realised that she had overdone the enthusiasm and helpfulness.

'I'm growing up,' she said, correctly divining that this would make her two older sisters laugh.

Baby and Becky glanced at each other and then started to chuckle.

Normally at this point Brona would have turned to her parents and moaned that they were ganging up on her. But on this occasion she had manipulated the scene to exactly where she wanted it to go, and to Baby and Becky's surprise she did not start her usual 'woe is me' speech.

'Where are the choccies you brought back with you, Daddy?' asked Baby. Her face was still pale, but the greenish tinge was gone and there was no trace of the almighty hangover she'd been carrying earlier. Two painkillers and a large glass of orange juice, together with three hours' sleep and a shower, had bounced Baby Dunville back almost to her former glory.

'I'll get them,' Brona said, and shot out the door.

She brought them back in a bowl.

'I threw out the packaging,' she said helpfully, by way of explanation. 'They're awfully pretty, don't you think?'

'I can't wait to have one,' Baby said.

'But we won't be having them until after Christmas,' Brona insisted. 'I mean, they're part of the decorations. We won't be eating the other decorations, so we can't be eating these.'

'The whole point of them is that they are edible, silly,' Baby responded.

The tree had taken shape, the lights were on, baubles were dangling, tinsel woven in among the branches, and the girls hung the final decorations on it – thirty-six foil-wrapped chocolates.

They admired their handiwork – none more so than Brona, who had quite literally hand-carved those last decorations, out of hardened elderly nougat.

It was a happy scene. The tree stood in front of the bay window with the curtains open, the fairy lights catching the silver and gold in the decorations. The girls seemed united in their pleasure at the magic in front of them (although one was a little nervous), and their parents sat back in their armchairs and surveyed the situation with contentment.

'I love these days coming up to Christmas,' Becky said. 'That smell of fir, and the warmth in here, and when you go out it is bitingly cold, but you know that you can come back in.'

'And what do you like, Baby?' John Dunville asked his eldest daughter.

Baby looked at the tree and smiled.

'I just love being here with you and Mummy,' she said, smiling lovingly at him.

'And how about you, Brona?' he asked his youngest.

'Brona's thinking about all the presents she'll get,' Baby said helpfully.

'Speak for yourself,' Brona snapped. 'I wasn't thinking about the presents or about the chocolate decorations, or anything like that.'

Becky giggled.

'No one suggested you were thinking about chocolate, Brona. *You* said it. That means that you were thinking about greedy things,' she said.

'Was not,' said Brona.

'Were too,' said Becky.

'I was not,' Brona said. 'Tell her, Daddy, will you?'

'Becky, stop sniggering,' their father said. 'And leave Brona alone. This is such a peaceful scene, I don't know why you have to spoil it.'

They had dinner in the dining room, which was a ceremonial occasion at the weekends, a throw-back to an Edwardian era, with an air of formality which both parents enjoyed. This night, as on many others, each of the girls had invited a friend over, and each was dressed up.

'I hate the way we have to dress up for dinner at the weekends,'

Becky said in her room to Gabriela. Unlike the others Becky did not have a close friend, although not for lack of trying. Her inability to closely connect with her peers embarrassed her, but she did sometimes manage to find someone to invite. This time it was, as usual, someone she had not invited before, and Becky knew that they had little if anything in common.

'Is fein,' said Gabriela, a fifteen-year-old German girl who was new to the school and who had not, as yet, found her feet. 'In mein country ve too dress for dinner.'

Becky, who had no problem about dressing for dinner in reality, had only made the comment because she was embarrassed about telling someone else that jeans would not do in the Dunville dining room.

'Is mein hair in ordnung?' asked Gabriela, peering into Becky's dressing-table mirror.

'Is fine,' said Becky, and then noticed that she had dropped her pronoun. Possibly in sympathy, she thought to herself.

Gabriela had two hefty blonde plaits, which she had wound around her head. The very thickness of them gave her a healthy look.

'Gabriela should be in a dirndl,' said Baby to Anne Marie, who, lying beside Baby on her bed, snickered in agreement.

'Straight out of *The Sound of Music*.'

'Did you recover all right?' Baby asked. 'From last night, I mean.'

'I slept it off,' replied Anne Marie. 'Thanks be to God and all that is holy,' she added, with a grin.

'More like thanks be to vitamin C and painkillers,' Baby responded.

Anne Marie laughed again. 'Nice guys, weren't they?' she said.

'Can you even remember their names?' Baby asked. 'Because I can't.'

'Yours was Jasper, I think. And mine was Richard, I think. No, Jasper I'm sure of,' Anne Marie replied. 'But surnames? No, I've no idea.'

Both girls were dressed in miniskirts, polo necks, and tights. Their boots were on the floor beside the bed.

'Did you tell Adam?' Baby asked. 'About him bringing me home in the middle of the night?'

Anne Marie nodded.

'What did he say?'

'Oh, just something about how he can hardly keep up with us girls, and next time to phone him. If he is there he will bring you home . . . something like that.'

'But does he know that he has to cover for me if anyone asks?' Baby persisted.

'Yes, he does. There's no problem there.' Anne Marie wetted a finger and ran it over her dark eyebrows.

Once upon a time Baby used to lust for Anne Marie's eyebrows. Now she just dyed hers, and instead Anne Marie lusted after Baby's thick dark lashes, which were also dyed.

In Brona's room, Rhona was lying on the carpet and Brona was on the bed, hanging over the side looking at her.

'Well,' said Rhona. 'Did you get away with it?'

'Yep,' said Brona. 'No bother. Nobody noticed a thing. We did a brilliant job, didn't we?'

'Sure did,' replied Rhona.

'Hey, Rho,' said Brona, eyeing her pal on the floor. 'Did you bring something to wear for dinner, 'cos you need to get changed now.'

'I forgot,' came the reply. 'I really did. You better lend me something.' Rhona was used to Saturday nights at the Dunvilles', and the rules of decorum.

'Take your pick,' said Brona, nodding towards her wardrobe. 'When I grow up, people can come to my dining table with nothing on them if they want. But you know what my parents are like. I'm sorry.'

'I think it's funny,' Rhona said, as she looked into Brona's wardrobe. 'God, it's a right mess in here. What happened?'

'That's the way I keep it. I like it like that. There's a system but it isn't clear to everyone.'

Rhona was still standing looking in amazement inside Brona's wardrobe.

'But everything is in a heap,' she said. 'How would I know where to find anything at all?'

'Oh, just haul it all out and choose what you want,' said Brona, rolling on to her back on the bed. 'You're beginning to sound like my mother.'

'I actually feel more like The Brush with Death,' replied Rhona, as she gazed in despair into the offending cupboard. 'Remember that day she looked in your desk and asked if she should call a priest for exorcism?'

Brona laughed.

'And I said, "Yes, Mother"!'

'And she sent you to her office.'

'That was so unfair,' Brona said. 'Irony doesn't work when nuns try it. I thought she meant it, about the exorcism, and I thought it would be interesting.'

Rhona laughed, even though she didn't know the word *irony*.

In Becky's room, Becky was looking doubtfully at the full-figured Gabriela, who was squished into a skirt of Becky's which would not zip on her.

'Hold on, Gabriela,' Becky said nervously, as she did not want her skirt to burst. 'I'll brave Baby on high and see if she has something to fit you.'

She scooted upstairs and looked uneasily at Baby's door, on which was pinned a sign which said ENTER AND DIE. She licked her lips and then knocked on Baby's door.

'Go 'way,' Baby called.

'Baby, please,' Becky said. 'Emergency.'

'What is it?' Baby asked.

Becky entered.

Baby and Anne Marie looked up from where they were lying on Baby's bed. Both stared at her with blank faces.

'Baby, please. Gabriela doesn't fit into my clothes. I need to borrow something. Please . . . otherwise it'll be awful . . . you know how Daddy will go, and it'll be so embarrassing.'

Baby and Anne Marie laughed.

'No dirndl here,' Anne Marie said.

'Dirndl?' Becky was momentarily puzzled. 'Oh, I see.' She grinned.

'Hey,' Baby said, looking at the goatskin rug on the floor by her bed. 'Borrow that for her.'

Anne Marie started to sing. '. . . the lonely goatherd . . .'

Becky laughed.

'Very funny, both of you, but please, I need help. Come on, Baby, I helped you earlier.'

'So you did,' replied Baby, acknowledging the fact that Becky had saved her. 'All right, she can have my checked skirt, but if she does anything to it, she'll pay.'

'In Deutschmarks,' Anne Marie added helpfully.

Becky slid Baby's wardrobe doors open, noticing the neatness with which everything was arranged.

'Could I borrow a polo neck or something to go with it?' Becky asked, as she unclipped the checked skirt from its hanger. 'She's wearing an orange thing on top and it won't go with the red and white checks in the skirt, and . . .'

'No,' said Baby. 'I'm lending you the skirt. Take it and go, and if you don't want it, then just leave it.'

Becky mumbled thanks and took the skirt and went.

Dinner was a formal affair. The gong was sounded and the girls appeared from their rooms on various floors.

'Boring,' Brona murmured to Rhona on the staircase.

'Look at it this way, Bro,' said Rhona. 'If you were boarding, you'd be sitting down to dinner now with The Brush with Death peering at you down the refectory, and a bowl of either under-boiled or over-boiled potatoes and cabbage. And there'd be silence while you chomped your piece of leathery liver. And then you'd be listening to some nunnyperson reading from the Lives of the Saints or the Gospels or something.'

John and Elizabeth had finished their sherries and came in to join the girls in the dining room.

'Had a good afternoon, girls?' asked John Dunville to the series of faces in front of him. 'And you must be Gabriela,' he addressed the German girl. 'So glad you could join us. You know I know your father from work?'

Gabriela shook hands with both of the Dunville parents.

'Mein vater he say haylow,' ventured Gabriela. 'He see you wit his mother tomorrow.'

'His mother?' said Baby in surprise.

'No, darling,' Elizabeth said quickly, as Gabriela's English had clearly a long way to go.

'Mit meiner Mutter, I mean,' said Gabriela, blushing.

Becky glared at Baby, as it was obvious that Baby was just trying to disconcert Gabriela.

Brona and Rhona glanced at each other with ill-concealed amusement.

'Much better than the Lives of the Saints,' Brona admitted to Rhona in a whispered aside as they stood behind their chairs for Grace.

'Baby, please lead us,' her father said.

Baby dropped her golden head and intoned, '*Bless us O Lord, and these thy gifts, which of thy bounty we are about to receive, through Christ our Lord, Amen.*'

Elizabeth and the girls blessed themselves, and then sat.

Chapter Four

Dinner was drawing to a close, and the girls were finishing their lemon meringue pie, when Mrs O'Doody, who worked every morning in the Dunville household and did dinner at the weekends as well as Sunday morning breakfast, came into the room.

'Coffee?' she asked.

'Yes please, Mrs O'Doody, for John and myself,' Elizabeth said. Both Baby and Anne Marie said they would have coffee too.

'For four then?' asked Mrs O'Doody, looking at the other girls.

'For you, Gabriela?' asked Elizabeth of the German girl.

'Oh, no,' said Gabriela. 'We do not have coffee at night time. It . . . how do you say? . . . speeds up de heartbeat and makes for difficult sleep, and in de stomach it—'

'Just for four, thank you, Mrs O'Doody,' said Elizabeth quickly, before further details could be shared.

Becky went and got the demitasses from the sideboard and placed them on the table, while Mrs O'Doody returned with cream and sugar and the coffee pot.

'We'll pour, thank you, Mrs O'Doody,' Elizabeth said to her. 'Do go home as soon as you're finished in the kitchen.'

Baby was about to bring her cup up to her mouth when she suddenly said, 'Oh, wouldn't it be nice to have a chocolate with this?'

'There might be some mint chocolates in the drawer,' Elizabeth replied, looking towards the sideboard.

'Could we each take one of the chocolate decorations from the tree?' asked Baby hopefully, flashing her white-toothed smile from parent to parent.

'That's a nice idea,' John said.

Brona and Rhona had stiffened slightly.

'Oh yummy,' said Brona as soon as she realised there was no way she was going to be able to redirect the course of history on this particular day.

'Go in and choose which ones you want,' Elizabeth said. 'And bring your father one too. But not for me though.'

So the girls trooped into the darkened drawing room and over to the lit-up tree, and one by one they each lifted a foil-wrapped decoration from the branches.

Rhona nudged Brona and gave her a worried look. Brona's response was just to glare at her and shake her head.

Back at the table the sweets were unwrapped.

'Oh, mine looks like nougat,' said Baby in disappointment.

'Mine too,' said Becky.

'Mine *is* nougat,' Anne Marie said. 'What's wrong with that?'

'I thought I'd bought chocolate,' John said in surprise. 'I mean, I'd never have bought nougat, knowing you girls don't like it.'

'They *were* chocolate,' Baby said. 'I remember looking at the packets the day you brought them home, Daddy. I'm sure of it.'

Becky was directed to go and check in the bin in the kitchen where Brona had dumped the wrapping earlier.

'Yes, see,' Becky said, holding one of the empty packets. 'It says "Schokolade".'

'That must mean nougat in German,' suggested Brona hopefully.

'No,' said Gabriela, their German guest. 'Is chocolate – always.'

'My nougat looks like it's been hacked into this shape,' Baby said, shrugging her shoulders.

'Very odd,' it was agreed.

The mystery was left unsolved and the younger girls evaporated towards their rooms with their friends in tow, leaving Baby and Anne Marie to sip their coffee with John and Elizabeth.

'That was very odd about the decorations, wasn't it?' John Dunville said to Elizabeth, lying in bed on the Sunday morning.

She nodded in agreement, her mind playing over again the strange scene after dinner the previous evening.

'I suppose they were just mispackaged,' she said. 'These things happen, don't they?'

'They do,' he replied. 'It's just not very German though, is it?'

In her bedroom, Brona woke with a slight feeling of unease. It took her a few minutes to recall what it was that had disturbed her usual early morning equanimity.

Then back it came with a rush. Gabriela had kept going on about it as the four of them went upstairs. 'Ve do not make mistakes like that in my country,' she said.

'Oh, it doesn't matter,' Brona had replied. 'Who cares?'

Becky glanced at her and said nothing.

'But ve do not,' said Gabriela, clearly disturbed by the event.

'Do not care?' asked Rhona.

'No, she means do not make mistakes like that,' Becky said. 'She's probably right too,' she added, looking at Brona, who started to feel very uncomfortable.

Now, lying in bed thinking about going to Mass with the others, Brona felt a pang of guilt. The chocolate had tasted so nice earlier on the Saturday, but she wondered whether it compensated for the nervousness she had felt when Baby had made the comment about the nougat being hacked, and the way Becky had looked at her on the staircase. She felt that Becky knew, but for some reason had decided to say nothing.

That morning, the Sunday before Christmas 1970, the Dunvilles went to Mass as usual in the sister chapel of St Martin's in the Fields. The three girls filed up to receive Communion.

'Not coming, Mum?' Becky asked Elizabeth, as she was about to leave the seat.

'Not this morning, darling,' her mother replied. She looked tired, as if she had not slept, and she shook her head a little as if the whole scene had nothing to do with her, more as if she were a disinterested witness, rather than a participant.

Becky knew that her mother often slept badly, and sometimes complained of nightmares, and she wondered if that was what was wrong. It was seldom that Elizabeth did not join them for Communion.

As Becky moved slowly up the aisle to the altar rails, the pictures in the Stations of the Cross along the walls caught her eye.

Morning and evening in this valley of tears, she thought. *Or is it mourning and weeping in this valley of tears? How odd, I can't remember. Consider the lilies of the fields, they sow not, neither do they weep.*

She herself was not feeling well. She had the sensation of being light-headed and slightly sick. As she walked up the aisle, the feelings increased, and as her conscious self became aware of the sensations and what she feared might happen, she struggled to find something to grasp on to in her mind. Words and phrases were what interested her most and it was these that she sought for, but as she walked with her mind going hither and thither, trying to hold on to quotes which at that moment seemed meaningless, she knew what was going to happen. She knew she was losing the struggle and she clenched her hands to try to feel something.

Brona too looked up in the slow procession and she saw the Station of the Cross which depicted Veronica approaching Jesus. It made her feel thirsty, and she wondered if Mrs O'Doody would have squeezed oranges for breakfast when they got home.

Baby, leading the way, glanced at Becky as they moved along the altar rails to kneel, and saw the pallor on her face.

Becky's hands grasped at the carved wooden rails which separated the faithful from the priest and his altar boys.

Just hang on, Becky thought to herself. He's nearly here. God, don't do this to me. Please don't do this. She felt Baby touch her arm. She saw the light shine through the stained-glass window, and the depth of red in the glass heart of the saint. Get me through this, she prayed silently.

In front of her the priest paused, the wafer between his fingers. '*Dominus vobiscum*,' she heard.

She closed her eyes, and opened her mouth, sticking out her tongue. Like in the dream, she thought. Searching for the milk on his finger. Oh God, forgive me for these thoughts.

The wafer rested on her tongue. She tried to open her eyes. It was as if her limbs had turned to water and had no substance. She could feel Baby trying to force her to her feet, and the whispered words roared in her head.

And then there was darkness.

Please, Dad, Becky thought a while later. Please, you're a doctor, can't you be kinder to me? I didn't mean to faint. I didn't do it on purpose.

She could hear her parents on the landing outside her door having one of their rare arguments.

'She has low blood sugar levels,' her father said. 'She needs to have food before she goes to church. This is at least the sixth time this has happened. And how do you think it makes me appear? Fine doctor I look, when my daughter faints regularly in church.'

'Hush, dear,' Elizabeth said gently to him.

'I won't hush,' he replied. 'I'm fed up with this. I don't know why she has this problem. Nobody else in this family has.'

'What are you implying?' Elizabeth said.

There was silence on the landing.

Becky listened. She could hear her heart pounding.

'Nothing,' he replied. 'Absolutely nothing.'

'That I'm a bad mother?'

'I'm not trying to imply that you're a bad mother.'

'How come I can hear a "but" coming?'

'You, as her mother, have got to relent on this one. If she is going to church, which I might point out is at your insistence, then she has to eat before she goes.'

'Well she can't,' Elizabeth replied.

'It's years since you asked that priest if she could eat before Communion. And he was a doddery old fellow. For goodness' sake, Elizabeth, these religious laws change. For her to fast from midnight is just . . . I don't know, nonsensical. It's cruel . . .'

Becky closed her eyes tight, and burrowed down under the covers. She wanted them to stop arguing over her. There was something very lacking in reassurance in what she was hearing. She felt hot tears prick her eyelids and trickle down her cheeks.

Don't let me cry, she thought. And don't let them come back in here. He'll get even more annoyed if he sees me in tears.

Downstairs, Mrs O'Doody was serving up bacon and eggs, sausages, tomatoes, mushrooms and fried bread.

'Yummy,' said Brona. 'My favourite day of the week. And the party this afternoon. Mrs O'D., I'm helping with the cocktail things, is that all right?'

'Yes, Brona,' said Mrs O'Doody with a smile. 'Now, I also have potato cakes to go with your breakfast. Would you like some?'

Squeaks of delight out of Brona reassured Mrs O'Doody that potato cakes would go down a treat.

The party started promptly with the arrival of the von Veckers. Herr Doktor, Frau Doktor, Friedrich, their eighteen-year-old son, and Gabriela arrived on the dot of three.

'They've got to be kidding,' whispered Brona to Becky. 'Imagine if Mum went around calling herself Mrs Doctor just because Dad's a doctor.'

Becky giggled.

'Mum's not pretentious, and it's not in our culture,' she replied.

'Hey, it's the lonely goatherd,' whispered Baby to Anne Marie at the sight of Friedrich, as the guests came into the drawing room and further introductions were made.

'We are punctual, no?' asked Doktor von Vecker of his colleague John Dunville.

'Indeed you are,' John replied.

Doktor von Vecker bowed his head politely as he met the family, then Friedrich made a beeline for Baby, who stood by the tree with an enigmatic smile on her face.

The room filled with chatter and laughter. Fur coats hung in the hall. The girls circulated with trays of food. The buzz in the room increased.

'Like some more champagne, Mr Robinson?' said Baby to the Australian attaché.

'Yes, yes,' he said, eyeing the ravishing eldest Dunville daughter, who topped up his glass.

'Here's to you, Mr Robinson,' she said to him, raising the bottle slightly.

'And to *you*,' he replied.

'Recovered from the bash in your car?' asked Baby, looking him straight in the eye.

'What's that?' he asked, straining to hear in the crowded room.

'Oh, there's Mrs Robinson,' Baby said, looking over towards the door, where her mother was chatting to Magda Robinson.

'While the cat's away,' he chuckled to Baby.

'The mouse can pay,' Baby replied.

'Play,' said Mr Robinson.

'No, I said "pay",' Baby repeated. 'You forgot to pay my sister Becky for babysitting.'

'Did I?' He seemed surprised. 'Crikey ... er ... will you give it to her?'

He reached into his pocket and pulled out a wad of notes. Peeling off a one-pound note, he handed it to Baby.

'That doesn't cover a kiss,' Baby said, looking at the note.

'Oh, do I get a kiss?' Mr Robinson smiled at her, looking at her very pink lips.

'I meant the kiss you gave Becky,' Baby said. Her mouth seemed to smile at him, but her eyes did not.

'Oh,' he said. 'Er ... that ...'

'Or does Mrs Robinson think that that's part of the job?' Baby asked. 'I must ask her.'

Mr Robinson surreptitiously peeled off two five-pound notes and handed them to Baby.

'I'm sure that will cover everything,' he said hurriedly, and turned away.

'Yes,' said Baby, looking at the money in her hand. 'I think it will.'

'Good thing my parents don't know your parents. The last thing we want is them all getting together,' Anne Marie said to Baby as they sipped champagne behind the folding doors between the two rooms.

'I know,' Baby replied. 'I was really afraid last night that Daddy was going to say to you to ask them along today. After Gabriela saying her parents were coming, Daddy was embarrassed, and I was sure he was going to say something.'

'But they know each other from the hospital, don't they, the von Veckers and your father, I mean?' Anne Marie asked.

'Oh, I know they do. That's why they've been invited. Though Daddy says it's a hoot the way they still talk in the German equivalent of *vous* to each other.'

'Doktor von Vecker looks like he has a poker up his arse,' Anne Marie said.

'My father is what?' asked Friedrich von Vecker as he put his head around the folding door and looked at the two girls, who both started to laugh.

'The Fitzgeralds have arrived,' said John Dunville to his wife, heading for the hall.

Becky was in the hall, hugging her Uncle James and Aunty Nancy.

'Hi, Eleanor,' she said to her cousin.

'Hello, Becks,' Eleanor replied.

Eleanor was a year younger than Becky, but a year ahead of her at school, thanks to the combined efforts of Aunty Nancy and Mother Immaculata.

The two girls looked at each other with a sense of something indefinable. Once, when much younger, they had stood in front of a mirror together and examined each other's faces and then each other's bodies. Their similarities were pronounced. Both were small and slight, with fine bones, tiny wrists and ankles, small feet, shy smiles, dark hair around their tiny sallow-skinned faces, although Eleanor alone was prone to freckles.

'You're a Fitzgerald,' Eleanor had pronounced. 'You've got all the Fitzgerald characteristics – just like me.'

'But Baby and Brona – how come I don't look like them?'

'Because they carry the Dunville genes – probably to excess,' replied Eleanor.

'But why are my eyes brown?' Becky persisted. 'No one's eyes are brown in my family – or in yours come to that.'

'I'm not sure about that,' Eleanor replied. 'Must be a throwback of sorts.'

Now, in the Dunville hall, some four years later, the two girls looked at each other and smiled. Their liking was mutual, but it was tempered by the pushiness of Eleanor's mother.

'And how are you, Rebecca?' asked her Aunty Nancy. 'What class are you in now, dear?'

Behind her mother's back, Eleanor grimaced and raised her eyes to heaven.

Becky smiled politely.

'I'm still a year behind Eleanor in school, Aunty,' she said.

'But she's a year younger than you.' Aunty Nancy feigned surprise.

'Now, now, Nancy,' John Dunville intervened. 'You know my policy on a full education. I don't want my girls skipping years. I had them start late so they would have more home nurturing. And I will have them finish late, so they will be more mature.'

He gave Eleanor a hug, and then kissed Nancy.

'Jeepers,' Eleanor said to Becky as they headed for the dining room. 'I'm sorry. She just can't resist it, you know.'

Becky laughed.

'I know.'

'Families,' Eleanor said. 'Who'd have them?'

'Given the choice, not me. At least you're an only child,' Becky replied. 'Can you imagine having Baby and Brona as sisters?' she continued.

'Well, I have them as cousins,' Eleanor said.

'Scary, huh?' said Becky.

'To be fair, Baby leaves me alone. In school she ignores me – so that's okay. And Brona just sticks her tongue out at me when she sees me.'

70

'Brona's problem is that you are held up as a paragon of virtue and industry,' Becky laughed. 'I think it gets her down sometimes.'

What Brona actually said was, 'Every time I see my cousin Eleanor in school, I want to puke,' but Becky decided not to repeat that.

'Do you want me to help with passing food around?' Eleanor asked hopefully. 'I hate just standing.'

Father Monaghan from St Martin's sister chapel arrived.

'Jeepers,' said Eleanor Fitzgerald to her cousin Becky. 'Look who's here.'

'I know,' Becky replied. 'Mummy insisted. So Dad then insisted that he invite the minister from *his* church.'

'Do you go to his church?' Eleanor asked in surprise.

'Yes, we do. Every so often. Mother Immaculata says it's wrong,' Becky whispered. 'She says it's the road to damnation! But Daddy says it's a matter of balance. And he always comes with us to Mass. And then now and again he brings us to his church, but of course Mummy won't come. Bone of contention.'

'I can imagine,' Eleanor said.

The girls separated with their trays of food. The door into the hall was slightly ajar, and as Becky passed it she heard her aunt's voice.

'Elizabeth,' said Nancy Fitzgerald, 'you'll never guess who we bumped into earlier.'

'Who?' asked Elizabeth, gin and tonic in hand.

'Why, John Delaware,' Nancy replied clearly. 'Remember John Delaware? James told him we were coming on here and suggested he came too.'

There was the sound of a glass falling and breaking in the hall.

Becky stepped back and looked through the partially open door to see her mother crouched on the floor picking up pieces of glass and lemon.

'I'll get a cloth and a dustpan and brush,' Becky said helpfully. 'Here, Mum,' she continued. 'Just leave it. I'll do it.'

Both her mother and Nancy Fitzgerald turned and looked at her.

'You're a good girl,' Nancy said, but her face said something different, which Becky could not quite read.

'Go easy on the bubbly,' Baby said to Anne Marie, as Anne Marie hiccupped and wobbled slightly.

'Mmmmm,' murmured Anne Marie as the room started to swim.

'She's pie-eyed,' Baby said to Friedrich von Vecker. 'Here, give me a hand and we'll get her out of here.'

'Pie-eyed?' asked Friedrich von Vecker with interest. 'New word for me. Explain.'

He put an arm around Anne Marie and frog-marched her out of the Dunvilles' party and into the breakfast room.

'She's on her ear,' Baby explained. 'Stay with her while I phone for someone to come and get her before my father sees her, or he'll never let me out with her again.'

Anne Marie sank into an easy chair.

'You are drunk, no?' Friedrich asked her.

She responded with a large and most unladylike belch.

Baby returned and surveyed the scene.

'She is not used to drinking alcohol?' suggested Friedrich von Vecker.

'God, no,' said Baby with her most innocent expression. 'We are convent girls – the only alcohol we get is the blood of Christ.'

'Do not give me this bullshit,' said Friedrich von Vecker with a snort. 'I too go to a Roman Catholic school.'

'Ooops,' said Baby. 'I forgot you are Gabriela's brother. Well, Anne Marie can't drink fizzy drinks – they do something to her, as you can see.'

Less than ten minutes later, Becky put her head around the door.

'Someone called Adam is here for Anne Marie,' she said.

'Give me a hand, Friedrich,' said Baby, and they hauled Anne Marie to her feet.

'Hold on,' said Becky, putting her head back around the door. 'Dad is in the hall – don't bring her out like that.'

'Hold on to her, Friedrich,' said Baby, and she went out into the hall in time to hear her father thank Adam for driving her back and forth on Friday night. They were standing in the doorway.

'My pleasure, sir,' Adam said smoothly, glancing at Baby. There was a courteous expression on his face as he looked at her father, but his lips moved in a tiny smile as he looked at Baby.

'Hello, Adam,' said Baby. 'Oh, Daddy, you're wanted in the drawing room – Mummy, you know ...'

Her father excused himself and went inside, and Baby hauled Adam into the breakfast room.

'We've to get Anne Marie out of here quickly before my parents see her. She's a bit drunk,' she confided to Adam.

He took Anne Marie from Friedrich and had her out in the car in less than a minute.

'Thanks,' Baby said.

'My pleasure,' he replied.

She watched him as he got into the driver's seat.

He half smiled at her.

Baby winked at him.

Adam leaned across the passenger seat and unwound the window.

'And what did you get up to on Friday night?' he asked.

'Friday? Nothing,' she said smoothly. 'What did you get up to?'

'You should be careful,' the chauffeur said. 'Bad things happen to bad girls.'

Baby leaned down and looked through the top of the partially open window.

'That's not the way it seems to me,' she said. 'Bad girls have more fun. Now mind you take good care of Anne Marie. Her father wouldn't like it if anything happened to her.'

'How are you, Elizabeth?' Father Monaghan asked the girls' mother as she worked the room.

'Good, thank you, Father,' she said gently.

'You've a big party,' he said.

She looked around vaguely. The room was quite full. She felt very distracted.

'The girls have grown,' he said to her.

'Unlike other girls of our age, who have all shrunk,' Brona whispered sarcastically to Rhona.

Rhona giggled.

'Did Rebecca recover from this morning?' continued Father Monaghan. He seemed unwilling to let Elizabeth Dunville move on. He held her by her elbow so that she was locked in place.

'She's fine now,' said Elizabeth, willing herself to grab the moment and to say to him, 'I really ought to see how she is.' But the instant passed and she was caught again in his inquisition.

Becky, coming back into the room with a fresh tray of food, caught her mother's eye and got the feeling that rescuing was in order, though she didn't know what gave her that idea.

'More people at the door, Mum,' she said to her mother as she offered food to the priest.

Elizabeth excused herself and disappeared.

'Feeling better?' said the priest to Becky.

'Yes thank you,' she said. 'I sometimes feel faint in the mornings. But I'm fine now.'

'Quite a disruption you caused,' he said. 'Yes, quite a disruption,' he repeated.

He sounded disagreeable and Becky felt he was implying she had done it on purpose.

'Sorry,' she mumbled, and was about to turn away when he put a hand on her arm.

'Is it that time of the month?' he asked her inquisitively.

Becky looked at him, a feeling of disbelief surging through her.

He couldn't have said that, she thought to herself. He couldn't have meant that. Could he?

She had no idea how to answer. It was horribly intrusive and she was speechless.

Suddenly Baby appeared beside her.

'Is what that time of the month?' Baby asked clearly. Her voice cut neatly between Becky and Father Monaghan, and carried sufficiently further that several people turned around.

'Christmas time,' said Father Monaghan hastily. 'It's that time of the month. Just a few more days until Christmas.'

His face had taken on a reddish-purple hue.

Becky backed away towards the door with her tray of food, noticing how his eyes were looking down at his glass, and Baby's stance, one hand on her hip as she stared him down. Briefly she thought of how she, Baby and Brona did on occasion step in to protect each other, but how those instances were rare. It's as if when the chips are down . . . she contemplated, but didn't finish the thought as she heard Baby clearly say, 'And do you like to have a bird at Christmas?' Baby's voice was steady, but there was a small, unpleasant smile on her full pink lips.

'Bird?' asked Father Monaghan, uneasily.

'Turkey,' suggested Baby. 'Or maybe something more refined. What was that bird which descended at Pentecost? A dove, was it? Pure, innocent, in need of protection, but sadly sent to earth . . .'

In the hall, Becky came upon a new guest, who was being greeted by both her parents.

'John Delaware,' her father said. 'My goodness. It's been a long time.'

'You don't mind my coming?' asked the tall man with the laughing brown eyes, who was taking off his scarf and overcoat.

'We're delighted, aren't we, dear?' John Dunville said to his wife.

'Of course we are,' Elizabeth said. She appeared slightly flustered.

Her father introduced Becky to the guest.

'This is our middle daughter, Rebecca – known to friends and family as Becky,' he said.

Elizabeth took the tray of food from her.

'Delighted to meet you, Rebecca,' John Delaware said, reaching out his hand to shake hers. His hand was large and firm and cold. 'Cold hand, warm heart,' he said to her with a laugh, as if he knew what she was thinking.

He had an English accent, very similar to John Dunville's.

'Your voice is just like Dad's,' Becky said, smiling up at him. Usually she would have been too shy to say something so personal, but it just came out.

'We were at school together,' her father said.

'We shared the war as well,' John Delaware added. 'And how old are you, Rebecca? Or maybe you're too grown up to be asked such a question.'

Becky smiled at him.

'Sixteen next month,' she said. 'Baby and I share a birthday. She's my older sister.'

'I remember her,' he said. 'She had blonde hair as a baby.'

'Still has,' Becky said.

'So gorgeous hair runs in the family,' he said, looking at hers.

She found herself smiling at him with pleasure. He was so open and at ease. Her father led him into the drawing room. At the door, he turned back and said to her, 'Brunette with a touch of the burnished copper.' She felt he had been looking carefully for the right words.

This was not how she had ever thought of her hair. She glanced in the hall mirror to see if she could see her hair the way he did. Dull, dark brown was how she had always thought of it.

She saw herself looking the way she supposed she always did. Her face was pale because it was winter. Her hair was full and rich around her face, neatly combed and slightly bouncy after being blow-dried.

Burnished copper, she thought. How exotic. The hall lights were catching her hair and she saw it as he must have. She felt incredibly pleased.

She became aware of her mother looking at her.

'Are you all right, Mum?' Becky asked her. 'Father Monaghan wouldn't let me get away from him either,' she added confidingly.

She would have liked to have told her mother what he had said, but it wasn't the kind of thing you could repeat.

'I'm fine, I'm fine,' her mother said. 'Just suddenly tired. All the preparations, you know . . .'

Becky took the tray back from her.

'Maybe you could sit down in the dining room,' she suggested. 'There are chairs pulled out there, and other people will join you if you do. Daddy always says that,' she added with a smile. 'You'll attract them with allure,' she slightly misquoted her father, who often spoke of feminine allure and how it charmed.

'Good idea,' her mother said vaguely, but headed for the kitchen instead.

Back inside, Becky took a look at the action. Father Monaghan was now propping up the mantelpiece.

I'll keep well away from him, she told herself, as she took a wide berth round that part of the drawing room, offering the tray of food to those she passed.

She saw John Delaware being introduced to Baby, and she watched Baby flirting with him, fluttering her eyelashes and pursing her very pink lips.

She glanced over to the right, and she saw Father Monaghan watching Baby.

If looks could kill, she thought.

At that moment, Baby turned slightly and looked at the priest. She raised an eyebrow and her top lip lifted slightly on one side.

A sneer, Becky thought. She sneered at him.

Becky was constantly stunned that anyone could be as in control as her older sister was.

In the dining room, Brona and Rhona were looking through a cabinet and lifting out LPs.

'We're going into the breakfast room to listen to some music,' Brona said to her. 'You can't stop us.'

'I wasn't going to,' Becky replied. 'Why would I?'

It's all so confrontational, Becky thought to herself, wondering where her cousin Eleanor had gone. She would have quite liked to join Brona and Rhona in the breakfast room, as she suddenly felt that she had had enough of the party.

Friedrich von Vecker appeared beside her.

'Hello,' he said to her.

'Baby's in the drawing room,' Becky said to him.

'I wanted to talk to you,' Friedrich said. 'I'll talk to Baby later. So, you are in class with Gabriela?'

Becky looked at him, puzzled. He had seemed to be all over Baby the last time she looked, but now she felt like he was moving in on her.

'Yes,' she replied briefly.

She didn't know what to say to him. Taking a better look at him, she decided he looked like a male version of Gabriela, with the same colour hair, even whiter blond than Baby's. He was also built like a male version of Gabriela, tall, with big bones, and a slightly arrogant tilt to his head.

'Your English is better than Gabriela's,' Becky remarked, and suddenly wondered if that was rude the way she had blurted it out.

'I came here earlier,' he replied. 'I've been boarding. My parents and my sister only came a few weeks ago. But this you must know, as she is in class with you.'

Becky felt bored, but didn't know why.

It is all so innocuous, she thought. So much small talk.

She felt she didn't have the patience for it, and yet she knew that this was life and the way people lived it.

And Baby thrives on it, she thought, watching her sister through the open folding doors as she moved on to Magda Robinson.

Becky would have preferred to have been in her own room, reading or scribbling.

Anything but this, she thought.

'Yes,' she said aloud. 'Gabriela joined us just a few weeks ago. And how do you like living in Ireland?' she added politely.

'I like it more now that I am no longer a boarding pupil,' responded Friedrich von Vecker. 'Home life suits me better.'

A bright idea occurred to Becky, and, restraining herself from giggling, she suggested, 'My other sister Brona and her friend Rhona are listening to music in the breakfast room. All of the young people will be joining them. Why don't you go on in there, and I'll catch you up in a moment.'

Friedrich smiled at her, and half bowed his head, just as his father did.

'Good,' he said. 'I'll see you in there soon.' He seemed pleased with himself, as he kept smiling.

'The breakfast room is through there and turn left.' Becky pointed to the door to the hall.

After he had departed in that direction, Becky surveyed the room again. She now found that she was really at a loss. She wondered if she should suggest to Eleanor and Gabriela that they could go to the breakfast room too.

And then what shall I do? she wondered.

The sanctuary of her bedroom called, but she was distracted by Baby, who seemed deep in conversation with Magda Robinson. She wondered what Baby could possibly find to say to her.

Several people had joined her mother and were seated in the dining room. Becky placed her tray on the table beside them, and then slipped out of the room.

Upstairs, she lay on her bed and thought about the things she dreamed of, of being with someone who would make her feel special, and who would understand her. Someone gentle, but grown up. Not like Friedrich. Someone who'll show me love and hope and promise. Maybe someone like Simon Carter. She thought about the school gardener. I'm like a weaver, she thought. Trying to weave a life for me. Maybe everyone does that. I don't fit downstairs. Baby does, though. Her thoughts were coming in short spurts. 'Maybe it's because she's older. But I don't think I'll ever be the type who can talk for a few minutes to people and then move on. It's so . . . trivial.'

Getting up, she rooted through her desk drawer, looking for a piece of paper, as words were coming to her and she wanted to jot them down.

'Dream weaver,' she wrote. 'That's me. Alone with my magic. Weaving and weaving a tapestry of dreams, colours slipping in and out of the loom.'

She wished they would all go home so that she could try the words, which were being conjured up in her mind, with the piano downstairs.

She scribbled frantically as the song formed in her head.

I sit alone with my magic
Looking out towards the sky
My loom is resting to me
My future I will ply

Dream weaver
Just see her
Spinning the thread
Of future lives

I smile as I see the future
Wondrous dreams for you and me
Limitless imagination
Across eternity

Come quietly now, my lover
Accept what I have done
For you the war is over
The die is cast – our dream is spun

Come pack your things, my darling
We'll set off across the sea
To our dream island where
I spin my dreams for you and me

Come quietly now, my darling
Across the waves we'll fly
We're going to make some magic
In the place where dreams are mine

Dream weaver
Just see her
Spinning the thread
Of future lives

The spinning wheel is busy
I weave a gentle song
Of love and hope and promise
Live now – before it's gone

My loom stands ready ready
At my shoulder – I'll begin
To weave the magic of our lives
Threads of colour in between

Light flickers as I weave our future
With laughter and much more
Let me enchant you darling
From here to the safest shore

Dream weaver
Just see her
Spinning the thread
Of future lives

Come quietly now, my lover
Accept what I have done
For you the war is over
The die is cast – your dream is spun.

Becky fiddled with the words a little until she was happy with it. Then, signing her name at the end, she blew little kisses into the air.

For you, she thought to herself. For my imaginary you, wherever you are. Out there, waiting for me . . . My first song, written for someone I have yet to meet.

Chapter Five

Elizabeth had had a worse night's sleep than usual, and when she woke on Monday morning, John spoke to her about it.

'Are you all right?' he asked.

'Just old nightmares,' she said.

'Do you want to tell me?' he asked, as he had often done over the years. She shook her head.

'We're going to Confession this morning,' she said. 'The girls and I. I'm sure I'll feel better after that. Thank you, though.'

'Good, good. I'm off to the hospital. Get a rest when you come back. You look tired.'

Elizabeth called the girls.

'Come on, time for Confession,' she said.

'I've nothing to confess,' Baby called down the stairs.

'Me neither,' Brona said.

'Well, if you think hard enough, I'm sure you'll come up with something. But we're going anyway. We always go in the week before Christmas,' Elizabeth said to them. 'And today is as good a day as any.'

'If we waited until tomorrow,' Brona said, 'maybe I'll have something to confess.'

Becky sighed. This argument seemed to take place at least twice a month, with different reasons being put forward. Their mother always won, but Becky sometimes felt that Elizabeth won because Baby and Brona didn't really mind. It was as if they felt this was a script, which had to be repeated fortnightly.

Baby went back upstairs and into her room to get ready. On her desk lay a notebook, which she had been going through carefully when her mother had called. She picked it up and slipped it under her pillow, then smoothed the pillow neatly before slowly descending the stairs.

Becky and Brona were already in the hall.

The three girls were dressed in skirts and sweaters, with knee-length boots. They took their coats from the hall cupboard.

'I hate my coat,' Brona said.

'Shut up,' hissed Baby and Becky simultaneously.

They knelt in a row, waiting to enter the confessional. Becky tried to concentrate, but thoughts about her song kept coming to mind. Glancing to one side of her, she watched Brona pick at a thread on her tights.

Bet she'll have a hole in it by the time she's finished, she thought.

Glancing to the other side, she could see Baby's perfect profile. Suddenly Baby turned and caught her eye. Baby smiled. Her face lit up, her pink lips separated and her even white teeth flashed at Becky.

She's really beautiful, Becky thought.

She was about to smile back when Baby leaned a little towards her and whispered, 'You going to mention Charlie Robinson's kiss in Confession?'

Becky looked startled and was about to respond, when Baby smiled evilly at her.

It's like the smile she gave Father Monaghan at the party, Becky thought. Sort of cruel.

She shuddered involuntarily.

'First step to losing your virginity,' Baby continued in the lowest of whispers.

You utter bitch, Becky thought, digging her nails into her palms and trying to keep her face impassive. You utterly lethal utter utter bitch.

She knew from experience not to let Baby see her reactions.

One by one they entered the confessional.

'Bless me Father, for I have sinned.' Brona rattled the words out. 'It's been two weeks since my last Confession. I teased my sisters, and I told a lie. For these and all the sins of my past life I am sincerely sorry.'

She was in and out in less than a minute and a half, wondering if she had beaten the record for the shortest confession which Rhona had clocked up the previous year. She wished she'd remembered to check her watch before going in.

Ah well, she thought. Next time.

In turn they went in.

'Bless me Father, for I have sinned. It's been two weeks since my last Confession. I was angry at my sisters.' She paused. 'Really angry. More than once.' Another pause. 'A lot of times actually. And I had an impure thought.'

'Often?'

'No, Father, just once. And I abandoned my parents' Christmas party because I got bored, and afterwards I told a lie. I said I hadn't been feeling well.'

Becky was so grateful that it wasn't Father Monaghan. She didn't think she could have gone to Confession if it had been.

The priest's head was lowered, his forehead resting in his hand. At no point did he look at her or even take a quick glance sideways.

So much easier, she thought, to confess like this.

'And will you try never to commit those sins again?'

'Oh, yes, Father.'

'Then say the Act of Contrition.'

He gave her absolution and her penance and she left with her head bowed.

Outside she went to the pew where Brona was now sitting. Once again Brona was picking at the thread in her tights. She was looking up at the Stations of the Cross. Becky followed her gaze and wondered if that was Veronica giving the sponge of vinegar to Jesus.

A sponge of vinegar? she thought. I must have got that wrong. No one could be so cruel.

'Bless me Father, for I have sinned. It's been two weeks since my last Confession.'

'Go on, my child.'

'I told the occasional lie.'

There was a long silence.

'Do you have any more sins to confess, my child?'

'No, Father.'

'Then say a Hail Mary as your penance . . .'

'Bless me Father, for I have sinned.' Elizabeth paused and swallowed.

'Yes, my child,' he said to her.

She could see his profile dimly through the latticed grid. She shifted slightly. The wooden board hurt her knees. As she shifted she felt the toes of her shoes scuff on the floor of the box.

'It is four weeks since my last Confession.'

'Yes, my child.'

She tried to raise some saliva to swallow again, because her mouth was terribly dry.

'Go on, my child.'

'Four weeks, Father,' she said again. 'And in that time I've done all the things one always does.'

'Tell me, my child.'

'Oh, Father, you know. The things you do and don't mean to – irritation, bad temper, you know . . . the things one does for which one is sorry. You know.'

'Go on, my child.'

'Father, I have sinned.' She paused. It was all so immediate. So inescapable. It was here and now. The opportunity to tell, to show contrition, to explain, to be absolved.

'My child, I feel you are troubled. Tell me your sin.'

'Father, I have sinned so grievously that there can be no absolution. I bring my daughters here every two weeks, and sometimes I just cannot come in to confess. I have come here a thousand times to cleanse my soul, to pray for forgiveness. I will never find forgiveness.'

'My child, all sins are absolvable. If you are truly contrite, if you ask God for forgiveness, then there is absolution. Then and only then can there be salvation.'

'Father . . . but Father, what if the sin has consequences – consequences beyond one's mere soul? What then?'

'My child. All sin has consequences. God is all-forgiving. You confess, and ask forgiveness, and your sin is washed away in his infinite mercy. And you must not say your "mere soul" – it is your *immortal* soul. It will live for ever. And you want your soul to go to God, don't you?'

'But Father. If one has done something so wrong that it cannot be righted, how could one get forgiveness? How could there be absolution?'

'My child, listen to me. If, for example, a man commits a murder and he confesses and has true contrition, then God will forgive him.'

'But is that right, Father? If you commit murder, if you destroy a life, and all the lives connected with that life, how can God forgive you? How can that be right? How can God forgive you? How can you forgive yourself?'

'My child, the courts in the land deal with the physical punishment – the judge and the jury deal with the crime – but until the murderer comes to God and asks God for absolution, he can have no peace. But when God forgives him, then his soul is cleansed and he can be at peace again.'

She was silent. She could see his profile, and his half-closed eye.

'There are sins, Father, that cannot be forgiven.'

'Oh, my child. There is no sin that God will not forgive. He is all-knowing, all-powerful, all-seeing. Atone, ask for absolution, and it will be granted.'

'But if I cannot forgive myself . . .'

'You are putting a value on yourself above the value of God – that is the sin of pride.'

'Forgive me, Father.'

'I cannot forgive you. I cannot give you absolution until you have atoned.'

Her slender hands wrung each other in her grief.

'Then there is nothing for me here,' she said. 'There is nothing . . .'

'My child, unless you confess and ask God for forgiveness, you are outside the Church, and there is no place for you in his heavenly Kingdom. You cannot receive the Sacraments. And you are not of God.'

'God help me,' she said, rising to her feet.

This is despair, she thought. And that too is a sin. There is no escape. What am I to do? I have everything, and yet I have nothing.

She knelt in the pew beside her daughters and her heart felt frozen.

I have covered the truth with lies, she thought, but only because it was the only way I could live with it. And now the lies I've woven seem greater than the whole of the rest of my life. She knelt there with her head bowed before the altar; aware of Baby on one side of her, and she thought of what she saw as the crime she had committed against her eldest daughter, and of the love she felt for her, and her need to always atone before her.

John loves me, she thought, trying to reassure herself. Surely all I have to do is to be a good wife and mother. Surely that is enough. But seeing John Delaware at the Christmas party had sent surges of other memories through her, the nightmare things she could never quite get away from. An afternoon long ago when he had knocked at the door and she had let him in, and he had ravished her. She remembered pulling herself to her knees after he had left, and finding that she could barely stand.

Her head had throbbed and shock seemed to have deprived her legs of motion.

'John,' she had whispered. 'John . . .'

Which John's name was she calling? Who knew? Was it in anger or despair? She did not know.

It was whispered so silently in the depths of her mind that even she was unsure whether it was her husband John whose help she now needed, or despair at having once loved the other John who could have done such a thing to her.

She had pulled herself across the floor and to the hall.

In the distance she could hear Baby give one last yell, and then there was an almighty crash before silence really did settle on the house.

She dragged herself up the stairs, step by step, the palms of her hands seeming to burn on the carpet's weave.

At the top of the stairs she lay half draped on the landing as she tried to get her bearings.

I must bathe, she thought. I must . . . wash this . . . away.

Running the bath, now on steadier feet, she remembered the now silent Baby, and leaving the bath water flowing, she went to look for her child.

'Baby,' she called. 'Baby.'

Her voice seemed to echo in the still house.

'Baby,' she shouted louder. 'Where are you, Baby?'

In Baby's room, the side of the cot was down – one of Baby's newer tricks for letting herself out with greater ease.

'Baby,' she called. And then she saw the small white wardrobe, lying on its front, and she recalled the crash she had heard.

'Oh no, Baby,' she said as she crouched beside the wardrobe.

Try as she might, she could not lift it, and she knew that Baby was caught inside with the door of the wardrobe now on the ground.

'Baby, it's all right,' she said. 'It's all right. I'll get you out. Hold on, I'll get you out.'

The water in the bath flowed over the side and out on to the wooden floor and down through the ceiling to the kitchen below, as Elizabeth Dunville struggled to release her silent child.

She pulled on a coat to hide the state she was in and rushed next door to the neighbours for help.

'There's been an accident,' she shouted, hammering on their door. 'Help me. Help me.'

And they did. They came running and assisted her in lifting the wardrobe off the floor and righting it on its legs again.

With trembling fingers she fumbled with the now bent key in the door, and the latch lifted, and there inside was a white-faced Baby, shaken, frightened and unusually silent.

While Elizabeth lifted Baby out and held her close, one of the neighbours, hearing the sound of running water, went and turned off the tap and released the plug.

'Was she hiding in the wardrobe when it fell over?' asked one of the women.

'Mine does that – hides in it, I mean, for fun,' said the other.

'Is that how you banged your head?' asked the first. 'When it started to topple? You poor dear. And you were about to bath Baby. Did she hide because she didn't want the bath?'

'Mine does that – runs when I'm getting her bath ready,' said the other.

And so, unwittingly, they give her a story to explain her afternoon, and the bruises on her face, but not the damage to her ... not the damage to her being, to her spirit, to her life force.

They wiped away the overflowed bath water.

They settled her with Baby, who, while being comforted, got a little colour back in her face, but still she didn't speak. Her large blue eyes looked from time to time in horror at her mother, as though she knew that something unspeakable had happened.

And when the women were gone, and another bath had been drawn, Elizabeth and Baby got into it together and Elizabeth bathed both her own and her daughter's face.

'It's all right, Baby,' she reassured the silent child. 'It'll be all right now. Mummy's here with you. It'll be all right.'

She knew there was a time lapse she could not explain. She could remember hearing Baby outside the drawing room door, but she could not remember the bang on her head. She knew something unspeakable had happened on her own drawing room floor – a violation beyond anything she could bear to imagine. She knew that somehow during this – presumably between the blow to her head and this violation, while the man she once loved penetrated her over and over – Baby must have crawled into the wardrobe. That was what she told herself.

It was unbearable. It was unspeakable. It was beyond the bounds of her mind.

They were bathed and freshly dressed when John Dunville came home.

'Hello, I'm home,' he had called cheerily just inside the hall door.

The house was very quiet. Entering the kitchen, he found to his surprise that his usually punctilious wife had not got the dinner ready. The table was not even laid.

'What the dickens?' he mumbled as he saw water dripping from the ceiling on to the floor.

Elizabeth appeared in the doorway, bruised and shaken, with a silent Baby in her arms.

'What happened?' he asked. 'For God's sake, what's happened?'

And Elizabeth fed him the story of Baby hiding from her bath and a series of accidents unfolding from there.

'My poor Baby,' he said, taking the silent Baby up in his arms.

'And then the wardrobe started to wobble, and as I rushed over, it tilted and hit me on the head before trapping Baby inside . . .' said the pale Elizabeth, with the brutal cut on her forehead.

'And Baby hasn't spoken since?' John asked incredulously. 'We need to bring her to a doctor. She may have hurt her head. Not to mention your head,' he added, looking in shock from one of his darling girls to the other.

'No, no, we don't need a doctor,' said Elizabeth. 'No doctor, you're a doctor.'

'For God's sake, Elizabeth. Of course you need a doctor. Someone who can be dispassionate.'

'I don't need dispassion – it's compassion we want.'

He brought them to the hospital where Baby had been born some fifteen months earlier.

'Shock,' said the doctor.

'Shock,' said the nurse.

'She'll be all right,' said the doctor. 'She doesn't even have a bruise. She's just traumatised from being trapped in the wardrobe. She'll be fine after a good night's sleep.'

He turned to Elizabeth.

'Now, let's take a look at this.'

The nurse took John Dunville and his daughter Baby outside while the doctor started to examine Elizabeth. He cleaned the cut on her forehead, then he noticed the bruise on her neck.

'Unbutton your blouse,' he told her.

She was shaking.

'Unbutton it,' he said again. His voice was gentler. 'Tell me what really happened,' he said.

She shook her head.

'Did your husband do this?'

'No, no, God, no,' she said. 'John would never . . . ever. He's not like that.'

'But somebody did,' the doctor persisted.

'No,' she said. 'No.'

'I can't help you if you don't tell me,' he continued.

'No one can help me,' she said.

'If you change your mind,' the doctor said, 'you may come back. If I'm not here, someone else will help you.'

'You won't tell my husband,' Elizabeth said, getting down from the bed.

'No, I won't,' he said sadly. 'I won't.'

So Elizabeth, John and Baby had gone home. They made a meal of sorts and John settled Baby for the night. In bed he reached for his wife and she froze.

'I'm not going to hurt you,' he said. 'I only wanted to hold you.'

She turned on her side, pulling her knees up and clenching her fists in anguish. In her head she could hear the sound of her own voice shouting 'No!' and far away Baby's angry cries echoing through her mind.

John, beside her in the bed, lay silent and puzzled, trying to piece together what had happened. It made no sense to him.

In the morning he saw the bruises on her neck, but he was afraid to let her know he'd seen them.

He waited until after breakfast, and when he went to give her his customary goodbye peck, he wrapped her in his arms and he could feel that she had frozen.

Their days passed.

Sometimes Elizabeth would look at Baby and wonder what, if anything, Baby knew; what, if anything, Baby had pieced together.

Baby wouldn't go near her wardrobe, and in fact she wasn't too keen on going into the drawing room either.

The following weekend, when John was leading Baby into the drawing room to play with her, Baby pointed at the door and said, 'Mummy whumped her head.'

'How did Mummy thump her head?' he asked her carefully, looking at the door.

'Man,' said Baby, going to get her favourite books off the bookshelf.

'And who was the man?' John asked carefully, taking the books from her.

Baby opened the first book.

'Look,' she laughed. 'Doctor . . . nurse . . .' and Baby's blonde curls bounced as she giggled in glee.

Four weeks later, Elizabeth Dunville looked at the calendar on the kitchen wall. She, who was always regular, was two weeks overdue. She could feel an icy hand enfold her heart and grasp it too tightly. She was pale and listless. The days hung heavy on her hands. Over and over she went in her mind, blaming herself for having ever loved such a man, blaming herself for letting him into their home that afternoon.

It's my fault, she thought.

She wished Nancy were there. Nancy would help her.

The outline of a plan formed in her mind. Vague and sketchy were the details. All she knew was that she had to get away from London. Invitations were coming in for parties; there was a limit to how many times she could find excuses and not rouse John's suspicions.

'John,' she said to him that evening as they sipped their sherry.

'Yes, darling girl,' he replied.

He could feel some resolve in her. Something had changed, although the frailty which had originally attracted him was even clearer now.

'Tell me what it is, darling girl,' he said encouragingly.

'John,' Elizabeth tried again. 'I was wondering . . . do you think perhaps, if by any chance, perhaps . . . we could live in Dublin?'

He was taken by surprise.

'In Dublin?'

'You liked it when we got married there. And Nancy and James are there . . .'

He could hear the hope in her voice.

'Yes, darling girl,' he said.

The hope in her voice was the only glimmer of optimism he had seen in her for four weeks. He still had not figured it out, but he knew not to pry. He felt that she would tell him when she was ready. He suspected that she felt guilty about Baby getting caught in the wardrobe, for he knew that she was a most careful mother. Occasionally he would tell her a story about accidents which he came across at work, and how a momentary lapse on the part of a good mother had caused a child to be burnt, or to run out on to the road. He told her these tales to reassure her that such things happened.

'At least Baby didn't suffer any long-term trauma,' he would reassure her, and she just nodded. He had been back to the hospital and had spoken to another doctor, who checked the file for him and said, 'Bang to the head, bruising on the right thorax, state of shock . . .'

Nothing he did not already know.

'I'll look into Dublin,' he said as they got into bed that night.

He watched her as she sprayed perfume on the hollow at the base of her neck, and dabbed it gently behind her ears. She ran her silver-backed hairbrush through her hair over and over.

'Will you love me again?' she asked as she got into bed beside him.

'I've never stopped,' he said.

'No, I mean . . . will you . . . you know?' and she lifted her mouth to him for kissing, and then she lifted her nightgown to be sure he got the message.

She had plied him with wine during dinner. She had given him two double brandies afterwards. He was woozy and agreeable and pliable, and he hardened quickly. She braced herself for his caresses and in a way she was surprised to find how reassuring he felt, with the familiarity of his touch, and the way he tasted and smelt. She had feared violation but it was not like that. Even drunk, he was gentle but masterful, kind and caring, and although she was frozen inside and did not want what was happening, she knew that she must, absolutely must, go through with this if she was to hide what had happened. And surprisingly she found herself soften and the frozen centre of her being almost melted.

And it worked.

They made love and she forced herself to respond so that he would complete what she needed him to do.

Four weeks later she told him that she thought she was pregnant. He held her close and told her of his pleasure, told her that things were looking good on the Dublin front, and asked her how she would feel about moving before the baby was born.

'The move might be too much for you,' he said.

They were sitting together downstairs, with Baby tucked up in her little bed to which she had suddenly willingly progressed.

'No, no,' she protested. 'It will be fine. I'd love to go back home. And Nancy will be there and she'll help with things on the Dublin front.'

'I wonder how Baby will feel about the new baby,' John thought aloud.

'Oh, I'm sure she'll love it. And there will be the excitement of the move as well, and the relatives at home. It will be wonderful.'

But he was concerned. Not about Baby, but about Elizabeth. He felt she was behaving like someone acting a part, as if the real Elizabeth wasn't really there. There was a forced brightness to what she said, a dismissiveness of the problems as he saw them. In quieter moments he sometimes saw a look of infinite sadness on her face, which she invariably denied.

'Just a bit tired,' she said. After all, she was four weeks more pregnant than he thought.

She lied about her dates when she went for her check-ups.

She wished Nancy were there. She would have liked to tell someone, but there was no one to tell. She considered the priest in Confession, but she could not bear to voice aloud what had happened and how she was going to have to hide it.

Just to be able to go to Confession and to confess all of this, she thought. And to have the priest say, one Our Father and three Hail Marys, or even ten decades of the Rosary – anything to assuage the guilt I feel. But I cannot get rid of it. This sin is growing inside me, and the punishment will last all my life . . .

She needed to tell someone, and yet she was afraid to.

She tried to sound out Nancy, touching on the past and on John and June Delaware.

'You're much better off with John,' said Nancy. 'Yours is the perfect marriage.'

'But do you never pine for an old love?' Elizabeth asked her older sister-in-law.

'No,' said Nancy. 'What I have is just fine. And certainly what you have is more than fine.'

But Elizabeth felt that there was something unspoken, some hint of disapproval, some suggestion that she should never look back. The idea of telling Nancy was so that she could assuage her feelings of guilt – but telling her became impossible, and the guilt intensified.

And so over the years she regularly went to Confession, sometimes toying with the idea of admission and absolution, sometimes pushing it to the back of her mind and just dealing with the other problems in her life. There were times she could not receive Communion because of the intensity of the guilt. She knew, though, that the depth of her sadness was resurfacing now because of the unexpected arrival of John Delaware in Dublin.

She and the girls came home from church.

'Nancy,' she said to her sister-in-law later that day on the phone, 'I never really talked to John Delaware at our party. What is he actually doing here in Dublin?'

'Oh, dabbling in something or other,' Nancy replied. Then, with a sudden insight, she added, 'Are you all right?'

'Of course I am,' Elizabeth answered. 'I just wondered if he were going to be here for long.'

'I don't really know. I don't think so. He was talking more about going backwards and forwards between London and here,' Nancy said. 'Elizabeth – that's all over, isn't it? That thing from long ago?'

'Yes, of course it is,' Elizabeth reassured her.

'Maybe I should not have told him to come along last Sunday,' Nancy said. 'It's just that James was being so expansive – and you know men, how they forget . . .'

'Don't worry at all,' Elizabeth said. 'John was delighted to see him. There's nothing to be bothered about. I only just wondered.'

And when she hung up, she went and lay down, and suddenly she remembered a day, shortly after they had come back to Ireland and she and John had bought their house in Ballsbridge, when she went alone to see a nun in her old school, a gentle woman with a serene and kindly face who still taught there.

'Sister,' she said, 'are our sins there, waiting for us to commit them?'

'No, child,' Sister Stanislaus with the serene face replied, looking at the troubled woman in front of her, and seeing her as she had been just a few years earlier, young and radiant and beautiful and full of optimism. 'There is no predestination. Everything is in God's plan. But it is not ordained. We have freedom of choice. It's just that God knows what that choice will be.'

I had freedom of choice, Elizabeth thought as she lay on her bed, and truth welled up in her, dispersing the web of lies she had constructed in her mind to help her live with what she had done.

Could it be that on that afternoon when John Delaware had knocked on her front door, and she had opened it, her heart had fluttered with pleasure at seeing him?

What were the words she tried to forget?

'Hello, gorgeous, got a few minutes to help restore a thirsty aviator?'

She did try to hold him at the door, but only briefly.

Then she had smiled at him.

'Come on in,' she said, and she had willingly poured them each a gin and tonic.

She sat on the sofa facing him, as he propped himself against the mantelpiece.

'God, you look edible,' he said.

And Elizabeth had blushed.

During the second gin and tonic, he came and sat beside her.

'Forgive me, Elizabeth,' he said, as he touched her hair.

She said nothing. Just looked at him.

'Forgive me for running off. I had no choice.'

And still she said nothing. She watched his face, and the dark hair on his head, and she longed to run her hands through it, just once, just once more.

When he brought his face down to hers, she lifted hers obligingly, and their lips met. The old passion was there.

She thought of Nancy saying to her, 'Puppy love. And he's a bounder.'

And she thought, I don't care. I don't . . .

Feelings stirred excitedly inside her.

Don't let this happen, she told herself. But I want. I want. Just once. Just this once, and then I will lay this ghost to rest. He will leave and go back to his wife, and John, my husband, will come home, and life will be as it was.

Her heart pounded. His lips became more insistent. They burnt on hers. Then they came to her neck, and his touch was magic on the velvet of her skin.

In the distance she heard the wail of Baby waking, Baby demanding. 'Wait for me,' she said. 'I'll try and settle her. Wait for me . . .'

Getting up, she almost slipped, her head spinning from the afternoon gin and the pounding of the blood in her veins from the kiss.

He helped her to her feet.

'Hurry back,' he said.

She walked to the door, and reaching it, she turned back to him for a moment, and she slipped as Baby turned the handle. Her head hit it as she fell, and she felt the pain of the impact and knew her skin was cut.

'God, are you okay?' he said, rushing over to her.

'I'm all right. Wait for me.' She got to her feet, and there was the furious wailing face of Baby looking at her.

'For goodness' sake, Baby,' she said, lifting the toddler into her arms and heading upstairs with her.

'For goodness' sake, Baby,' she continued. 'I want you to sleep a little more. Please. Just another rest for Mummy. Please.'

But Baby pounded furiously with her fists on Elizabeth's chest.

'Don't do this, Baby,' she hissed.

She wanted to be back downstairs, she wanted just once to do this one thing, to 'go all the way' with this man whom she had once loved and for whom she still felt such passion.

Looking around Baby's room, she tried frantically to see a way to distract Baby, to keep her occupied for however long it would take.

She scooped up Baby's bedding and put it in the wardrobe.

'God forgive me, Baby,' she said. 'Just this once, settle down in here.'

And she put the startled Baby into the wardrobe and locked the door.

Back in the drawing room, she had hesitated as she came through the doorway. He was standing waiting for her. She could feel her knees buckle slightly, and her head hurt where she had banged it. He didn't seem to notice. His fingers opened the tiny pearl buttons on her blouse, and slipped it off, and then they were tearing at the rest of her clothing, and he had placed her on the sofa, and the rest was history.

Busy sperm fought against the tide and worked their way upwards, ever upwards, her egg being first prize for the speediest.

John left hurriedly, and she, after he was gone, panicked at the state she was in, at the yells of the furious Baby above in the wardrobe, at the blood on her forehead, the bruises on her breasts and neck, the torn silk undergarments scattered on the floor, and the wet patch on the sofa.

With wobbly legs she made her way to the staircase, where she heard the crash, and then the silence.

'Oh God, what have I done?' she had asked aloud. 'Oh God, what did he do to me?'

I participated, she thought now. I got what I wanted – and what a price I've had to pay.

Chapter Six

Dear Diary,

If I were Anne Frank I would be writing this to Kitty – and it would read 'Dear Kitty', but the only Kitty I know is Kitty O'Dowd, and I don't somehow think I would address her either verbally or in writing. Kitty O'Dowd belongs to a different group altogether, and anyway she's a class ahead of me.

I got this diary as a Christmas present from my sister Brona.

Brona is a born-again pain, but having said that, this is undoubtedly the nicest present she has ever given me. It is a five-year diary, but I have so much to write in it that I'll probably need a page for every day, so it'll end up being a one-year diary, and if it's found by someone in the future they will be amazed to discover how action-packed my life is – and when I become a famous author maybe it will be presented to some university for their archives. Anyway, the diary is bound in red leather and has a lock on it, and a little key, which I am keeping in the fireplace in my room. The fireplace, I should point out, is not used for a fire, and if you put your hand up into the chimney, you find a little recess, and there I will keep the key for safety. When we first moved to this house I was seven, and sometimes we had fires in the bedrooms if one of us was ill. But then my mother said it was too expensive to get all the chimneys cleaned (there are bundles of them), and so we had to stop having fires. Which is a pity, because I really liked sitting in front of the one in my room. Actually, now that I think about it, I think the problem was that we only had one fireguard and there was a row about who should have it. And Dad said, 'Right, that's that. From now on, there will be a fire in the drawing room only.' And so we all lost out. 'We all' means myself, ghastly Brona and malevolent Baby. Yes, I'm sorry now that I gave out such a stink because Brona had a fire on a particular day and I didn't. Never mind, at least Brona doesn't have a fire now.

Dad says that if he knew he was going to end up in a house with four females he would have stayed in the Air Force.

So it's just as well he didn't know, because then I wouldn't have been born and that would have been dreadful – both for mankind and for me ... though come to think of it, Brona wouldn't have been born either, so that would have been a blessing.

But then I wouldn't have known about Baby and Brona and so I wouldn't have known that the planet was a better place because they didn't exist.

So maybe it's as well that they were born, because now I know that if Dad had stayed in the Air Force and not married Mum, and not had Baby and Brona, then the world would have been better.

So their existence makes me appreciate the fact that their not existing would have been preferable.

I'm planning on studying Philosophy when I go to university and I try to practise my logic whenever possible. There's the gong for dinner so I had better lock this up.

Becky replaced the key up the chimney and headed down the stairs to the dining room.

At the dinner table, dressed in black velvet, Brona smiled at Becky – more of a sneer, in fact.

She's learnt that look from Baby, Becky thought to herself.

Brona passed the potatoes to Baby, missing out Becky.

'What about me?' said Becky.

'Oh, sorry,' said Brona, thrilled that Becky had walked into her trap. 'I assumed you were on a diet, and wouldn't want any.'

'Why did you assume that?'

'Well, if I were you, I'd be on a diet,' said Brona, piously pushing back her brown hair from her face .

'If I were you,' snapped Becky, 'I'd get my hair cut.'

'Why?'

'Because it's so dull that if there were less of it, there would be less dullness at the table,' replied Becky.

'That's enough, Becky,' said her parents at the same time.

Brona smiled.

Fifteen–love, she thought. No, thirty–love, she amended, as she thought about Becky's diary and how she would get to read it the next time Becky was out, as she had retained the second key when giving it to her sister for Christmas.

I hate you, Becky was thinking. You are the most horrible, conniving sister anyone could ever have had.

'I think you girls are definitely ready to go back to school,' their father said.

It was just another Sunday evening, ten days after Christmas, with school restarting the following day. Back in her room Becky packed her bag for school, including her new fountain pen. Getting out *The Prelude* by William Wordsworth, which she had asked for for Christmas, she lay on her bed and opened it again. What puzzled her about it was the fact that the extracts she still liked the most were the ones which had been read in class, while the rest, including the interlinking pieces, had little resonance with her.

Did they choose the best bits to put in our English poetry book? she wondered. Or is it because we have analysed them so thoroughly that I can relate to them? But in that case, surely if I just read other bits over and over until I get the pictures in them, then I will feel the same about them.

She turned the pages slowly, trying to find something that would spark her interest, and then in desperation she returned back to one of the familiar passages.

There was a boy, she read.

Change that to 'girl', she thought.

There was a girl, ye knew her well, ye cliffs and isles of Winander.

Maybe if I rewrote the whole of this piece and put in places I know ... in fact, if I rewrote the whole of *The Prelude* from my perspective ... and it received literary acclaim ...

Her mind wandered to a podium somewhere austere – perhaps a university hall – flashlights from the auditorium, recognition, interviews afterwards from handsome, lanky journalists with lean, hungry faces – or maybe just one journalist with slender artistic fingers whose brown hooded eyes would respond to her ...

In the next bedroom, Brona was reading the instructions on a bottle of hair dye, wondering what the reaction would be if she dared. She unscrewed the cap and sniffed it.

I should have done it just before Christmas, she thought. They'd never have noticed and they'd have had time to recover from it by now. Why, oh why, didn't I do it then?

98

Glancing at the clock on her bedside table, she reasoned she would still have time to do it now. It had to stay on her hair for half an hour, then be washed out and her hair dried.

'I'm going to have a bath, Mum,' she shouted down the stairs, knowing full well that she could not be heard in the drawing room, where her parents were listening to Strauss, and Baby was playing with Meccano in front of the fire.

Well, they can't say I didn't tell them, she thought self-righteously, taking a towel from the airing cupboard and going into the bathroom with her clock and the bottle of dye in hand.

In her room Becky, overhearing her sister, thought, I wanted a bath. Not fair that she got there first. She was aware on some level that her father was right, and that it was time they got back to the routine and discipline of school. She knew she had had enough of playing happy families, although she did not think about it in such terms. As the days had worn on, the constant rubbing of the three girls against each other had started to fray nerves, and she felt irritable towards the other two.

With that thought she returned to *The Prelude*, wondering what would happen if you put a rowing boat on the River Dodder in Ballsbridge. Mentally she abandoned Wordsworth in favour of Tennyson.

Well, it would surprise everyone from the Bank of Ireland down to the Swastika Laundry, she thought. Me rowing downwards towards the sea.

She smiled.

> *Out upon the banks they came*
> *Knight and burgher, lord and dame*
> *And round the prow they read my name*
> *Becky of Dunville.*

Hah. That'd get their attention all right.

In the bathroom, Brona used the hand shower to wet her long hair thoroughly, while hanging over the side of the bath. She poured the bottled liquid over the top of her head, and rubbed it into her hair, bringing up a lather and scooping her hair upwards until it sat as a congealed frothy blob on top of her head.

Twenty minutes like this, she thought, reaching for a towel off the rack. Wiping her hands and face on the towel before swinging it around her neck, she got the very definite feeling that it didn't feel like a towel should feel.

She opened her eyes to take a look at what was around her neck, and to her horror discovered that it was Becky's pink sweater, which her sister had been wearing at dinner.

Not only was it Becky's pink sweater, but it was also Becky's best sweater, and Becky's favourite sweater, and indeed a sweater which she, Brona, had coveted for the previous ten days – ever since it had arrived on Christmas morning from her parents.

Oh God, she thought in dismay.

Then, with perfect younger-sister self-righteousness, she thought, Well, she shouldn't have left it in here on the towel rail. Anyone would have mistaken it for a towel.

In her bedroom Becky lay on her bed rewriting an old favourite.

> *By the shores of Dodder River*
> *By the shining deep sea water*
> *Stood the dull and hapless Brona*
> *Daughter of the dogs, Brona . . .*

The rhythm wasn't working too well. She sighed, wondering what Brona was doing in the bathroom, as the bath water had not run for very long at all. Then she wondered what Baby was doing down in the drawing room. Sucking up, no doubt, she thought. Probably playing with the Meccano again.

She sighed again, then rolled over on to her back and looked at the ceiling.

Pity it's so high up, she thought.

The previous year all the girls' bedrooms had been painted, and Becky had chosen blue for her walls and navy for the ceiling, with the intention of painting stars on it – in the correct constellations. However, to date she had done nothing about this other than to lie admiring the navy blue and thinking what the stars would look like when she finally got around to them.

Unfortunately it was always night time by the time she got around to thinking about doing it. On top of this, she knew what her parents would say if she lugged a ladder through the house and up the stairs. And anyway, she thought, I still haven't got around to buying silver paint.

Thinking about dragging the ladder up the stairs made her think about going up to the top storey of the house, which she duly did. She did not usually go up there. Her pre-Christmas ascent to get a skirt for Gabriela had been the first trip in a long time, and she had not been up since. On the right was Baby's room, which now had a black skull painted on the door along with the warning ENTER AND DIE.

Becky hesitated. It was tempting, but on second thoughts she decided against and instead opened the other door. There were various pieces of furniture stacked against the walls, rolled-up remnants of carpet, two trunks and a row of suitcases. It looked like Mrs O'Doody had not been up there in a while, as there seemed to be a film of dust over everything, and Becky could taste it in her mouth. She recalled Baby saying that she would keep the top floor clean to save Mrs O'Doody, but clearly Baby had not meant this room.

The different angles of the ceiling right under the roof always interested her. They seemed to bear no relation to the roof from the outside, and yet she knew there must be some connection. She looked at the ceiling as she always did, and decided it had to have something to do with the chimney pots. But what exactly, she didn't know.

Approaching the window, she looked out over the bright lights of the city and smiled. She shifted one of the curtains, and a cobweb floated by her face. Reaching out a finger, she caught it as it drifted slowly downwards. She opened the window and let the web float out into the night sky. It stuck to her fingers, and she blew at it until it dislodged and disappeared in the darkness.

Out flew the web and floated wide

She smiled in glee. This was perfect.

All I need is a mirror to smash, she thought, wondering if it was bad luck to actually break a mirror, or bad luck for the person who owned the mirror. She knew Baby had numerous mirrors in her bedroom.

The mirror cracked from side to side

Hah! she thought. I don't have to actually break it, just sort of crack it a little.

The curse has come upon me

Well, that's true enough, she pursued the thought. Both ways, that is. The curse of being born a Dunville, and the middle one at that. And I have my period. What more does the poet need?

101

Cried Becky of Dunville.

She closed the window, but stayed there looking out across the bay at the twinkling lights. The fog horns blared.

Must be fog coming, she surmised, turning and going out of the room.

The fog crept in across Sandymount Strand. In thin tendrils it curled and twisted up across the sand, greyish green and thick. It reached the sea wall and climbed slowly up and over it. Spiralling gently over and over itself, it headed across the road, the tendrils thickening and lengthening to become gigantic tentacles.

In the bathroom, Brona, yawning, checked her watch and counted out the last seconds until she could rinse her hair clean. She noticed that the pink sweater seemed to have yellowish streaks on it, so she popped it into the bath, thinking that her shampoo would wash the marks out of it.

The shampoo did not.

After she had finished her hairwash, she squeezed the pink sweater out and put it back on the electric towel rail, hoping that Becky would think that the heat from the rail had scorched it.

Downstairs, Baby looked up dotingly at her parents. Her father smiled at her as she put the last pieces of her Meccano crane together. With one eye she glanced at the clock on the mantelpiece.

Another hour, she reasoned, before the parents go to bed.

They always went early on a Sunday night. From the kitchen came slight clinking noises, and she knew Mrs O'Doody was clearing away the last of the good service and would shortly leave.

God, but time goes slowly when you want it to go quickly, she thought. She tidied away the Meccano neatly into a large box.

Brona was feeling slightly uneasy as she looked in the bathroom mirror. She used a towel to wipe the condensation from the mirror to give herself a better look at her hair.

They mightn't notice, she thought hopefully. If I dry it and tie it back, maybe . . . She thought she'd better get Becky on her side, totally forgetting the ruined pink sweater now squeezed out and hanging back on the bathroom rail.

'Becky,' she called gently, as she came out of the bathroom.

There was no reply from Becky's room.

'Becky,' she tried again.

There was a grunt from behind the door.

'Hey, can I come in?' Brona asked.

'No,' was the reply.

'What do you suppose Baby is doing?' Brona tried again. It was the one point on which she and Becky were not at odds.

'Playing Meccano and pretending to be wonderful,' Becky replied, unable to hold her silence at the chance of joining forces against their older sister.

'Mmmm,' said Brona outside the door. 'Pretending to be the longed-for son and heir?'

'No doubt.'

'Pretending to be half if not quarter her age?'

'Probably,' came from the bedroom.

'Please can I come in?'

Becky looked at the door and wondered what Brona was really up to outside it.

Curiosity won.

'Okay,' she replied, pulling herself up on her bed and eyeing the door with a certain degree of interest.

The door opened, and Brona entered.

Becky gasped.

'Oh, Jesus,' she said.

'It's not that bad, is it?' Brona asked, rushing over to Becky's dressing table and peering in the dim light into the mirror.

'Mother of God,' Becky said. Her initial amazement at Brona's blonde hair now gave way to momentary glee. There would be hell to pay, she knew.

'The nuns will go mad,' she said.

'Come on,' Brona wheedled. 'It's not that bad. And anyway, you said my hair was dull, that's why I did it.'

'Don't you dare try and blame me for this,' Becky said, now sitting bolt upright on the bed. 'I only said that because you said I should be on a diet.'

Brona bit back a catty comment because she really did need Becky on her side.

'It's only because you have such lovely hair, and that bitch Baby too, with her long blonde curls. That's why I did it. Please, please tell me it's all right.'

'Look, I can tell you it's beautiful, or amazing – which it is – until I'm blue in the face, but can you see Mother Immaculata's face when you trundle in tomorrow? Not to mention the parents when they see you.'

'What am I going to do?' asked Brona, now in a panic.

Becky eyed her sister's hair again.

'Maybe if you tie it back?' she suggested. 'And wear a hair band, then not that much will be on display.'

She came and stood beside her sister and they looked into the mirror together.

There were no similarities between them. Becky, a year older, was smaller, with dark straight brown hair, brown-eyed, petite. Brona was taller, with stronger bones, longer-legged, blue-eyed like Baby, and in Becky's opinion becoming more positively evil by the day.

But not quite as evil as Baby.

'What'll I do?' Brona asked.

'You need the parents on your side,' Becky said. 'Otherwise when Mother Immaculata phones home tomorrow, the mater will go mad.'

Baby came upstairs and, hearing voices in Becky's room, waited outside the door. She knew immediately something was up, as Becky and Brona seldom conversed, and it was virtually unheard of for Becky to permit anyone, let alone Brona, into her room. To pass time until they emerged, as she could not work out through the heavy door what they were talking about, she went into the bathroom. Seeing Becky's sweater on the towel rail, she picked it up in amazement.

'Hey Becky,' she shouted. 'What happened to your jumper?'

'I spilt gravy on the cuff at dinner,' Becky shouted back. 'So I rinsed the arm. Don't you touch it,' she added, coming out on to the landing.

There was momentary silence as she looked in disbelief at her once pink sweater, and then she started to yell at Baby.

'What have you done to it? You goddamn cow, what have you done to my pink . . .' She was almost sobbing.

Their parents appeared on the stairs, their father taking them two at a time; he grabbed Becky and pulled her off Baby, who was shouting that it wasn't her fault.

There was bedlam on the landing as Baby made a dive for Becky.

In Becky's bedroom, Brona made a moue into the mirror and sighed.

Not my fault either, she thought.

Their mother was holding Baby and their father was restraining Becky when Brona made her appearance.

Both parents, catching the blonde shininess of her head out of the corner of their eye, dropped the other two screaming girls and turned to look at her.

'What do you think?' said Brona hopefully.

Even Baby stood there open-mouthed, while Becky grabbed her ruined sweater and started to cry.

'Oh shut up, Becky,' Baby said. 'Even you must be able to see what's happened to your silly pink jumper. It almost matches Brona's hair.'

'I thought it was just normal shampoo,' Brona tried again.

Dear Diary, Becky wrote an hour later.

Somehow I managed to get blamed for what Brona did to her hair, and for what she did to my sweater. Seemingly I shouldn't have said her hair was dull over dinner, and I shouldn't have left my sweater in the bathroom. Someone tell me if this is fair? Because it doesn't feel like it. If I starved myself to death because Brona said I should be on a diet, do you think they'd blame her? Well, they jolly well wouldn't. This family doesn't work like that. And it's not my fault. It's not.

Her eyes were red and swollen, and her face hurt from sobbing. The sweater was in hot water in the wash basin in her bedroom.

If only I had tried to dry it in here, she thought. But there's no heater here, and that's why I put it on the bathroom rail.

She got undressed and climbed shivering into bed, pulling the covers up over her head, and there she started to cry again.

Silent, shaking sobs, the last tears of childhood.

In her bedroom, Brona lay under her covers, with her new blonde hair spread out on the pillows and her mother sitting on the edge of the bed holding her hand.

'It's all right, darling,' Elizabeth said. 'I know it's difficult growing up. But your hair was lovely too. It's just different to your sisters' hair. And you have other attributes.'

105

'But I just wanted to have pretty hair like they do,' said Brona cleverly.

'Well, you have blonde hair now. And it's . . . well, it's . . . different. No, no, don't start to cry again. It's lovely, darling. It's just that I always loved your brown hair.'

'Mouse-brown hair,' Brona said sadly. 'It was mouse brown. Baby said that. And Becky said it was dull.'

'Now, now, darling. It was lovely. And it's lovely now too.'

'But Mummy,' said Brona with a sob, 'what if Mother Immaculata doesn't like it?'

There was silence from her mother. Elizabeth Dunville had not a doubt in the world about what Mother Immaculata's sentiments were going to be.

'Supposing I write you a letter, darling? I'll explain it was an accident and that it will wash out. It will wash out, won't it?' she added, getting up quickly and going into the bathroom to find the culprit bottle.

Coming back in to Brona in her yellow bedroom with her yellow hair, she shook her head.

'It won't wash out. But it will grow out,' she said to her daughter. 'I'll write you a letter, but I suspect Mother Immaculata may not take this lightly.'

Upstairs on the top floor, Baby was getting ready to slip out once the house was asleep. Black eyeliner was being assiduously applied, and Baby surveyed herself in the full-length mirror on her wall. She would have liked to iron the curls out of her hair as she sometimes did, but it was not part of the plan of sitting and playing 'baby' at her parents' feet in the drawing room. And anyway, seeing what Brona looked like with her straight bleached hair, Baby was happy enough to head off into the night curly as she was.

In fact, she concluded, I don't think I'll ever iron my hair again.

She was mouthing to herself about the trouble which had taken place on the landing earlier – it had delayed everyone going to bed and she was concerned that Hugo, her boyfriend, would not wait up for her; that after perhaps an hour he would give up and go to bed. She was afraid he wouldn't hear her knock on the door, as he had no bell and no knocker.

And I haven't seen him for fourteen days, she thought, her mind returning to their fond farewell on the evening before school had closed for Christmas, and Hugo Mombay Humphries had returned to London for the seasonal festivities with his parents.

Hugo Mombay Humphries stood six foot two inches tall, his build being such that he would have made a fine sportsman had he been so inclined. Baby had been drawn to him because she fancied his English voice and because he was the best-looking male at the disco the night she first saw him. *Veni, vidi, vici* was Baby's motto, and she moved in on him using her looks and her maturity as the wiles to attract him. And Baby always got what she wanted. She enjoyed his company, but nonetheless used the time he spent at his other home in London to do her own thing. Missing him when he left, she simply went and did the things she would have done had she not known him, assuming that he was probably doing the same. Being older than she and already in university was part of the attraction. She had no interest in boys her own age, and was normally drawn to men a good deal older than she was. Her ability to change her appearance from Daddy's girl to vamp assisted her in her activities. But with Christmas over, and long days spent at home being a good girl, except for the occasional relief of going out with Anne Marie, she was very ready for Hugo's return.

Her coat was rolled up in a cupboard in the breakfast room, along with her shoes, so that she could silently descend the flights of stairs in stockinged feet, carefully avoiding the creaking floorboards well known to her astute mind.

The fog had crept up through Sandymount, Irishtown and Ringsend to Ballsbridge by the time Baby Dunville let herself out through one of the breakfast-room windows, and carefully pulled it down behind her. She was surprised to find herself enveloped in thick, almost suffocating dampness when she lowered herself into the back yard. She wondered how far she could get if it was going to be like that.

Out through the yard, down the passageway to the back garden, carefully lifting the latch on the back gate, and pressing the button so it would not close in her absence, Baby Dunville walked slowly and carefully down the pebbled driveway, keeping one hand on the house wall and then on the front garden railing as she headed for the footpath.

On a ferry on the Irish Sea, Hugo Mombay Humphries and his parents were stationary, listening to the foghorns blaring in Dublin Bay which held them arrested some miles out.

He was exasperated beyond words, and frustrated, because for most of the previous fourteen days he had been contemplating what he was going to do both to and with Baby Dunville when he got his hands on her that night.

The very thought of her aroused him beyond belief, and he was forced to wrap his coat around himself to hide his condition, as he headed for the Gents.

Becky switched her light back on. Something had disturbed her through her sobs. She checked the time on her bedside clock – it was 11.35 p.m., and the foghorns were still sounding in the bay.

Becky slipped out of bed and put her dressing gown on over her pale blue pyjamas. Gently, with practised care, she opened her bedroom door and, like her older sister before her, crept out, avoiding the creaking floorboards on the landing and the stairs. She descended to the breakfast room, where to her surprise, having turned on the light, she saw the window into the laundry yard was slightly open.

Not a bit like Dad, she thought, as she went over to push it down the last inch and lock it.

Taking a tangerine in blue foil from the bowl on the table, she curled up on the rug in front of the dying embers of the fire and slowly unpicked the paper. The tangy smell of orange was at first only faintly apparent, but once her thumb penetrated the skin, she got the taste of it in her nose immediately. She sniffed it over and over – always finding it comforting, reassuring, tied in with memories of early childhood, sitting just so in front of a fire, feeling safe. She threw the skin into the grate, and slowly it started to brown and smoke, and wafts of tangerine came her way, reinforcing her memories of childhood love.

She let no thoughts enter her mind, just the waves of happiness caught in the smell and then in the taste of the fruit. The tangerine skin burned, and finally disappeared to ash. Becky, hugging her knees, watched the last traces of ember die.

Some ten minutes later she was back in bed – the tears long gone – and sleep came quickly.

In their bedroom, John and Elizabeth Dunville had moved quickly into their usual Sunday night routine. John, in bed first, watched his wife as she undressed and hung her dress in the wardrobe, as she removed her make-up and her jewellery, as she smoothed cold cream on to her face, and finally slipped into a white lace nightdress. Hands behind his head, he smiled at her, happy to forget the argument which had taken place among the girls on the landing a little earlier.

Elizabeth, after saying goodnight to Brona, had gone to her desk at her bedroom window and had written Mother Immaculata a letter of apology over the bleached blonde hair. Now she rubbed hand cream into her elbows and down her arms, thinking of the girls and how they so quickly flared up.

She sighed and said aloud, 'Poor Baby, getting dragged into that. And of course, poor little Brona, so worried because of her dyed hair.'

She thought to herself, as she often did, Thank God I have three girls – and not any boys. And yet she knew that once, long ago, she had wanted a boy, but that was before Baby's arrival.

Thank God, she thought again, her mind running over the faces of her friends' children, and how the boys sometimes had a look of their father; whereas when she looked at her three girls, she just saw the bits of herself reflected in them.

She felt a wave of fear wash over her and she looked at her husband.

'Come,' he said, lifting the covers for her, and she slipped in safely beside him.

Brona turned on her side in her bed, already in a deep sleep, her unconscious mind journeying down the pathway to dreams. A place where tinsel glistened on a Christmas tree, and snow fell softly outside, and all her presents were stacked from floor to ceiling waiting, just waiting, for her to open them.

Elizabeth Dunville moved lovingly in the safety of John Dunville's arms. And further down Lansdowne Road, Baby Dunville, who could see only some four or five feet ahead of her, wished she had a white cane like a blind man, so that she could tap her way through the thick darkness into Hugo Mombay Humphries' arms.

The streetlights hardly penetrated the fog at all, casting instead a dull glow through it. The sound of the foghorns was momentarily drowned out by the noise of a car, and then there was silence.

Chapter Seven

A t Assembly the following morning, the first school day in the
New Year, Mother Immaculata addressed the girls in forbidding tones.

'Girls of St Martin's.' The gimlet eyes looked over the top of her
spectacles as she perused the hall from her vantage point on the stage,
upon which many a school play had been and would be performed.

'Girls of St Martin's, you are welcome back for the start of a new
term, and a new calendar year.'

The year had turned – it was January in the Year of Our Lord
nineteen hundred and seventy-one.

'When I say you are welcome back, I refer, of course, to those of
you who are here.'

Becky was about to nudge Helen McKeever, but changed her mind
at the last minute.

Lordy, she thought. If she has managed to notice in twelve seconds
flat who the absentees are, she's bound to notice me nudging Helen.

At that moment Helen McKeever nudged Becky instead.

'For those of you who did not give your best last term, now is your
chance to undo the damage . . .

Mother Immaculata's voice did not change, but the message was
clear.

On she went, through the various forthcoming events, a reference
to the school play, which was traditionally held the Friday prior to
the commencement of Lent, and an introduction to the new singing
master, who, if Mother Immaculata was to be believed, and few would
dare not, was indeed an acquisition for the school, despite the fact that
he was male.

'Mr Jones, our first male teacher ever at St Martin's . . .' Her
intonation being anything to go by, Mr Jones sounded like he would
also be the *last* male teacher ever at St Martins. 'He will bring you
girls to new heights . . .'

This brought a giggle from some of the assembled pupils, quickly hushed as Mother Immaculata's gaze fell on the unwitting culprits.

'Although part-time, Mr Jones will be the class teacher for fourth year, as Sister Joseph is very ill. You will include her in your prayers, both before each class and at night. You may now proceed to your classrooms. Brona Dunville, you are excused from class and may go and wait for me in my study. Helen McKeever, stay back when the others have left.'

'Oh, feck it,' Helen whispered to Becky. 'She must have seen me.'

'Of course she saw you. She is as God, omnipresent, omniscient, omniwhatever. Just say you're sorry,' replied Becky, relieved that she had not been the one to nudge, and also quite pleased that on the first day of term Helen McKeever had bothered to nudge her.

Brona, leaving the hall and heading for Mother Immaculata's study, pushed past Becky and raised her eyes to heaven.

Becky genuinely felt sorry for her. But the truth was, however bright the hair had looked in the shadows of the landing late at night, it was nothing to what it looked like at nine o'clock in the morning in the unforgiving light of the school hall.

'Brona Dunville,' said Mother Immaculata, eyeing the girl with distaste. 'What happened to your head? Is that a wig?'

Brona shook her head.

'No, Reverend Mother, it's not a wig. It . . . er . . . it was a . . . well, a sort of a . . . an accident,' she stuttered, fumbling in her tunic pocket and pulling out the letter from her mother. 'My mother sent you this,' she added hopefully, as she passed the letter across the nun's desk.

'Your mother? Are you saying that your mother is aware of the state of your head?'

For Pete's sake, thought Brona. Do you think I forged the stupid letter?

'Yes, Reverend Mother,' said Brona, in what she hoped was a tragic voice.

Mother Immaculata looked at the envelope lying on her blotter, and with long, thin fingers reached out and took it. She examined the front and the back of it carefully, before picking up a letter-knife and neatly slitting the top of the envelope. The contents – a single page – was removed, and all the while she kept her eyes on Brona's face. Finally she shook the folded piece of paper open and read it.

111

'Where is your sister Barbara this morning?' she enquired.

For a moment Brona wondered whether Barbara was referred to in the letter, and then she realised that this was Mother Immaculata's form of interrogation, a skill which the older girls said had been perfected while the head nun was a leading force in the Gestapo.

'My sister . . . Barbara?' said Brona.

'Yes,' said the nun in icy tones. 'Your eldest sister – Barbara Dunville. You do recall her?'

'She's in class, isn't she?' said Brona, now slightly bewildered.

'Do not play games with me, my girl,' said Mother Immaculata, looking back over the top of her spectacles at the unfortunate girl in front of her. Her glasses were perched fairly low on her aquiline nose, and both eyebrows were raised. Her eyes seemed icy cold.

'I don't know,' tried Brona carefully. 'I mean, I thought she was in class.'

Oh, Christ, she thought. Where is my bloody sister?

Mother Immaculata placed the letter on the desk.

'You may go and get your coat, Brona Dunville, and home you will go. You may return to St Martin's when your head has returned to its normal state.'

For a moment Brona wondered if there were indeed something wrong with her head, or if it was the hair that Mother Immaculata was objecting to.

'But, Reverend Mother . . .' she tried nervously.

'Are you arguing with me? Is there something you don't understand? Is there something you would like me to elucidate? Do not go near your classroom, do not speak to any girl in the school, take your coat from the cloakroom, and go directly home.'

Brona shook her head.

'Yes, Reverend Mother,' she said. May I pass Go? she wondered silently. May I collect two hundred pounds?

'Then what are you waiting for?'

'Nothing, Reverend Mother,' Brona said, turning and leaving the study.

Mother Immaculata lifted the receiver of the phone on her desk and pressed the button which connected her to Sister Rodriguez.

'Has anyone phoned in to explain Barbara Dunville's absence?' she asked into the microphone. 'Then confirm for me that Barbara Dunville isn't in school this morning.'

112

I can kill two birds with the one stone, she thought to herself as she released the button on the intercom.

Brona headed for the cloakroom, where her coat hung among the others. Her bag was in her classroom but she was afraid to go and collect it. She found a pencil on the floor of the cloakroom, and tore a sheet of paper from a copybook lying on the window ledge.

I've been sent home, she wrote, *because The Brush with Death is jealous of my hair.*

This she stuffed into Rhona's coat pocket, and off she headed out of the school. Halfway down the steps she wondered briefly where Baby was. Now that she thought about it, she could not recall seeing her in Assembly.

Oh hell and damnation, she suddenly thought, as a disturbing idea occurred to her. Did Becky ask me to waken her?

Sister Rodriguez put her head around the door of the fourth-year classroom.

'Excuse me, Sister,' she said, addressing the nun who was endeavouring to teach the girls. 'Rebecca Dunville. A word, if you please.'

Becky looked at the teaching nun, who nodded at her, and then stood up and headed for the door. She thought it might be to do with Brona's hair. She was wrong.

'Rebecca Dunville,' said Sister Rodriguez.

Becky looked around to see if there was another Rebecca on the corridor from whom Sister Rodriguez might be differentiating her.

'Yes, Sister,' she said meekly.

'Your sister Barbara.'

'Yes, Sister?' Becky was puzzled.

'She isn't in school today?'

Becky was silent for a moment.

'I thought she was, Sister,' she said. 'She came in ahead of Brona and me.'

'Well, she does not appear to have arrived,' said Sister Rodriguez, dismissing Becky by turning and walking away.

Becky shrugged and went back into the classroom. As she sat down, she wondered what Baby could be up to.

Oh, bother, she suddenly thought. Brona did call her, didn't she?

Becky's mind wandered during the rest of the history lesson. She could remember her father waking her.

'Becky,' he had called her from her door.

'Mmmmm, morning, Dad,' she had replied.

'Morning, Becky,' he had said. 'Look, your mother isn't feeling well. She's having a lie-in. You girls can get up by yourselves. I've to go in early. Give the other two a call for me, and save me . . .'

Becky knew the reason he was asking her was because she was the reliable one, the one who would get up and not fall back to sleep.

'Yes, Dad,' she said.

'See you tonight,' he called.

She had heard his footsteps going down the stairs, and then the hall door closing. She dozed a little before pulling herself out of the bed.

'Hey, Brona,' she called. 'We've to get up by ourselves. Can you hear me?'

Brona grunted.

'Look, you call Baby,' Becky added, 'and I'll make the tea.'

'What time is it?' Brona asked.

'Ten to eight,' Becky replied. 'We need to hurry.'

With that the first hooter went off in the Swastika Laundry just up the road. The Swastika Laundry was situated halfway up Shelbourne Road, and their hooters went at 7.50 and 7.55, which was perfect timing for the girls.

Mrs O'Doody had arrived as Becky and Brona were about to leave for the bus.

'Where's Baby?' she asked Brona, as she met the two girls in the hall.

'She must have gone ahead,' Brona said.

Becky wasn't paying attention. She was thinking about her mother, who had been lying asleep when she went in to say goodbye. When she had bent to kiss her, her mother had jumped, startled, suddenly wide awake, and she had looked at Becky in utter fear.

'It's all right, Mum,' she had said. 'It's just me. Becky. Just saying goodbye. Off to school now.'

Her mother had held her close for a moment.

'Have a good day, darling,' she said.

Becky thought about that look on her mother's face when her eyes had first opened. She must have been having her nightmare, she pondered. I thought it had stopped, but it must be back. That's why she's lying in.

And now, sitting in class, she wondered if Brona had indeed gone and woken Baby.

*   *   *

114

This was roughly the same thought that Brona was having.

Did Becky tell me to call Baby? Did I call her? She simply couldn't remember. From the moment she had woken, all she could think about was her hair and what Mother Immaculata might say if she noticed.

And now she knew what Mother Immaculata would say.

She headed down the steps of the school, and wondered if the people passing by knew she had been sent home. It took her almost ten minutes to get to the bus stop, and then she had to wait for a bus, which seemed to take for ever to come. She kept hoping she looked like a girl on a mission of some sort. But she had the horrible feeling that people would know that she was homeward bound because her hair was bleached.

On the bus, the conductor said to her with a laugh in his voice, 'Have you been expelled?'

She froze him with what she hoped was an icy look, and wished she had her schoolbag with her so she could pretend to be reading.

Then a woman on the bus said to her, 'That's a St Martin's uniform, isn't it? I'd know it anywhere. The girls next door go there.'

And Brona thought, You silly old bat. If you'd know it anywhere, why are you asking me?

Brona nodded at her.

'And where are you off to?' asked the woman agreeably.

'There has been an outbreak of rats in the school,' said Brona sadly. 'And it has been closed. We've all been sent home.'

'Good God,' said at least three members of the public perched on their seats on the bus.

'How dreadful,' said the woman. 'And did you see any?'

'Oh, yes,' replied Brona, warming to her theme. 'There were dozens of them at Assembly this morning. They swarmed over the stage in the hall.' She almost added that they were disguised as nuns, but decided against at the last minute.

And so it was that the people who heard her passed her story on, and Mother Immaculata was inundated with phone calls from parents and from the press as the day wore on. By the third phone call she began to smell a rat, so to speak, but it was too late to trace where the rumour had started as the story was already third, fourth, fifth hand. However, she did have her suspicions.

*   *   *

115

Brona Dunville, blue-eyed, bleached hair, arrived home. She went around the back, and let herself in the rear door, which was unlocked. She was hoping to avoid Mrs O'Doody. She slipped in through the pantry, into the kitchen, through the breakfast room and into the hall, where Mrs O'Doody was polishing the Benares tray with a remarkable degree of gusto for one so old.

'Hello, Mrs O'Doody,' Brona muttered. 'Is Mum around?'

Mrs O'Doody, getting deafer in her old age, nearly jumped out of her skin.

'Brona, I didn't hear you,' she said.

'I'm sorry,' Brona said. She hadn't meant to startle Mrs O'Doody, on whose side she endeavoured to stay, as Mrs O'Doody did miraculous things around Brona's bedroom, and regularly brought it to a state almost comparable to Becky's, although the tidiness she imparted to it never lasted for long. 'Sorry,' she repeated. 'I was wondering if Mum is here.'

'She's still in bed,' Mrs O'Doody said.

'Has Baby been around?' Brona asked carefully.

'No,' said Mrs O'Doody, with a shake of her grey-haired head. 'She left just before you girls this morning.'

That could be hearsay, Brona thought to herself, and she scooted up the stairs on silent feet. On the landing she paused, wanting to go in to her mother, but then decided to postpone that while she checked if Baby was in her room.

She nipped up the next flight of stairs and stood on the tiny top landing, looking at Baby's door with its forbidding notice ENTER AND DIE.

She tapped gently on the door.

'You there, Baby?' she whispered.

There was no reply, so she tried again, a little louder. There was still no response, and so bracing herself, she put her hand on the doorknob and turned it.

The door swung open.

There was no sign of Baby. Her bed was made, and the clothes she had worn to dinner the previous evening were strewn over the end of the bed. Her wardrobe door was open, but otherwise the room looked much as it had done the last time Brona had dared to take a peek.

Her plants seem to have come on a lot, thought Brona, running her eyes up and down the room and noticing how the plants had grown.

She hesitated and listened carefully at the doorway to check that there was no one coming upstairs, before going to the bed and looking under the pillow. Experience had taught her that that was where people placed things they didn't want other people to know about.

There was a notebook, and two envelopes, one with an Irish stamp, the other with a stamp from Great Britain.

Brona flicked through the notebook, which seemed to contain figures and nothing else. She slipped the envelopes into her tunic pocket to read the contents later in the comfort of her own room.

Then, carefully repositioning the pillow, she left the room.

Becky, heading out of the classroom at the first break, saw Baby's closest friend.

'Is Baby in?' she asked Anne Marie.

'Who?' said Anne Marie.

'My sister, Barbara,' Becky replied. Your best friend, she thought, but needless to say she didn't add that.

'Nope,' Anne Marie said, and walked on.

I swear to God, thought Becky, when I'm in my final year I'll be nice to girls in the classes beneath me.

She thought about phoning home, but it meant getting out of the school, and the call box around the corner would probably be out of order. It usually was.

Helen McKeever caught up with her.

'Cheer up,' she said. 'It mightn't happen.'

'Sorry,' Becky said. 'I'm just puzzled as to where Baby has got to.'

'If I were you,' laughed Helen, 'I'd be counting my blessings that she isn't around. At least she can't make your life miserable.'

'Mmmm, true,' replied Becky uncertainly. Because the truth was that even in her absence Baby was making Becky uneasy, if not quite miserable.

Back at home, Brona wondered if Mother Immaculata had phoned. In fact the head nun had tried to ring, but Mrs O'Doody had disconnected the phone in the hall so that it wouldn't disturb Mrs Dunville, and so Mother Immaculata had been unable to get through.

Brona went to her mother's door and tapped gently.

'Mummy,' she said as she went in, 'can I get you a cup of tea?'

Elizabeth Dunville was lying looking out of the window at the greyness of the January day.

'Oh, you're home. Is it that time already?' she asked in surprise.

'Well, no, Mummy. It's only ten o'clock, I think. Mummy, Mother Immaculata didn't like my hair,' she said sadly.

'Oh.' Her mother took her in properly and seemed to remember what had happened the previous evening. 'Oh dear,' she said.

'Can I get in beside you?' Brona asked.

'I really should get up,' her mother said. 'I've had a good lie-in. What did Mother Immaculata say?'

'She sent me home.' Brona seemed on the verge of tears. 'She said that I couldn't return until my hair was normal again. It's not fair,' she added, as she threw herself down on the bed. 'I mean, coming from a nun who probably became a nun because she hadn't any hair.'

'Now, darling. I don't think that's why people become nuns,' said Elizabeth Dunville vaguely. For the life of her she couldn't think why anyone *would* become a nun, but she didn't say that.

'What am I going to do, Mummy?' asked Brona piteously.

'Oh dear.' Her mother looked at her again. 'I suppose I'd better phone the hairdresser. No, that won't do, it's Monday – they never open on a Monday.'

'I'll make you a cup of tea,' Brona said, suddenly seeing at least one more day off school in the offing.

'Rebecca Dunville to the study.' Sister Rodriguez put her head around Becky's classroom door for the second time that day.

Becky glanced at Helen, who raised her eyes to heaven.

'Your home telephone appears not to be working,' said Mother Immaculata over the top of her spectacles. 'Your sisters Barbara and Brona cannot hide from me,' she added.

Becky tried to look appropriately impressed but had the awful feeling that a giggle was about to rise inside her.

Suppress it, she thought. Don't, don't, don't laugh.

And in her head she envisaged Mother Immaculata as God, hunting her quarry ... *I fled them down the nights and down the days*, she thought, quoting from Francis Thompson's *The Hound of Heaven*.

'Are you listening to me, Rebecca Dunville?' enquired Mother Immaculata.

'Yes, Mother. Yes, of course, Mother.' All fears of an offending giggle disappeared.

'Good. Then you will give this letter to your parents on your arrival home. Do I make myself clear?'

'Oh yes, Mother,' said Becky, taking the letter from the nun. Their fingers accidentally touched as the letter was passed across, and Becky was startled at the icy coldness of the other's hand.

Somehow, on the bus home, Becky felt that she was going to be incriminated in the day's happenings, even though she was the only Dunville girl not to be in deep water. At that time, although she didn't know the phrase *don't shoot the messenger*, she had an idea about the sentiment.

And so the day wore on. Between Mrs O'Doody deliberately disconnecting the phone and then forgetting to reconnect it, and Brona in due course forgetting about Baby's absence from school, it was going on five thirty in the evening before Becky got home with Mother Immaculata's letter.

Becky was uneasy as to which parent to give the letter to. On the one hand, her mother had not been well in the morning, so maybe it should be kept for her father. On the other hand, her father might blame her for Baby not turning up to school, seeing as he had asked her to call his eldest daughter.

'What did Baby say?' she asked Brona.

'What did Baby say when?' replied Brona, peering into the hall mirror and wondering if her hair had grown at all during the day.

'About not being in school.'

'What?' Brona spun around. 'Oh. Well, nothing. She didn't say anything. I mean, I didn't see her. She'd left by the time I got home. Did she never turn up in school?'

Becky shook her head. They stood in the hall, looking at each other, their mutual dislike momentarily quelled as they contemplated the absence of their elder sister.

'Did you check her room?' Becky asked. 'I mean, she did wake up this morning?'

'Well, she's not dead in her bed if that's what you're wondering.'

Some vague memory flickered in the back of Becky's mind but she couldn't think what it was. All she knew was that it added to her feeling of unease.

Elizabeth Dunville came into the hall.

'Hello, Becky, how was the first day back?' she asked her middle daughter.

Silently Becky handed over the letter, and Elizabeth Dunville said, 'Oh dear,' as she took it.

'Should I read it now?' she asked. 'Or wait until your father gets in?'

'Oh, I'd leave it,' Brona said, at the same moment as Becky said, 'Maybe you should look at it now.'

They glared at each other. Brona ran her eyes unpleasantly down the length of Becky with a sneer on her lips, and Becky turned away.

Their mother opened the letter, and pulled out the sheet of paper inside.

Brona thought how differently her mother took the letter out, so unlike Mother Immaculata that morning. Becky was thinking how pale her mother looked. As she watched, Elizabeth's face changed from a look of tiredness to one of extreme puzzlement.

'What does she mean, "Barbara" isn't in school? I thought this letter was going to be about Brona's hair. What does she mean?' she asked. Both girls shuffled slightly, and then admitted as one, 'We don't know.'

'Did Baby not go in with you this morning?'

The disconnected telephone was discovered when Elizabeth Dunville went to call her husband. Becky and Brona retreated to the breakfast room, where they usually dined with Baby from Monday to Friday. The table was set for three.

Brona plonked herself down in Baby's place.

'You can't sit there,' Becky said.

'Why not? She's not going to be in for dinner.'

'How do you know? Anyway, it'll upset Mum,' Becky replied.

Brona scowled, but for once did not argue.

'How do you know she won't be in?' Becky pursued the question. 'Is there something you're not saying?'

Brona did not bother to answer. After a few minutes, Becky got up and went and got their dinner from the oven.

'Give me a hand,' she called in to Brona.

'Why should I?'

'Because I think we should get on with things,' Becky replied, lifting out the Pyrex dish with shepherd's pie in it.

'Mum always does that.' Brona sounded sulky.

'Well, it looks like she's not going to this evening, so let's just do it ourselves,' Becky said.

John Dunville arrived home shortly afterwards. They heard his car on the gravel of the driveway. Usually one of them would have gone out and opened the gates at the top of the drive so that he could swing into the back garden. Neither girl moved. They picked at their food. There was a sense of doom at the table, intangible but nonetheless real. Their father came to the front door and so they knew he had left the car in the drive. They could hear murmured voices in the hall as their parents conversed, and then their father taking the stairs two at a time as he headed up to Baby's room at the top of the house.

'I can't eat,' Brona said, pushing her plate away.

This time Becky did not answer. They looked at each other, and in a rare moment of mutuality and a recognition of the other's need, Becky said, 'It'll be all right.'

'Will it?' Brona asked her.

They held each other's gaze for a moment longer before both looked back at their plates.

The door opened and their father came in.

'You've got to help us here, girls,' he said.

There was no customary peck on the cheek, no smile, nothing.

They both looked at him expectantly.

'When did you last see her?'

It was the first of many moments of truth, and the need to lie was strong, but neither did.

'Last night, on the landing,' Becky said.

'Me too,' from Brona.

'And this morning? When you called her?' He addressed Becky. 'Did she answer?'

'I didn't call her. I should have, but I didn't.'

Brona, grateful for not having been shopped, glanced at her sister. 'Maybe *I* should have called her,' she said. 'I think Becky told me to, but I didn't. I . . . I must have fallen asleep again, or something.'

He looked at them both. His face was a mixture of fury and anxiety.

'Did she say anything? Did she mention anything . . . anything that she had to do? Anywhere she had to go, or to see someone? Please, think.' His voice was more urgent than they had ever heard it.

They were both suddenly afraid. They shook their heads.

'Finish your dinner,' he said. 'I'm going to call the O'Mahonys.'

'Dad, I asked Anne Marie in school, but she said she hadn't seen her,' Becky said.

He was silent.

'Fine. I'll call the police.'

And he was gone.

Elizabeth Dunville sat in the drawing room on the sofa, holding her husband's hand. From time to time she seemed to have a problem breathing. He kept one arm around her shoulders as they faced the two detectives, who sat at opposite sides of the fire in armchairs.

'Can you give us an approximate idea of the time?' one asked. 'The last time you're sure you saw her?'

'Ten, ten fifteen, last night. It could have been ten minutes after that,' John Dunville replied. 'Not later than ten thirty.'

'And the circumstances?'

'How do you mean?' he asked.

'Was there a row? Bad feeling? Something that might have sparked her off into running away?'

'She hasn't run away,' Elizabeth answered. 'I know something has happened to her. I just know it.'

'Look,' John replied, 'there was a row, but not with her. It was between her sisters. She was unwittingly involved, but only briefly. It wasn't important. And I'm sure she wasn't upset by it. It was just a blow-up between the younger two. Nothing important. It isn't relevant.'

'Is there a boyfriend?'

Elizabeth Dunville started to sob.

'No, no boyfriend,' John replied. 'Yes, of course she went out. You know, parties, dances. She wanted to go to a club, but we didn't allow her. Next year is time enough for that. She's got her Leaving Certificate this year.'

The older detective addressed Elizabeth.

'Mrs Dunville, I know this is difficult, but we have to explore every avenue. It's very hard on you, but no matter how sure you are that she hasn't run away, we still need to look at it as being a possibility. Now what was the argument about?'

And so the details of the bleached hair and the pink sweater were

122

gone over and teased out in public, and both detectives nodded and listened and then asked to talk to Becky and Brona.

Becky, white-faced, and Brona, tearful, sat at the kitchen table and tried to answer the questions put to them as best they could.

'Was she upset by the argument?'

They shook their heads.

'No, not Baby,' Becky said, not liking to add that Baby thrived on arguments, that there was nothing Baby enjoyed more than she and Brona tearing each other's hair out. 'No, definitely not.'

'Does she have a boyfriend?'

Both girls were not quite so sure.

'No,' said Brona after a momentary pause.

'You wouldn't really know with Baby,' Becky said. 'I mean . . . well, she's older than us. She was very private about a lot of her life.'

She heard herself saying 'was', suddenly putting Baby into the past tense, and she felt cold fear.

'I mean "is", I mean Becky *is* very private. You know . . . her room is off limits to us. She takes the same bus as we do to school, but she sits apart.'

'We all do,' Brona added. 'Sit apart, I mean.'

'Well, do you think she has a boyfriend?' the detective tried again.

'I don't know,' Becky answered, as honestly as she could.

'I saw her with someone outside school before Christmas,' Brona said. 'I think he was waiting for her on the corner. But that's not unusual,' she added hastily. 'I mean, that's where boys wait for the girls, as the nuns won't let them near the steps.'

It all seems so ridiculous, Becky thought. Here we are discussing Baby's disappearance, as if she really has disappeared. And she can't have. Things like this don't happen. Not to us. Not to people like us.

One detective glanced at the other.

'Girls, we need a photo of her – a recent one. And then we'll check her room.'

Becky fetched a photo from the wall in the hall, and both men looked at it. There was Baby, some two or three months earlier. It was in black and white, but her blonde curls showed clearly. Her skin glowed, her mouth was smiling, her neck was long and her good bone structure clear. Her mouth, slightly open, revealed even white teeth.

'Without the school shirt and tie,' one of the detectives said to the other later, 'she'd pass for twenty-one or more.'

'And a beauty too!' the other said.

'That face is the face of an angel,' said the first one.

'But we're not dealing with an angel, are we?' said his partner.

By the time they had this conversation, they had been to Baby's room, and seen the general tidiness of it, the clothes neatly hanging in her wardrobe, the previous day's clothing lying on her bed, her shoes paired neatly on the floor of her cupboard, and the five marijuana plants carefully watered in front of the window.

'You cannot be serious,' John Dunville said in the drawing room, when they told him of their find. 'You cannot be serious. For God's sake, Baby wouldn't know a marijuana plant from a banana tree.'

But the evidence was there. The marijuana plants were carried carefully downstairs and removed from the house, and John Dunville stood in the hall, staring in disbelief.

'But Baby . . .' said Elizabeth. 'Baby wouldn't . . . Baby couldn't . . .'

Conor O'Connor, the younger of the two detectives, a burly man with dark curly hair, sat beside her in the drawing room.

'Kids nowadays,' he said, trying to connect with her. 'Sometimes parents don't know the half of what is going on.'

'But we did. We do,' she said. 'We have a very close relation- ship with the girls – and Baby, well, she's our first – obviously our relationship with her is excellent. We're very close. All of us. Especially Baby and me. And Baby and her father.' She was gab- bling out the words as she tried to make some sense of what was happening. 'Baby couldn't have known what they were,' she said. 'That's what it is. She wouldn't have known. She must have bought them somewhere, or maybe got them as a Christmas present. She didn't know.'

John Dunville, coming back into the room, sat down heavily in an armchair and stared at his wife and the detective.

'Tell him, John,' Elizabeth said. 'Tell him. Baby didn't know what they were. They weren't hers. She wouldn't have known. And this is just distracting everybody from the fact that she is missing. That's what's important. Something has happened to her. We've got to find her. The plants aren't relevant.'

'Do you know how long they've been up in her room, Dr Dunville?' Conor O'Connor asked John.

'Of course I don't,' he answered. 'Did you know they were there, Elizabeth?'

'No,' she said. 'You know how Baby looks after her own room. Dusts it, vacuums it – everything. To save Mrs O'Doody.' She turned to the detective. 'Mrs O'Doody is getting on in years. She does for us – she's our household help, and she cooks as well, at the weekends. And Baby wanted to save her the journey to the top of the house, so she said that she'd look after her room herself, that there was no need for anyone to go up there.'

'And when did you last go up?' she was asked.

'I don't know,' she said. 'I'm not sure. I'd have no reason to go up. Baby brings her own laundry down, and when it is washed and ironed, she brings it back up. It could be weeks and weeks since I was up there.'

She looked at John for help.

'It seemed innocuous enough at the time,' John said slowly, his eyes thoughtful. 'It was like a girl finding her way into young womanhood. Wanting her space. Her privacy. She never gave us any trouble – there was no reason to be concerned.' He looked at his wife as if he were trying to piece the whole picture together.

'It's surprising sometimes what goes on,' Conor O'Connor said. 'Even in close-knit homes like yours clearly is,' he added carefully.

'Close knit?' John echoed. 'We're closer than that. We know where the girls are, and what they're doing, and the times they're due home, and when they get in. We're on top of the situation all the time. This just is not possible.'

'It does throw Baby's absence into a different light,' suggested the detective.

'It doesn't,' Elizabeth said unsteadily. 'I know that when John first phoned the police station he was told to leave it until tomorrow – that she would probably come back later this evening. But Baby isn't like that. None of the girls are. And certainly not Baby. All that's happening now is that you're calling her disappearance an absence – and that's not the case. It's not. It's important that you go out and look for her. That's what's important.'

She started to cry.

In the hall, John and Conor O'Connor spoke quietly out of earshot of Elizabeth, who had been joined in the drawing room by Becky and Brona.

'I had a problem getting you to take Baby's disappearance seriously at this early stage.' John Dunville said. 'I've had to pull strings – use every contact I could think of – to get you to come out at all. I'm asking you not to go off on a tangent because of the plants. I can see that there is much more to this than was at first apparent. But please don't put her disappearance on hold while you're investigating the plants, or whatever you're planning on doing.'

He knew that he needed time to think, to clarify in his head what was or what might be going on, but the last thing he wanted was for the police to back off the disappearance angle, when clearly all his and Elizabeth's instincts were that something had happened to Baby.

Chapter Eight

During the night, Becky heard her parents on the stairs. Their footsteps hovered on the landing, then ascended to Baby's room. She lay in bed, shivering. Then her door creaked slightly as it opened.

'You awake, Becky?' Brona whispered. 'Please can I come in?'

Becky moved over and lifted her bed covers and Brona slipped in under them.

'I never saw Daddy looking like that before, did you?' Brona whispered.

'No,' Becky said, feeling a strange comfort at having her sister in the bed beside her.

'What do you think has happened?' Brona continued.

'I don't know,' Becky replied. 'I don't know.'

She felt an infinite sadness wash through her, as if, somewhere far away, the waves of a sea passed over her and the waves carried grief and fear and desolation.

'It'll be all right,' she whispered fiercely to Brona. 'In the morning, Baby will come back. Then it'll be all right.'

'Mummy thinks something terrible has happened, doesn't she?' Brona asked. She started to cry.

'Don't cry,' Becky said. 'Please don't cry. It's not going to help. And your nose will get all blocked up and you'll feel even worse.'

'But what if she doesn't come back?'

'Of course she'll come back. Of course she will. And we'll all be fighting again in no time. And Mum and Dad will forget that she's gone and caused all this trouble, and she'll be their favourite, and you and I will laugh when we remember this,' Becky said.

She almost believed it when she said it. How could it not be so? she thought to herself. Baby'll turn up tomorrow, looking beautiful, and this will all be just a bad dream.

'You don't mind if I sleep here?' Brona asked.

'No, of course not,' Becky whispered.

And that in itself is extraordinary, she thought. Brona and I haven't been in a bed together since ... God, I don't know. Ten years? More?

She shivered, and the girls moved closer together, giving each other warmth and comfort.

'It'll be fine in the morning,' Becky whispered again. 'Just wait and see.'

Come morning, they woke early and lay there side by side, each waiting for the other to move, waiting for words of reassurance, waiting to hear Baby's solid step on the stairs, and her confident voice calling, 'Dad, Mummy, I'm back ...'

They opened their eyes, and in the darkness of the early January morning tried to make out each other's features.

'Do you think she came home during the night?' Brona asked.

'I didn't hear her,' replied Becky.

'Go and see, will you?' Brona begged. 'Please.'

Becky slipped out of bed and on to the landing.

Dear God, she thought. If Baby is back, I'll never fight with her again, or say anything bad about her, and I don't care about my pink sweater. I'll be good for ever and ever. I'll do anything, anything you ask. Just please let Baby be back.

She hesitated on the landing. The house felt strangely desolate, as if there was a life missing from it. She stood quietly and listened – for a movement, a sign, something that would reassure her.

Her parents' door was open. Putting her head around it, she looked in at their empty bed.

Let her be back, she prayed again.

She slipped quietly on bare feet up the next flight of stairs to Baby's landing.

Baby's door was open.

The room was empty.

Down in the breakfast room, her parents sat holding cups of coffee. Her mother's face was drawn and white, with dark circles around her eyes, and her eyes were full of fear. Her father looked up as Becky came in to them.

She raised her eyebrows hopefully, questioningly to him. He shook his head almost imperceptibly.

128

'Can I make you some more coffee?' Becky asked

'No,' John Dunville replied. 'I'm trying to get your mother to go to bed for a while. She needs sleep.'

'How can we sleep?' Elizabeth asked. 'How can we do something as mundane as sleep while Baby is missing? How can you suggest such a thing?'

Becky looked from one to the other.

'You must be terribly tired,' she said. 'Why not both lie down for a little? Brona and I will sit and wait. I'm sure Baby will be back soon.'

They waited all that morning, moving slowly from one room to the next. The family doctor was called and Elizabeth was persuaded to lie down on her bed, and was given tablets to make her sleep.

'You'll be no use to anyone if you don't sleep,' said Dr Moody.

'But I need to be awake. I need to know . . .'

'No, you must sleep.' Dr Moody held her hand. 'It will be all right. First you sleep. You'll be called as soon as there is news. For now, you just sleep.'

In the drawing room he talked to John Dunville.

'You don't mind my calling you?' John asked. 'I could have given her a shot myself, but under the circumstances . . .'

'No, right thing to do, John. Now, what is happening?'

'As far as can be seen, Baby left here the night before last, late, and didn't come back. The police are being helpful, but they seem to think that nothing has happened to her, that she left of her own volition, and that her absence is by choice.'

'Is this based on anything?' asked Dr Moody.

'They found stuff in her room . . . I don't know. Elizabeth is absolutely sure that something has happened to her.'

'And you?' persisted Dr Moody. 'What do you think?'

'Richard, I just don't know. If they hadn't found this stuff in her room, I too would be sure that she's been abducted or had some kind of an accident. But I'm full of doubt now. Nothing is clear. Obviously all the hospitals have been checked. The police are going to follow up on friends tomorrow if she doesn't return today.'

Dr Moody nodded.

'May I ask what was found in her room?' he asked.

John Dunville hesitated.

'I may regret it later if I tell you,' he sighed.

'Only tell me if you want, but remember, we're friends, colleagues. Anything you say I'll treat in the strictest of confidence.'

'They found marijuana plants. Five of them . . .'

'Anything else?' asked Dr Moody. 'I wouldn't worry too much about the plants. Between you and me, my son was growing the very same in our conservatory and my wife was watering them. It wasn't until we had friends over for dinner . . . well, you can imagine. A Californian cousin over on holidays admired how well they were doing.'

They both smiled.

'Thank you,' John said. 'For some reason that is reassuring in an odd way. I have this fear about some drug underworld and Baby involved in it. Though the alternative – the not knowing – that is terrifying in another way.'

Dr Moody nodded.

'What now?' John asked.

'You'll have to wait. She may come back today or tomorrow, but in the meantime get the younger two back to school, keep the show on the road. Yes, I know, easy for me to say.' Dr Moody looked at his friend. 'I'm at the other end of the phone if you want me. You know that, just pick up the phone and ring.'

'I don't want to go back to school,' Brona said. 'Anyway, Mother Immaculata won't let me in the front door of the building, not until my hair has grown out. Please, Daddy, let me stay home until Baby is back.'

John Dunville turned to Becky.

'Take her into town, to a good hairdresser – I don't know who, use your imagination, or your feminine intuition, or whatever. Get her hair dyed to a normal colour. No, don't argue,' he added as Becky opened her mouth. 'It's back to school tomorrow.'

'I wasn't going to argue, Dad,' she replied. 'It's just . . . how can we go to school with Baby missing? I mean, how can we go in and pretend everything is normal?'

'I know, I know,' he replied. 'Come and sit here, girls.'

They came and sat on either side of him on the sofa.

'Baby may come home today, in which case, once this is sorted out, life will just go back to normal. Or she may not come home until tomorrow or the next day. So the most sensible thing we can do while we're waiting is to behave just as normal. Insofar as we can, that is. I know this isn't easy for either of you, but I need you to think in terms of the broader picture just for now. For my part I have patients to see, hospital rounds to do – people who need my help. People who would be very sympathetic if they knew our predicament, but who nonetheless need my assistance. And that is what I have to do.'

'And Mum?' Becky asked.

'Your mother is a different story. I know that. This is terrible for her. What I'm going to do is phone your aunt Nancy. Mrs O'Doody is here in the mornings, and tomorrow I'll see if Nancy can come over. We'll take it a day at a time.'

White-faced, frightened, Brona looked up at him.

'But Daddy, you're making it sound like this could go on and on . . .'

He shook his head.

'I don't think that, dear, not for a moment. But right now, this is the only way this can be handled. We deal with it one day at a time, and before we know it, Baby will be back.'

Brona bit her lip, trying to hold back the tears. Becky reached across and took her hand.

'It's going to be all right, Brona,' she said. Her voice was stronger. 'You and I are going to go into town now and we'll get your hair sorted. We'll do just what Daddy says. It's the right thing to do.'

John Dunville caught Becky's eye, and nodded.

'Go now,' he said. 'There are some detectives coming over late afternoon, and I want you back in case they need to ask you anything.'

'But we don't know anything,' Brona wailed.

'It's all right, Brona,' Becky said reassuringly. 'Honestly. They may think of some brilliant question that only you and I know the answer to, and that'll help them find Baby.'

'That's right,' her father said.

The two girls took the bus to town. Becky kept wanting to phone home to find out if there was any news, but knew she must not. She knew that each time the phone rang their parents would jump, knew their feeling of hope, knew their disappointment, their frustration, their anguish.

'I don't want my hair to go back to mouse-brown,' Brona said firmly.

'What colour would you like that both you and Mother Immaculata can live with?' Becky asked her reasonably.

'I can't have another shade of blonde?'

'No. You can't. Mother Immaculata won't let you back. You know that.'

'But with Baby missing, maybe she will be understanding,' Brona tried hopefully.

'I have a feeling Reverend Mother won't see it like that,' Becky said, her voice firm, although she was really trying to be gentle. 'Let's not risk it.'

They settled for a dark brown and a cut.

'You're going to have a terrible problem,' the hairdresser said. 'Your hair is going to split – this kind of stuff shouldn't be put in on top of bleach. I don't know . . .'

They prevailed upon her and she did the job. Afterwards, in Bewleys, Brona had two Mary cakes and a glass of orange. Becky had her first cup of coffee. The coffee made her feel grown up. She cradled the cup in her hands and looked across it at Brona. Neither said anything. Brona ate her cakes and then looked up at Becky.

'Well, what do you think?' she asked.

'She'll be back today,' Becky said.

'No, I meant about my hair,' Brona said.

Becky looked at her. She wanted to shout, 'Stop being so selfish. Cut it out. This isn't about you. No one cares about your hair.'

But looking into Brona's face, she saw vulnerability. There was fear in her eyes. And hope too. Hope that Becky would say something nice to her, something that would reassure her at least for a little while.

'It's lovely,' Becky said. 'I didn't think it could come out so nice. The girl did a lovely job on it. And the way she has layered it – it makes it look really soft on your face. You look older too,' she added.

Brona beamed, and stretched her hand across the table to Becky.

'Everything is going to be all right, isn't it?' she asked.

Becky looked around the restaurant. There was something so familiar about being there – the clanking of cups on saucers on glass-topped wooden tables, the comfort of the plush booths, the rich smell of coffee hanging in the air. And yet, she thought, this is different. Instead of us all sitting together, I am in our mother's place across the table, and Baby isn't here. I am the adult now. How strange. How unlikely. And instead of Brona and me fighting and saying mean things to each other, I am playing the role of the older and wiser sister. I am the reassurer. She nodded at Brona, and touched the fingertips which were reaching out to her across the table.

'Yes,' she said. 'It will be all right.'

For a moment it felt that it would be. For a moment she felt hope, optimism, an achievable aspiration for safety and the return to normality.

It may not be the same, she thought. But somehow it will be all right.

And then the dull thud of fear returned and with it the memory of the sense of desolation in the house, which was completely different to when her grandparents had died. That had been the course of nature, she thought as they walked down Grafton Street. This was different. This was frightening.

Brona suddenly touched her arm.

'Becky,' she said. 'Do you feel strange? I mean, looking at people as we walk down the street – everyone looks like they are living normal lives and no one knows that Baby has disappeared.'

'Yes,' Becky said. 'I know what you mean. As if they are living a reality and it isn't ours.'

She had this feeling of things rushing past her, and that she and Brona were moving in a dream side by side. Brona moved closer to her and looked at her, and Becky thought how they looked like other people on the street, younger maybe, because girls their age were at school, and yet they were not the same. There were all these women in gloves and scarves, moving in some sort of unison with a plan outlined for how they would fill their day, but she and Brona were just going through the motions, like unreal people. The feeling of detachment was so strong that Becky shivered.

They sat together on the bus going home, Brona beside the window. The glass was covered in condensation, and with one gloved finger, which had a hole in the tip, Brona wrote the word BABY on it.

Becky, seeing what she had done, moved slightly closer to her and kept her arm pressed against Brona's as the bus left town.

'Whatcha think they're all doing in school?' Brona asked.

'Some of the nuns are probably losing their vocation because of Mr Jones,' Becky said.

Brona started to laugh.

'That's so funny,' she said when she caught her breath.

'Well, I think he's quite nice-looking,' Becky said defensively, as Brona had laughed so hard she'd banged her head off the window and yelled, 'OUCH!'

'No, I'm not laughing at what you said,' Brona gasped. 'It's just the fact that *you* said it. *You*, I mean. I didn't think you'd have a thought like that.'

'It was the way Mother Immaculata said yesterday, *"Mr Jones will bring you to new heights".*' Becky giggled as she did the imitation.

Both girls laughed until they nearly cried. And when they stopped, they looked at each other, and suddenly there was this strange feeling of guilt.

'How could we laugh like that when Baby is gone?' Brona said, and tears sprang to her eyes.

'It's not wrong to laugh,' Becky said. 'It's not. Baby would have laughed too, had she been here.'

'But she never saw Mr Jones,' Brona said, wiping her tears away with the back of her hand.

'She'll laugh when we tell her,' Becky said.

They looked at each other, thoughts falling over each other in their heads. The fear that Baby would not come back for them to tell her this shared joke. The knowledge that if they did tell her this joke, she would be amazed that these two had shared a real laugh together sitting side by side on top of a bus, and she would probably sneer.

Where are you, Baby? Becky thought as they walked the last stretch of their journey home. How could you do this to Mum and Dad? How could you do this to Brona and me? Though you probably can't imagine that Brona and I would miss you. And it's not that I miss you, it's just that I want you back. I want everything back – the way it was two days ago. I want to hear you being superior and supercilious and mean. I want to hear Brona making nasty digs at us both. I want things the way they were. How could I want those awful things? And yet I do.

'Your father had to go in to the hospital for an hour, so I popped in for a bit,' Aunty Nancy said when they got home.

The house seemed different with Nancy Fitzgerald in it. It felt strange, but more reassuring than it had felt before. Nancy fussed over them in a way neither Becky nor Brona was accustomed to, but it was better than the way things were earlier.

'Is there any news?' Becky asked her.

She shook her head.

'Don't forget, no news is good news,' she said emphatically.

'And Mum?'

'She's still in bed. Best place for her at the moment.'

'What'll we do?' Brona asked.

'The best thing you girls can do,' said Nancy with determination, 'is to act as normal. School tomorrow. Tidy your rooms now, get your books ready for tomorrow. Give your mother as little trouble as you can. Act normally.'

Dear Diary, wrote Becky, lying on her bed.

Since I last wrote to you, Baby, my older sister, has gone missing. No one has any idea where she is or why she's gone. My aunt Nancy says that Baby has a mind of her own, and she'll come home when she's ready. Mummy thinks something has happened to her.

People from the newspapers came and Brona and I had to sort out recent photos of Baby.

Uncle James, who is a lawyer, came over and he answered the questions for the press. He says it's good that her picture will be in the papers tomorrow – it will help to jog people's memories. But it was very foggy on Sunday night, and I don't think too many people could have seen her in the fog.

Brona says that she thinks Baby has been kidnapped and that maybe they don't have the right address for the ransom note. Uncle James said we don't have the kind of money that would make a kidnapper interested. Daddy keeps saying that she'll come back. He said that she had been playing with her Meccano on the Sunday night, and that there is no way she was planning on running away.

When he said that to Uncle James, Uncle James said, 'She was doing what?' And I suddenly thought that it was an odd thing to do. I mean, she's nearly eighteen. It's just that she's always played with her Meccano because she knows that Daddy enjoys her doing that, and we were so used to it that we never really thought about it. But now suddenly it seems a very odd thing to do. Meccano – a construction game for a child, and anyone I know who has it in their house has it there for a brother, not for themselves. It makes me think of Baby scheming – she was always scheming, but I hadn't seen it like that with her and Daddy and Mum.

Isn't it strange how people do things in one family and not in another, and you just take it for granted and don't see it as being peculiar until you see a look of surprise on someone else's face. And you can't really explain it to someone else. Baby has always done things like that. And thinking about it now, she did it to keep the parents' attention focused on her. When we were little I think she did it to upstage us. I remember Brona playing with building blocks, and Baby moving in front of her so that she would be the centre of attention, bringing some construction kit to the hearthrug and asking Dad for advice, and little by little she manoeuvred Brona back out of the limelight.

If it was the limelight she was looking for, she certainly has got it now.

I feel so angry this evening. Having felt sad all day, I now feel like screaming. If she comes back this evening I think I'll kill her.

Aunty Nancy was great with Mum, but after she left Mum started shaking and crying again. I don't usually like Aunty Nancy much, but I really liked her being here today. She made us all have a meal this evening after the detectives had been. Mrs O'Doody stayed on, and Aunty Nancy helped her in the kitchen, and we all sat down in the dining room (which we never do on a Tuesday), and she just kept talking. Normally that is so irritating, but tonight it wasn't. It sort of balanced the emptiness in the house, and every so often she'd get Mum's attention even if it were only for a minute or two.

But after she left, Mum said to Dad that she couldn't stand Nancy being here and that she didn't want her to come tomorrow. Daddy just said, 'We'll see, dear,' in his noncommittal way.

I hope Aunty Nancy comes back tomorrow. I'm dreading going to school. Uncle James said that it will be easier when people know. They'll see it in the papers tomorrow.

He told Brona and me what Baby was growing in her room. I couldn't believe it. I was sure it was a mistake. But Uncle James said it wasn't. He asked us how long the plants had been there, and of course we didn't know because Baby didn't let anyone into her room.

Becky rolled on to her back and turned off her light.

Baby, where are you? she wondered.

She tried thinking very, very hard about Baby, and Baby's presence, feeling that maybe she could in some way conjure up an image of where Baby was and what she was doing. But there was nothing.

The most she could come up with was an image of Baby opening her Christmas presents and smiling with glee at her parents.

'I love it, I love it,' Baby had said, opening a slim box which contained a gold watch. Becky could see her rising from her knees

136

and throwing herself into her father's arms. 'Oh, Daddy, thank you,' she'd said.

The image faded and was replaced by Baby looking slightly maliciously at Becky after the pre-Christmas party.

'How much did you expect the Robinsons to give you?' she had asked Becky.

'Fifteen shillings – that's what I'd hoped for,' Becky said.

'You're in luck then,' Baby had replied, handing over a pound note. 'And so am I,' she added, after Becky had expressed her gratitude. 'I thought you were going to be looking for a split on the rest of the money I got from him.'

'How do you mean?' Becky asked.

'Well, I got another ten pounds off him, and you're more than happy with one pound,' Baby said, with a satisfied cat smile.

'Oh, sure,' Becky replied, not knowing what Baby was talking about.

Baby smiled at her, waiting for Becky to take in what she had said.

'He gave you ten pounds?' Becky said in surprise a few seconds later, as the meaning of Baby's utterance dawned on her.

'He gave me eleven – a pound for your babysitting, and a tenner for his kiss.'

Becky looked aghast.

'You mean he mentioned that . . . Oh, that's awful,' she said. 'And he paid for it? That's disgusting.'

'No it's not,' Baby said. 'And he didn't mention it. I did.'

'You did what?' Becky exclaimed. 'But I told you in confidence. How could you? That's awful.'

She had felt really furious.

'Why should he get away with that?' Baby had said. 'A grown man. He was lucky. I could have told his wife.'

Becky shivered. She could see Baby's face quite clearly as she ran this conversation through her mind now. It was as if Baby saw things from a different perspective.

It's not as if I ever wanted to babysit for them again, Becky thought. But how can I look at him knowing that she blackmailed him over that disgusting slobbering . . . and then wouldn't even give me the money?

And then there was the image of Baby on the landing, sneering over the pink sweater, and looking like a tigress when Becky tackled her.

And Baby in her school uniform, her tie perfectly knotted, her shirt so white, singing in the choir. Although she was in the back row because she was one of the taller girls, she always seemed to stand out.

Those blonde curls, Becky thought. And her face – it seemed to radiate beauty ... I wonder what Mr Jones would have made of her ... will make of her, I mean, she corrected herself quickly. I mustn't think like that. It's destructive. Think positively. That's what Uncle James said.

Her mind wandered to Mr Jones.

Hmmm, she thought.

Mr Jones was tall, with fair hair. She wondered what it would be like to sit on his knee.

Later, when she did sit on his knee, he tipped her backwards and kissed her on her lips. His kiss was different to Mr Robinson's.

His lips seemed firm on hers, and she felt hers soften and weaken.

Mr Jones had taken them for singing that Monday morning after Christmas, before they knew that Baby was gone. Blushing, Becky cringed when he picked her out.

'You're just opening and closing your mouth,' he said to her. 'Why aren't you singing?'

'I can't,' she replied with embarrassment. 'I'm tone deaf.'

'She makes an awful noise,' said Helen McKeever helpfully.

'What's your name?' he said to Becky, ignoring Helen.

'Rebecca Dunville,' she replied, feeling terribly humiliated.

'Well, tell you what, Rebecca Dunville,' said Mr Jones, who had introduced himself to the class as Christopher Jones, 'why don't you come up here to the piano? I'll show you the chord— Do you play the piano?' he interrupted himself.

'Yes,' she nodded.

'Better and better,' he said with enthusiasm. 'Rather than have you getting stress lines on your face from pretending that you're singing. Up you come. You can give the chord to start and count them in.'

Becky's blush of embarrassment turned to one of pleasure. She made her way up the room to the piano. Mr Jones rested his hand on her shoulder as he showed her what to do, and a furious class looked on hoping she would make a mess of it.

She didn't.

*   *   *

'Why don't you call me by my first name?' he asked her later, after he had kissed her, and his fingers moved to unknot her tie.

''Cos I like calling you Mr Jones,' Becky said. She was a little older then, but she still looked much the same as she had done that first day in his singing class.

'Shall I call you Becky?' he asked. 'Like your friends do?'

She shook her head.

'No, Mr Jones. Please call me Rebecca Dunville. In that voice you used in class. Remember, after you learned everyone's names, you called us by both names, like the nuns do, only it was your voice, your intonation – I like the way you said my name.'

He put his hand on her bare knee and with one finger traced around the top of her white knee-length school socks.

He smiled at her. It was a flickering smile. It seemed to pull her into collusion with him. She was enticed by it, entranced, enchanted. It was not like the smile he had used in class, or the one the day of the bomb, when he had been so gentle.

The Dunville house settled that Tuesday night. The waiting game was on, learning how to live with expectation, learning how to keep the doors to optimism open, how to pass time.

Brona Dunville was in her bedroom, which Mrs O'Doody had worked on during the day and which was looking reasonably tidy, bar the clothes which Brona kicked across the floor that Tuesday evening. Brona was in her pyjamas under her covers with her now darkened hair splayed across the pillow. She thought about going into Becky again for comfort, but sleep came while she was still contemplating leaving the warmth of her own bed.

John and Elizabeth Dunville lay together, their door ajar so that they could hear if the hall door opened during the night. There was quite a gap between them in the bed, and it seemed to be widening. They dozed fitfully, waking suddenly, holding in their minds one moment of peace before remembering that something terrible was happening, and full memory came flooding in.

Becky Dunville, in her dark-blue room, with her starless ceiling, rubbed herself gently and let images of Mr Jones standing beside her at the piano dance in her mind, and long before orgasm she too, exhausted, nodded off.

Chapter Nine

B ecky and Brona went to school by car on the Wednesday morning. They sat in the back, Brona beside a window, and Becky perched in her usual place in the middle.

'Move up,' Brona whined, sticking her elbow into Becky.

Becky shifted a little to one side.

'Move right over,' Brona insisted. 'There's plenty of room.'

'I don't want to sit in her place,' Becky said grimly, looking straight ahead.

'For God's sake,' John Dunville snapped, 'will you two stop squabbling. Don't we have enough problems?'

Becky moved over to the other window. Her face was very pale.

'Daddy,' she said, 'Mother Immaculata won't see you. She—'

'She will see me,' he replied firmly. 'There is no way that I will not be seen.'

At the school, he led the way up the steps, where he was halted by Sister Rodriguez.

'Good morning, Dr Dunville,' said Sister Rodriguez. 'I see you've brought the girls in today. Is one of them missing?'

'Good morning, Sister. I want to see Mother Immaculata,' he said, ignoring her query. His voice was like ice.

'You two go on ahead,' he said calmly to the girls. 'I'll look after everything.'

As Becky and Brona moved down the hall, they heard Sister Rodriguez intoning as in a liturgical chant, 'Mother Immaculata doesn't see parents without an appointment.'

'I would like to see her now.'

Becky hovered at the end of the hall, hoping to hear what the outcome of this confrontation would be. Putting down her bag, she slowly straightened her socks.

'Mother Immaculata has Assembly in ten minutes,' replied Sister Rodriguez, standing firmly in front of him.

Like Charon at the gates of hell, Becky thought.

'In which case we'd better hurry, hadn't we?' said John Dunville, looking at his watch. 'I've to be in the hospital in twenty minutes and my time is short.'

At Assembly, Mother Immaculata was missing.

Brona, three rows in front of Becky, turned around and looked at her sister. Becky grimaced at her. It was supposed to be a gesture of solidarity, but it was misinterpreted and Brona stuck out her tongue. Then Sister Rodriguez walked on to the stage to take Assembly.

'Mother Immaculata has been unavoidably detained,' she told the expectant girls in irritated tones.

'Oh, goody,' said Rhona to Brona under her breath. 'The police have finally caught up with her.'

It was not a good joke under the circumstances, but Rhona didn't know that.

'Love your hair, Bro,' she whispered. 'Is that what you were doing yesterday?'

Brona nodded. It all suddenly seemed terribly difficult. She wondered if Becky were feeling the same.

Becky was thinking about Baby's photo in the newspapers that morning, and wondering how many of the girls had seen it before coming to school.

Most of them are boarders, she thought. And how many of the others get the papers delivered? It could be tonight before everyone knows. I wish Uncle James had told us more about what to say.

She was feeling awfully nervous, as well as upset.

She looked up at the assembled staff and noticed that Mr Jones was looking directly at her. For a moment she thought that he might be thinking about singing class on Monday, and then suddenly she knew from his face that he had seen the paper, and had read the article, and knew that she was one of the sisters mentioned in it. She felt tears well up in a moment of self-pity, and she imagined that he was feeling sympathetic towards her. Then she swallowed the tears. Why would he be feeling sorry for her? The article had made it clear that the police thought Baby had run away, even though she had been reported as missing. Or maybe it hadn't. Maybe Becky was just picking that up from her father.

But in the corridor on the way to class, she saw Mr Jones looking at her again, and the expression on his face was not unkind.

Helen McKeever dug her in the ribs as they went in their class-room door.

'Fancy him?' she asked.

Becky looked surprised and shook her head.

'It seemed a very soulful look to me,' pushed Helen McKeever, peering into Becky's face questioningly.

Becky shrugged. She did not want this. She could not handle this. She felt now that Mr Jones' look was one of pity, and it made her feel very vulnerable.

Eleanor Fitzgerald, who was a boarder, found her at break.

'Daddy phoned last night and told me,' she whispered to Becky. 'Are you all right?'

Becky nodded. It was awfully difficult not to cry.

'What do you think has happened?' Eleanor asked.

'I can't imagine,' Becky said. 'I just don't have a clue. You know what Baby's like. She's so in control, doing her own thing . . . I don't know. Mummy is convinced something terrible has happened. I don't know.'

Eleanor, a year younger, small and slight like Becky, looked into her cousin's face and held her arm for a moment.

'I'm here if you need me . . . if I can do anything,' she said.

'Thanks, Eleanor,' Becky mumbled.

She hid in the cloakroom during the rest of break, as she could not face the others. And after break there was extra Assembly. This was virtually unheard of. The girls trooped expectantly into the hall.

This can't be about Baby, Becky thought. They wouldn't do this to us, hold such an Assembly in front of Brona and me. Would they?

They would.

Becky watched Brona lift her chin defiantly, and so Becky lifted her chin too, but she could not maintain her stance, and she found herself dropping her head as several girls turned to look at her and Brona while Mother Immaculata told the school that Barbara Dunville had disappeared.

'The police . . .' She said the word as though it were one with which she was not hitherto acquainted. She paused lengthily and then continued. 'The police are . . . involved. Later this morning, detectives will be coming in to the school and if anyone has anything that could throw any light on this particular situation, they would be advise to come forward.

'Barbara Dunville is a mere seventeen years old. We will include her in our prayers today, and each day until she returns,' Mother Immaculata finished.

Until she returns, Becky thought. Yes ... Dear God, please let her return.

It was the first real moment of hope. The idea that all these nuns and all these girls would pray together – surely prayer could move mountains. So many thoughts directed one way. So much force in the prayers of the nuns. How could Baby not come back? How could God not answer?

And then Becky heard a voice in the back of her mind asking her, 'What if there is no God?' It was like the echo of someone else's voice, but she knew it was hers. Over and over it went in her mind.

Mother Immaculata led them in a decade of the Rosary.

'Hail Mary,' she intoned, 'full of Grace, the Lord is with thee, Blessed art thou amongst women, and blessed is the fruit of thy womb ...'

Becky felt completely numb as the girls responded. She noticed that Mr Jones was not praying.

Does he not pray ever, she wondered, or does he think there is no point? In a godless world, what does one do?

She forced herself to join in the prayers.

What else can I do? she thought. Without prayer there is no hope.

And while she prayed, she saw the girl in front of her take a tangerine from her pocket. Seeing the tangerine sparked the tangy smell of it in her mind, and she suddenly remembered the open window in the breakfast room. A cold and horrifying sense of shock went through her.

My God, she thought, Baby left the window open – she left the window open because she was planning on coming back. And in that moment she knew that her mother was right and that something had happened to her sister.

She could not breathe. It was like a hand around her throat.

Dear God, if there is a God, she prayed. It was a new prayer for her. 'Deliver Baby back to us, we beseech Thee.'

'Becky, Becky.' It was Brona calling her, pushing through the throngs of girls, who were strangely silent. Their curiosity was clear, but somehow their usual whispers were muted, and they just turned and stared at Becky and Brona as they passed them.

Becky stopped and turned and faced her sister. Brona's face was scared and her hands were shaking.

'You look awful,' Brona said to her.

So do you, Becky thought. She wanted to tell Brona what she had recalled, but suddenly saw no point in adding to her sister's terror when clearly there was something happening Brona's end, so instead she said, 'What's up?'

'Come here.' Brona pulled her down the corridor. 'Something awful has happened.'

Becky was dragged along behind her and Brona took her to the hollow under the stairwell.

'Becky, the most awful thing. Don't be angry. Please, please don't be angry, but look what I've found.'

And Brona pulled the two letters from her pocket.

'Becky, I forgot. I took them from Baby's room . . . from under her pillow on Monday morning. Remember, when The Brush with Death sent me home from school? I found them then, and I put them in my pocket and I forgot until now. I just forgot.'

Brona's anguish was real, and Becky took the letters from her.

'Have you read them?' she asked her shaking sister.

'No. I only just found them. I'd forgotten. I put my hand in my pocket at prayers and there they were. What'll we do? What if they're important?'

In a remote way, Becky noted how Brona had both involved her and deferred to her over and over now that the chips were down.

'It's okay,' she said. 'You've given them to me. I'll pass them on. Don't worry.'

They looked at each other, and Becky clasped her sister's arm in a gesture of comfort, just like Eleanor had done earlier to her.

'Now, keep your chin up,' she told her younger sister, 'and go to class.'

Slipping the two letters into her pocket, she headed for the cloakroom, which was out of bounds during classes. She momentarily put aside her urgent need to impart the information that she had closed the window, and in so doing had locked Baby out.

The first envelope was postmarked in Dublin with an Irish stamp. With nervous fingers she drew the sheet of paper out and opened it.

Dear Barbara,

I gave you my number – phone me. I'm thinking about what we did. Let's do it again.

Love

C

Who's C when he's at home? Becky wondered. And what did they do?

The cloakroom door opened and Becky stepped back quickly between the rows of coats, shoving the letters into her pocket as she did so.

'What are you doing, Rebecca Dunville?' asked Sister Rodriguez, looking at Becky with narrowed eyes.

'Sorry, Sister,' Becky replied, hoping the nun hadn't seen her sudden movement, and that the corners of the letters weren't sticking out of her pocket.

'I'm waiting,' said Sister Rodriguez.

'I felt funny after the Rosary, Sister, and I wanted to be by myself for a few minutes,' Becky lied.

Back in her classroom, Becky kept wondering about the other letter. All she had taken in was that it was postmarked London, and the date was possibly the twenty-seventh of December. It had been slightly blurred and she couldn't be sure. She tried to remember the post arriving over the Christmas period, but with lots of letters every day, even after Christmas, someone always just sorted them and laid them on the Benares tray in the hall. There were lots of late Christmas cards, she thought, so no one really asked about each other's mail.

Now the London envelope was like a gigantic weight in her pocket.

Those detectives are due in, she thought. She wondered if she should just hand the letters over to them, but then she thought no, that she had better read the second one. At least that way I'll know, she reasoned, and the more I know, the better. She had this feeling that she wasn't being told everything at home. There were conversations behind closed doors and information coming through seemed diluted.

Sister Rodriguez gave her no peace during French class, and seemed to have no understanding that her concentration was off.

'Rebecca Dunville,' she snapped time and time again. 'Pay attention.'

At one point Becky nearly shouted, 'Shut up,' at her.

This is not like me, she thought, casting her eyes down to her book. I don't feel like me. I can't stand this. This is unbearable.

French verbs swam around her head, and all she could think of was the other letter in her pocket.

I know it holds a clue ... I just know it. It may even have the answer, went the thoughts in her mind.

But she was afraid to ask if she could leave the room, and she had to wait until the class ended before heading for the toilets.

Darling B,

It's been one party after another since we arrived here, but that doesn't mean that I haven't missed you. In fact, all I can think of is getting back next week. Snip a little more of your pubic hair for me and send it post haste – I'm afraid I cut the last curl very finely and rolled it in a joint and smoked it on Christmas night. Water those plants, and keep some for me.

Never had a high like it.

Love

H

Becky read this twice in complete disbelief. If what she had seen the milkman do on the television coming up to Christmas had startled her, it was nothing to what she felt now.

Who is H, she wondered, and what in God's name does he mean? And obviously he knows about the plants. Maybe they're his. Maybe Baby was minding them for him.

She read the letter over and over, and eventually folded the sheet of paper and put it back in its envelope, and replaced it with the other one in her pocket. God, she thought, what'll I do with this?

Heading back down the corridor, she realised she must have been longer than she thought, as the corridor was empty and she could hear voices behind the various classroom doors.

'Are you all right?'

She spun around and found herself facing Mr Jones. He didn't look angry, she thought, trying to read the look on his face.

She nodded.

'I'm late for class,' she said.

'That's all right,' he replied. 'I'm late too. And it's my class you're late for.'

'Oh,' was all she could muster.

'Are you sure you're all right?' he repeated. 'You're terribly pale.'

'I found something,' she said. 'I've remembered something. I ...

I . . . don't know what to do.' Her voice faltered and wavered and she could feel herself on the verge of tears.

'That's all right,' he said to her. 'You're the missing girl's sister, aren't you?' He had his hand on her shoulder now.

She nodded miserably.

'Look at me,' he said to her, and reaching out he touched her chin. 'Can I help you?'

His voice was intense and she felt he was totally focused on her.

'I don't know,' she said. 'I don't know what to do. My other sister found letters of Baby's – letters she'd taken from her room and forgotten about – and I've read them, and I don't know what to do . . . and . . . and I remembered something awful. I don't know what to do,' she repeated.

'Do you want to talk to one of the nuns?' he asked her kindly.

'Oh no,' she said in horror.

'That's all right,' he said, slightly surprised at her vehemence. 'Look, we'll go into class, and afterwards stay behind and you can tell me, if you'd like. You can think about it during class, as you won't be singing anyway.'

He smiled at her, and she felt an incredible wave of reassurance as he steered her down the corridor.

'Okay?' he said, with his hand on the doorknob.

She nodded. He patted her lightly on the shoulder and then opened the door.

The class sang and Becky Dunville played the chords. When the bell rang for lunch, Mr Jones dismissed the class, calling on Becky to remain.

'Rebecca Dunville, please stay a moment while I give you some sheet music so that you can practise at home. You do have a piano?'

Becky nodded assent. Helen McKeever stuck up two fingers at her as she left the classroom with the rest of the girls, many of whom turned back to look at Mr Jones standing beside Becky at the piano. He looked through sheets of music until they were alone.

'Now, can I help you?' he asked.

'Yes,' she said. 'I know that I need to see the police when they come in, and I know that Mother Immaculata will be there, and I don't want her to see what I have to give them. And I'm afraid to wait until this evening when I get home.'

Standing up, she removed the two envelopes from her pocket. She held them for a moment while she looked at them again, and then she handed them over to him. He took them from her.

'May I read them?' he asked.

She looked away as she tried to imagine what he would make of the second letter, and then she nodded.

'You said there's something that came back to you,' he said gently to her.

Again she nodded, endeavouring to find the words to explain what she had remembered.

'This is awful,' she said. 'Really awful, and the police have to be told. I'd ask Mother Immaculata if I could phone home but I know she'll say no, and I wanted to tell my dad. And if I slip out to a phone box and get caught ... you know ... and the local box is always broken ...'

'Tell me,' said Mr Jones.

Becky knew that she was very pale, and suddenly she could hear his voice from a great distance. He was saying something like, 'You've got to talk.'

She tried to hold the words as they moved in her head. Glancing at the piano, she saw the keys very clearly outlined and then they started to blur.

Oh, no, she thought. No, not this. Not here.

'Faint,' she tried to say, trying to warn him, suddenly realising she had had no breakfast and remembering her father's words about her blood sugar levels, and then there was something cold washing through her, and her words and her thoughts were very loud as they roared in her head, and the floor seemed to come up to meet her.

'What do you think you are doing, Mr Jones?'

These were the first words which Becky heard as she started to come to. She moaned slightly to try to let Sister Rodriguez know that she was ill, but her moan added to the nun's belief that she had caught Mr Jones and one of her pupils in flagrante. Becky became aware of the floor under her, and that she was cradled in the arms of the crouching Mr Jones.

'She fainted,' said Mr Jones evenly to Sister Rodriguez. 'Can you assist me, Sister?'

Sister Rodriguez reassessed the situation. Within a few seconds Becky could feel the flapping of hands in front of her face, as Sister Rodriguez endeavoured to revive her.

'I'm okay,' Becky mumbled.

'No slang, Rebecca Dunville,' said Mother Immaculata, whose sudden appearance in the classroom had something vaguely miraculous about it. 'You are a girl of St Martin's, and "okay" is not in our vocabulary.'

'Yes, Reverend Mother,' murmured Becky as she started to feel the texture of Mr Jones' jacket against her cheek, and realised that one of his hands was stroking her hair.

'Poor girl,' said Mr Jones.

Becky was unsure whether this was addressed to her or to the head nun, but either way Mother Immaculata made a noise which sounded like *pshaw*.

'She's terribly pale,' continued Mr Jones. 'And this situation with her sister missing must be a terrible strain. Shouldn't she be brought to sick bay?' he asked.

Becky could see Mother Immaculata considering the possibilities before agreeing.

'I'll carry her,' added Mr Jones, scooping Becky up in his arms. 'She's no weight at all. Please lead the way,' he said to the Reverend Mother, who immediately responded, '*I* will lead the way,' to show that it was she who was in charge.

'You'll be all right,' Mr Jones whispered to Becky as he carried her from the classroom.

Two thoughts went through Becky's head. One went along the lines of, I hope no one can see my knickers, and the other thought was, I hope everyone can see me being carried by Mr Jones.

The safest thing to do, she reasoned, was to close her eyes and just enjoy the feel of being carried in his arms at speed through the school. She could hear the swish of the nuns' robes and the mumblings of pupils as they passed down the corridors and through from one building to the next. Then she could feel that he was ascending the staircase, as she seemed to bob up and down a little in his arms.

Then suddenly she was being lowered on to a cool bed, and her head felt the depth of a pillow beneath it.

'You may leave us, Mr Jones,' announced Mother Immaculata.

'I'll take her shoes off first to save you doing it, Mother Immaculata,' he said, in those same even tones.

Then Becky felt her shoes being released from her feet.

Thank God I don't have smelly feet like Helen McKeever, she thought as she opened her eyes and smiled at him.

149

'You'll be all right now, Rebecca,' he said. 'You're in safe and caring hands.'

She wondered whether she could hear an edge in his voice.

'Were you being sarky?' she asked him later, much later. 'That day I fainted, remember, and you carried me to sick bay. Were you being sarcastic when you said that I was in safe and caring hands?' There was not a word that he said which she did not retain in her schoolgirl's mind.

'Sarcastic?' he teased. 'Me? About the good nuns? Never.

'You were so pale,' he continued. 'I was worried.'

'And the Raven thought we were up to something,' giggled Becky.

'Good thing she can't see us now,' said Mr Jones, as he undid Becky Dunville's school tie.

In sick bay, Becky dozed fitfully until Sister Sick (such was the name the girls had given to the nun in charge of sick bay) brought her in a tray. 'Mother Immaculata spoke to your father, and he said to give you tea and toast, said Sister Sick, peering at Becky. 'You are very pale, my girl,' she commented as an afterthought. 'After your tea you can rest a while before going back to class.'

Glancing at the clock on the wall and noticing the time, she corrected herself. 'You can rest until the end of classes and then go home.'

Becky slept after Sister Sick left, and somehow got forgotten. When she woke it was four thirty and school was well over.

Getting out of bed, she slipped on her shoes and tried to tidy her hair before leaving sick bay. The school was strangely quiet as she headed through the corridors to collect her coat and bag.

They must be at prep, she thought vaguely.

She felt a bit better, but there was an eerie feel to the place as she let herself out the main door and pulled it closed behind her.

The cold winter air hit her, and she buttoned and belted her gabardine before descending the steps and setting off down the street. It was already dark and her breath clouded in front of her. The street lamps were flickering and she suddenly remembered with horror that she had not yet told anyone about how she had closed and locked the breakfast room window on the Sunday night; that that was still there to be dealt with.

I better hurry, she thought. The sooner I get home and tell them, the better.

It was slightly foggy and she shivered in the cold as she hastened towards the corner of Sutherland Street to head in the direction of the Square.

'Do you need a lift?' a voice said to her from a car window.

She jumped in surprise, as she had not even seen the car, let alone registered that there was someone in it.

Mr Jones looked up out of the window of a dark blue Mini.

Becky hesitated. He was so incredibly kind to her, and there seemed to be a lack of kindness in her life. She nodded.

'Are you feeling better?' he asked.

'I slept,' she said. 'I'm fine now, thank you.'

She felt embarrassed that he had seen her faint, and although she wished that she hadn't fainted, she loved the way he had held her and carried her.

Getting into his car, she was terribly aware of him sitting in the driver's seat, and how long his legs seemed, and how his hands moved the steering wheel.

'I passed the letters to the police,' he said. 'They came in while you were in sick bay.'

'What did they say?' she asked.

'They took them and read them, and asked how I'd come by them. There is nothing for you to worry about.'

'Did any of the girls go in to see them?'

'I gather that a few did, but Sister Rodriguez seemed to think that they were just attention-seekers. Mother Immaculata agreed that several of Baby's closest friends should be interviewed. But more than that I don't know.'

'I see,' said Becky.

It felt so strange to be sitting in Mr Jones' Mini, driving through the darkened streets towards home.

Strange? she thought to herself. More like unbelievable.

But she was grateful for both the warmth and the company, and she knew that these moments with him would be taken out that night in bed to be gone over and over.

'In the corridor before class, you said you'd remembered something. What was it?' asked Mr Jones as they pulled down Lansdowne Road.

'I closed the window,' Becky said. 'I locked Baby out.'

Mr Jones listened as she explained what had happened.

'Go in and tell them,' he said. 'Do you want me to come in with you?' he added.

'No thank you.' She shook her head. 'I'll be all right now,' she added. 'Honestly,' she said, because he looked so dubious. 'And thank you.'

'That's okay,' he said, adding with a small laugh, 'I imagine I'm allowed to use the word *okay*, not being a pupil of St Martin's.'

Becky gave him a small smile, then she opened the door and got out slowly, reluctance showing in her movements.

'Look,' he said, leaning across and looking up at her through her still open door, 'it strikes me that you're in a very difficult situation. If you need to talk . . .'

The open-ended sentence rang in her ears as she walked up the drive. The cars outside on the road belonged to detectives, she knew that instinctively, and it was with fear that she took the key from under the flowerpot, and went in.

Brona came down the stairs and looked at her.

'What happened to you?' she asked. 'You look dreadful.'

Becky shrugged. 'Long story,' she said. 'Who's inside?' She jerked her head towards the drawing room.

'Aunty Nancy is there, and Mummy and Daddy, and three cops, no robbers. Oh, and Uncle James is there too. He just arrived in the last few minutes.'

'What's up?' asked Becky. 'Is there any news?'

Brona scowled and shook her head before heading for the kitchen.

'No news and no food either,' she muttered. 'Maybe Mrs O'Doody will have left us something.'

Hovering in the hall, Becky looked at her face in the mirror. She did look pale.

Pale and interesting, she thought hopefully, wondering how Mr Jones saw her.

Her uncle James appeared behind her.

'Hello,' he said. His voice was kind, and so were his eyes.

'Is there any news?' she asked, trying to put as much optimism as she could into her voice.

He didn't need to answer. It was written all over his face.

'A couple of letters have turned up,' he said. 'It's hoped they'll throw some light on things.'

Becky nodded.

'I passed them on,' she said. 'And Uncle James, there's the most awful thing . . . something I'd forgotten.'

'What is it?' he asked.

'On Sunday night,' she said, 'you know that's when Baby . . . disappeared . . . I came downstairs to get a tangerine. I only remembered today when I smelt one in school, and the window was open. The breakfast-room window, I mean. And I closed and locked it. I locked her out.'

The words came out in a rush. There was guilt and panic all over her face.

He could hear it in her voice. 'Look, you did nothing wrong. If you find a window open, you close it. There's nothing to be worried about. But we do need to tell them inside. Right away. Now, what time do you think this was at?'

'What time was this?' asked Conor O'Connor, the junior detective. 'Can you pinpoint it at all?'

Becky shook her head. 'I'm not sure,' she said. 'I sort of think something disturbed me . . . maybe I heard something . . . I don't know. Midnight? That's the best I can do. Maybe a little before. I'm just not sure.'

'This is good,' he said to her. 'And you haven't done anything wrong,' he reassured her, just as James Fitzgerald had done.

'I should have remembered,' she said.

'Why? Why should you? You closed a window. Any other time it would have had no significance. This time it does,' said Conor O'Connor. 'You didn't do anything wrong.' His voice was reassuring.

Everyone in the room could hear the fear and self-recrimination in her voice as she reiterated, 'But I locked her out.'

'If she was trying to get back in,' said Aunty Nancy firmly to Becky, 'then she would have. Now that's enough of that. Have you had anything to eat?' she asked, and she took her niece firmly and kindly by the arm and led her out of the room.

'Shouldn't I stay?' Becky asked.

'You've had enough for one day,' Aunty Nancy said.

'Don't you think Aunty Nancy is awfully . . . nice?' said Becky to Brona later that evening. 'She's really considerate. Not the way I usually think of her at all.'

'I think she's awfully interfering,' Brona said. 'And so does Mummy.

I heard her talking to Daddy about it. She doesn't want Aunty Nancy around at the moment.'

'I wonder why,' Becky said thoughtfully. 'I mean, if it weren't for Aunty Nancy ... well ... I don't know.'

They were on the landing, hovering before going to bed. They seemed to be trying to prolong these late night moments together.

'You weren't on the bus coming home,' said Brona.

'I wasn't well,' Becky said, 'and I ended up in sick bay and when I woke it was really late.'

Brona looked at her closely.

'Becky,' she said.

'Mmm,' replied Becky vaguely, as she was suddenly thinking about Mr Jones.

'Becky, you know the way I teased you about being fat?'

Becky bristled and narrowed her eyes.

'Becky, you're not fat. You're very, very thin. Aunty Nancy said it to Mummy and Mummy went mad.'

'I'm fine,' Becky said. 'And I'm going to bed now. Good night.'

In her bedroom she lifted her pyjama top and looked at her ribs.

I'm fine, she thought. But maybe ...

She didn't finish the thought. She wanted to get into her bed, and to think about Mr Jones carrying her through the school.

Like Lancelot, she thought. *He moved a little pace ...*

But in bed she found her thoughts going back to downstairs and the various happenings of the evening. She thought about Conor O'Connor, the detective. He was a burly man, big, dark, and a good bit younger than her father, but nonetheless fatherly. There was something kind about him. He seemed to have taken them under his wing.

Just doing his job, I suppose, she thought.

At one point she'd been in the hall and he'd come out from the drawing room, and she'd asked him if he had got the letters all right.

'Mr Jones passed them to you?' she asked, knowing that he had, but wanting to make contact with him.

'Yes,' he said. 'Did you read them?'

She thought of lying, because she didn't want him to ask her about the contents. In fact she couldn't bear to think about the one from 'H'. However, lying didn't seem a very good idea, so she just nodded at him.

'Don't worry about them,' he said to her. His voice was kind. 'Other people will look after them now.'

'Did . . . did you show them to my parents?' she asked hesitantly.

'To your father, yes,' he replied. 'Not to your mother, not yet. There is nothing in them that is going to make it easier for her, and they're handling enough today.'

But *I* have to handle the contents, she thought. And I don't know how to.

'I've discussed them with your uncle James,' continued Conor O'Connor, as if he could read her thoughts. 'So if you need or would like to talk to him about them, then you should. Or to me,' he added. 'If you want to ask me anything, you can.'

She shook her head.

'Did Baby never mention any boys to you? Never?' he asked.

'Never,' Becky said. 'Never ever.'

'And you have no idea who the letters might be from?' he asked.

'No. I assume from boys, but I don't know who they might be. I don't know what boys Baby might have known.'

'And do you have a boyfriend?' he asked her.

She shook her head, but she was thinking of Mr Jones.

She was still thinking of Mr Jones as she fell asleep.

Chapter Ten

During the night Brona woke, legs flailing under her bedclothes. Clambering out, she headed across to Becky's room and slipped into bed beside her.

'Becky,' she whispered.

Becky emerged with a jolt from her dream world, a place where people were smoking the strangest things, and she was playing music to accompany them.

'It's the wrong chord,' she said to the surprised Brona.

'What is?' asked her younger sister.

Becky looked through the darkness in surprise as she recognised the feel of her sister in the bed beside her.

'What do you want?' she asked.

'I had a nightmare,' Brona whispered. 'I don't want to be alone.'

'You're okay now, go back to sleep,' Becky said.

'I'm afraid I'm going to disappear,' Brona said, as she snuggled down in the bed.

Yes, thought Becky. I know what you mean. I know that feeling. I had it in sick bay this afternoon. A strange, scary feeling, finding myself all alone and wondering was it I or they who had disappeared. I'd forgotten. She recalled that instant of wakening in the strange bed with its white counterpane, and the white walls of the room with just a crucifix hanging opposite the bed, with its tortured Christ gazing down. And in the silence of the room, as awareness started to sink in, she wondered if she were the one who had vanished without trace . . . and then memories started to filter through, and with them came the fear again.

'Go to sleep,' she said aloud as her mind churned through the day and the days gone by.

I wish I hadn't closed that window, she thought. No matter what Aunty Nancy says. I wish I hadn't. What if Baby came back, running scared, and headed for the window and found it closed, and whoever was chasing her caught her . . .

The thoughts and fears were terrifying.

What are we supposed to do? she wondered. How do we pass the time? Like today – the awfulness of today ... pretending ... not knowing ... not knowing what people were thinking. And by tomorrow everyone will know what was in the paper. And what did it sound like, what Mother Immaculata said? How could Baby be gone?

She lay there beside the now sleeping Brona and stared into the darkness. 'It's early days', that was what Uncle James had said. What on earth does that mean? she wondered. When will it be late days? When will time be up?

She shivered.

I wish I had a best friend, she thought. Even a Rhona Brophy thinkalike, or someone like Anne Marie O'Mahony with whom I could share.

She wondered if the police had talked to Anne Marie. How could they not have? She would know more about Baby's activities than anyone else would.

There were so many frightening thoughts inside her head. She thought about her own classmates – Helen McKeever, whom she often sat beside, but she couldn't talk to her, and Gabriela von Vecker ... and how every time a new girl arrived, which wasn't very often, she hoped that just maybe she'd find a special friend.

No one to talk to, she thought. Really only Brona, but she needs my support, not my worries.

She closed her eyes tight, and there was Mr Jones patting her knee in the car. He'd said something about this, something about if she needed to talk. She thought about his hair and the way it was so straight, and his eyes were grey with tiny flecks ... she was almost sure there were tiny flecks in them ... of a darker grey maybe ... and his tweed jacket felt nice against her cheek ... and he had taken off her shoes ... so romantic ...

Three o'clock in the morning, and Elizabeth Dunville, lying in her bed, stared blindly at the ceiling. Deep inside her she could feel what she was convinced was the agony of Baby. Added to that was the extreme frustration that no one would listen to her or believe her. She knew that something had happened to Baby, as surely as if it had happened to her. She could hear John's even breathing as he slept.

How can he sleep? she wondered. How can anyone sleep when this is happening? Please God, give us Baby back. Baby, wherever you are, know that I am with you. I'm holding you in my arms and in my heart as surely as if you were here.

The previous evening the police had asked for a description of the clothes Baby was wearing when she went missing, and she and Becky had gone up to her eldest daughter's room to try to work out what was missing.

After searching through and through her things, Becky said that Baby's newest jeans were missing, and her black boots.

Elizabeth had knelt there on the floor, looking at the wardrobe and how neatly Baby had kept her clothes.

And this is all that is left of her, she had thought. Standing up again and leaning into the cupboard, she could smell the fragrance of Baby in it. Picking up a sweater, she buried her face in it, and it was as if Baby were there.

Now in her bed she longed again for that sensation – the feel of Baby in her senses – and she eased herself out of the bed and, slipping out of the room, went up the stairs to the top floor.

In Baby's room she took the same sweater from the cupboard, and lying down on Baby's bed, she held it close to her face, and the feeling came stronger that Baby was somewhere terrible.

She wanted to cry but she bit back the tears because she was afraid that in crying she would no longer be able to breathe Baby in.

When she woke it was to find John lying beside her on Baby's bed, holding her close, and she knew that he was trying to connect with her, but she pushed him away.

'We've got to talk,' he said.

After the girls had gone to school he tried again.

'But I can't talk to you,' Elizabeth said. 'There is no talking to you. You won't listen. I know that something has happened to Baby. I know it.'

'Listen to me,' he tried. 'Just listen. You may well be right. In fact I think you are, but all the evidence is showing that Baby had a life of her own – one we knew nothing about. There's that notebook, and I must admit I can make no sense of the figures and letters in it. And the marijuana plants. Elizabeth, unless we can come up with something other than mere feelings—'

'Mere feelings,' she shouted at him. 'Mere feelings? You call these mere feelings? Oh God.'

There was despair then in her voice.

'Oh, go to work,' she said dismissively.

'I'll go when Nancy comes,' he replied.

'I don't want her here.'

He got up in frustration and went to make coffee.

'She's just impossible to get through to,' he said to Nancy when she arrived.

'Don't worry,' Nancy said. 'You go on to work and I'll take over.'

'She's not that keen on you being here,' John said tentatively to his sister-in-law.

'I'll talk to her,' Nancy reassured him. 'Someone has to be here . . . in case there's news . . .'

In school Rhona gave Brona a dig in the ribs.

'You're quite a celebrity,' she said. There was slight envy in her voice.

'Well, I'll swap places with you if you like,' Brona said fiercely.

'Where do you think Baby's gone?' Rhona asked.

'Don't know,' Brona replied. 'Mummy thinks something has happened to her. I think the police think she's run off or something. I don't know.'

'And your dad and Becky,' persisted Rhona. 'What do they think?'

'Don't know,' Brona said. 'God, I hate this place. All this praying. It's driving me mad. And if it isn't praying, it's French verbs. Fat lot of good they are.'

'Well, if Baby has run away to France,' said Rhona helpfully, 'she might find them useful.'

Becky saw Conor O'Connor in the main hall as she headed to her classroom. Checking quickly that there were no nuns around, she approached him.

'Hello,' she said.

'And how are you today?' he asked.

'I'm fine.' She brushed the query away. 'Have you . . . well, have you spoken to Anne Marie O'Mahony?' she asked him. 'I keep thinking she's the most likely person to know something.'

'That's why I'm here now,' he said. 'She was absent yesterday. I called to her house but there was no one there. If she's in today I'm going to see her here, and otherwise I'll head back to her home.'

'I'm sorry,' Becky said. 'It sounds like I'm interfering, or telling you what to do.'

'No,' he said kindly. 'Any assistance is welcome. Any thoughts that you have . . .' He left the sentence unfinished.

'Baby will be all right, won't she?' Becky asked.

In her classroom she thought about that encounter. He hadn't really answered her, she realised. With that sinking feeling that she was getting used to, she lifted the lid of her desk and pulled out her books.

'I'm supervising you for this period,' said Mr Jones as he walked up the aisle between the desks. 'Sister Rodriguez has been detained.'

There were a number of sniggers at him using the word 'period', but a look from him quietened down the stirrings in the class.

Then, just as he reached the top of the class, Becky looked up and met his eyes. His mouth moved slightly in a smile of something she could not quite define. Complicity, she thought? Or maybe understanding, maybe comprehension. She felt that he knew the leaden weight inside her.

She watched him standing in front of the mantelpiece with the coal fire burning in the grate, saw the way the winter light came through the windows in shafts, and how he moved his long musician's hands. Behind him the statue of St David stood with its perfect face and she had the feeling that time was standing still.

For one brief second everything in the room seemed outlined clearly, and then there was the most horrifying sound of an explosion, and the windows lifted from their frames and came shattering in on the screaming girls.

'Down, down, under your desks,' yelled Mr Jones, and the twenty-five terrified girls covered in glass shards slipped to the floor and crouched beneath their desks, shaking.

It was as if time stood still, Becky wrote later in her diary. *It was impossible to know what had happened first. As if the sound of the bomb reached us after the windows lifted. When we got back up and saw the damage and realised that no one was actually hurt (a miracle, as Mother Immaculata said), the candle in front of the statue on the mantelpiece was still lighting, and the only difference was that there were no windows. The classroom hadn't been too cold because of the fire, but suddenly it was freezing.*

Mr Jones was wonderful. He made us stay under the desks until we were given an all-clear. Then we were ushered out the back of the school into the freezing cold because there was still the fear of another car bomb on the street.

The car had been further down the street from the school, closer to Sutherland Square. At first it was unclear where the bomb had actually been placed, because every vehicle parked there had gone up in the explosion. Becky's classroom windows were the only ones in the school which had caved in.

Sister Rodriguez said that that was a sign that there was evil among us, and that it was the statue of St David which had protected us, wrote Becky in her neat hand that night. *Uncle James said, 'A load of cobblers' when I told him, and we both laughed. Then later, when we were absolutely freezing, we were allowed into the refectory and given tea. Most of us were shivering both from the cold and from shock. Mr Jones was great. He was very organised and yet gentle. He smiled so gently at me. He checked that each of us had tea and those who were really shaking, he said they should put extra sugar in their cups. Helen McKeever said he could put extra sugar in her cups any day, and she patted her chest. How juvenile. Uncle James said that whoever put the car there probably got the wrong Square and that it should have been down beside the British Embassy, and that everyone was very lucky that there was no one on the street.*

But later that evening, while Becky was writing in her diary, the army experts putting the pieces together from the bomb discovered that there had indeed been someone caught in the explosion.

Because of the damage to all the vehicles, it was at first unclear which car she had been in, but the broken body of a girl was found, burnt and fragmented beyond recognition.

The phone rang at ten thirty p.m., and Becky, who happened to be in the hall, answered it.

'Have you any comment to make?' asked the voice at the other end of the phone.

'About what?' Becky asked in surprise.

'About the girl whose body was found near the bomb?'

Becky stood beside the phone, the receiver having fallen from her hand as she tried to understand what was being said.

'What is it?' asked Uncle James, coming into the hall.

She looked up wildly at him, her mouth open, but no words coming out.

Uncle James picked up the phone but the line was dead.

A few moments later, Conor O'Connor arrived at the front door. He knew from their faces that they'd already been told.

'I came as fast as I could,' he said. 'But there's always someone faster.'

James Fitzgerald brought him into the drawing room, where they were all gathered.

'It's not certain,' Conor said to them. 'It's only a possibility. It's a young woman, roughly . . . well, roughly the right height, but more than that is unclear.'

'Is she dead?' asked Elizabeth Dunville, pacing in front of the fire. Her voice sounded choked.

'Yes, yes, she is,' he replied. 'Death would have been instantaneous.'

'It isn't Baby,' Elizabeth said. 'Baby isn't dead. I can feel her. She's in a terrible situation, but she isn't dead. You've got to find her. Please.'

She looked around wildly.

'Time is running out. Please.'

'Come and sit down, Elizabeth,' Nancy said to her. 'Come and sit.'

'Oh, stop it, Nancy,' Elizabeth replied. 'It doesn't matter if I'm standing or sitting. That isn't Baby, and nobody is doing anything about finding her. Please will someone find her.'

'What hospital?' asked John Dunville of the detective.

'She's been brought to yours,' was the reply.

'I should get in there straight away.'

'I've a car outside for you,' Conor O'Connor said. 'But you know they won't let you in on the—'

'I need to see her,' John said. 'I'll know at once.'

'You won't know,' Conor said. 'Trust me. You won't know.'

He took John aside, and Becky could just make out the words 'dental records . . . only possibility . . .'

'Who's with her?' John asked.

'There's a German doctor who's doing it,' said Conor O'Connor, 'together with a pathologist and forensic experts.'

'Good,' came the response. 'Von Vecker is good . . . very good. But I need to go in there.'

*   *   *

162

In the drawing room, the others sat as characters in a play. As Becky watched them, it occurred to her that both her uncle and her aunt must be going through their own pain with regard to their niece's disappearance, and yet they seemed to be detaching themselves from that so as to support her parents and Brona and herself. She wondered if that was what being a grown-up was, if that was what it meant, if that was how everyone behaved, or if they were exceptional.

But we don't know how to behave, she thought. Brona and I, we don't have a clue. We're going through the motions of normal days and school. And Mrs O'Doody is coming in and doing the cleaning and the laundry and the ironing as if it were all normal. But it isn't. It's the middle of the night, and there's been a bomb just beside the school, and now there's a girl dead and they think it is Baby. She heard an almighty sob and looking up she realised that it had come from her.

'These girls should go to bed,' she heard Aunty Nancy saying. 'Look at them. They need sleep.'

Brona was sitting staring at the picture on the wall above the fire. Her eyes were red-rimmed, and every few minutes tears would start to trickle down her cheeks. Then they would stop. She just sat there.

Baby dead, Becky thought. How could Baby be dead? Baby with her blonde curls and her big blue eyes, with her vivacity and her strength, how could that be? she wondered.

And like her mother the previous night, she remembered that fragrance of Baby coming from her wardrobe.

How could that be there, if Baby were dead? she wondered. What will happen to it? Will it fade until it disappears? Until there is nothing of Baby left?

It was almost midday on the Friday before Doktor von Vecker pronounced that the girl in the bomb was not Baby Dunville.

Thank God, Becky thought.

'Now will you get out there and look for her,' Elizabeth said, frustration, anger and exhaustion in her voice.

I'll kill you, Baby, when you get home, Becky thought, biting her lip, and biting back her fury.

'You looked so angry,' Brona said to her afterwards. 'Were you angry that it wasn't Baby?'

'No – not angry that it wasn't Baby,' Becky replied slowly. 'But I am angry that she is putting us through this. How about you?'

'I'm afraid,' Brona said. 'Afraid that this is going to go on and on and on. And I don't know what I'm supposed to do.'

Looking at her, Becky wondered if this was the same feeling that she was having. Because with the anger, there had of course been relief. Relief that Baby had not been in one of those cars. Relief that Baby was not broken and destroyed beyond identification. And then fear too.

I am afraid too, Becky thought. Fear . . . that is the over-riding feeling.

John Dunville broke down in the hospital in sheer relief, but knowing as he did so that the nightmare wasn't over, that it had simply taken a different turn.

'Eleanor is home for the weekend,' Nancy said to Elizabeth. 'Let us have the girls to stay. They'll be company for each other, and—'

'No,' said Elizabeth.

In the hall, Becky and Brona could hear them clearly as the door was open.

'What do you care about Becky and Brona? You . . . you . . . God, you dump your only daughter as a boarder so you don't have to look after her.'

'That's not quite fair,' they heard their aunt Nancy reply in a relatively even tone after a slight pause. 'You know we feel that Eleanor is better as a boarder so that she will have company. Otherwise she would be rattling around in our house on her own.'

'Oh, for goodness' sake,' said Elizabeth. 'That's just an excuse so that you don't have to spend time with her.'

This time there was a tightness in their aunt's voice as she responded. 'I'm going to ignore this, Elizabeth. We both know that not everyone is able to have two or three children. Or even one for that matter. And we consider ourselves lucky to have had the one. So please don't be unkind. All we're trying to do is to help.'

'I'd quite like to go to Uncle James and Aunty Nancy's for the weekend,' Brona whispered to Becky.

Becky didn't reply. She didn't know what she wanted. She just knew that where she was was unbearable.

They were putting on their gabardines and getting ready to go in for afternoon classes, as both parents said they would be better off in school rather than sitting around the house.

Better off? wondered Becky. What on earth can they mean? We can't concentrate. We haven't slept. We're going in to sit and wait.

'I'm glad they said we've to go into school,' said Brona. 'I can't bear being here.'

Maybe they're right, Becky thought. Maybe the distraction of school life is the easiest way to pass this time.

They both hovered in the hall, wondering if there would be more forthcoming from the drawing room, but a silence appeared to have descended from that quarter.

'We'd better say goodbye,' Becky muttered, as she headed in.

'We're off,' she said to the two adults. 'Mummy, if it's easier for you, Brona and I would be happy to go to the Fitzgeralds' for the weekend.'

'What do you mean, *easier* for me?' her mother snapped at her.

'I'm only trying to help,' Becky said.

'Help? Haven't you done enough already?' Elizabeth all but spat at her.

'How do you mean? I *am* only trying to help,' Becky said, aghast.

'I mean closing the window and locking Baby out,' her mother said with a sob.

Becky looked at her. She wanted to cry, but she would not.

'That is unfair, Elizabeth,' Nancy said, seeing the look on her niece's face. 'As well as being unkind ...'

'Maybe it is fair,' Becky said quietly. 'Although I didn't know she had gone out, I did close and lock the window. And I'm sorry.'

'It's not your fault,' her aunt said. 'Your mother is just exhausted, and terribly worried. She's not blaming you.'

'That makes a change,' Becky said bitterly, and left the room.

On the bus, Becky had the distinct impression that Brona was crying again, but her face was turned towards the window, and even in the reflection she could not be sure. She also had the feeling that roles within the family were being switched. Brona the aggressor, the tease and tormentor seemed so vulnerable, so unable to handle what was happening.

Not that I can handle it, Becky thought. But somehow I seem to be doing a better job of it. Or am I imagining that? And Aunty Nancy, who always tries to make us feel not as intelligent as Eleanor, seems to be pulling out all the stops and behaving in the most supportive way. Uncle James too. Not a bit like how they used to seem to me.

And Daddy, who is always a bit remote, now seems even more so. But in the past he always seemed on top of things, and now . . . well, now, he's not. And Mummy . . .' She couldn't bear to think about her mother. She looked so ill, and was so . . . Becky couldn't find the words.

'Chin up,' Becky said to Brona as they headed up the steps of St Martin's.

In school they reported in for late arrival, and Mother Immaculata for once did not demand a detailed explanation.

'We don't have a note,' Becky said. 'I'm sorry. It was impossible to ask for one.'

Mother Immaculata looked at the two girls standing in front of her, and merely asked, 'Any news, Rebecca?'

Becky glanced at Brona, who was hanging her head.

'Only that the girl in the bomb wasn't Baby, Mother,' Becky replied.

'We're praying,' the Reverend Mother said to them both. 'We're praying for Barbara and for your parents.'

Becky wondered if those prayers had changed the identity of the dead girl. She wondered for a moment if the girl had been Baby when the bomb went off, and then was metamorphosed into some other female. She said nothing.

She wanted to say 'thank you', but no words came out.

Just pray a little harder, she thought.

When school ended and she was going down the steps, Anne Marie O'Mahony caught her up.

'There's someone who wants to meet you,' Anne Marie said.

'Me?' asked Becky.

A nod from Anne Marie confirmed this.

Becky looked around for any sign of Brona, but there was none, so she followed Anne Marie down to Sutherland Square. They had to go the long way around, as part of Sutherland Street was still closed off after the bomb. As they walked through the gate into the Square, Becky got the feeling that she was entering a different world. The Square was out of bounds to the girls, and she never went into it, although she knew that other girls did. She was now taken with its sense of order. It was like a pure and perfect Dublin winter scene, the trees bare, the hedges thin, the cold winter grass cut close to the earth.

Ahead of her, sitting on the first bench, was a young man.

As they approached, he stood up and looked at them both, first of all nodding to Anne Marie, who just said, 'This is Becky,' and then turned and left.

Becky stood in front of him, taking him in. He was tall, with dark wavy hair, lean-faced, slim, quite pale, with dark brown eyes.

'Hello,' he said. 'I'm Hugo – Hugo Mombay Humphries, a friend of Baby's.'

H, she thought. This must be H.

He had a very nice and cultured English accent.

'Hello,' she said nervously. She'd wondered what he would be like, this mysterious H, and she was surprised at how nice he looked, at how he took his hand from his pocket as if he were going to shake hers, and then changed his mind.

'I'm so sorry,' he said.

'Sorry?' she asked.

'About what you must all be going through,' he replied. 'Is there any news?'

She shook her head.

'Have the police found you yet?' she asked. 'You know they're trying to place you.'

'I saw them this afternoon,' he said. 'I didn't know until last night, when I saw the papers.'

'But your letter said you missed her,' Becky said. She could hear something like petulance in her voice. 'Why didn't you try to contact her?'

'We were due in on Sunday night on the boat . . . I've told all this to the police,' he said. 'But I want to tell you too. Look, let's go somewhere where we can have coffee. It's freezing here, but it was the only place I could think of when I spoke to Anne Marie.'

They walked down to Trinity College, neither really saying anything. They entered the college through Lincoln Gate, and they walked side by side in silence until they got to the Buttery. From time to time she looked at him from the side and she could see how attractive he was. He had a good profile and he held himself well. She found she couldn't concentrate. Everything seemed to distract her, as though she'd lost the facility to move her thoughts forward. The closely cropped grass of the frosted playing fields reminded her of the grass in Sutherland Square.

'It's quite empty,' she said. 'I thought it would be packed with students.'

'Term doesn't start until next week,' Hugo responded.

In the Buttery he pointed at a table.

'Take a seat,' he said, 'while I get us something hot to drink.'

She looked around with interest. It was her first time there and she felt a sense of excitement. She drank in the layout and the atmosphere. The ceiling was low in the underground restaurant.

Like in a cave, she thought, looking around at the alcoves and pillars which seemed to divide it up. She felt self-conscious sitting there on a small stool, waiting for him to return, but no one seemed to notice or to look at her in any odd way. She wished she wasn't wearing her school uniform.

'Maybe you'd have preferred tea,' he said, putting the mug of coffee in front of her. 'I forgot to ask how you take it, so I put in milk. Do you need sugar?'

She shook her head.

She kept thinking that if Baby weren't missing, this would be terribly exciting, but because of the over-riding feeling of fear and unease, the right ingredients for real excitement were absent.

'Are you a student here?' she asked.

'Yes,' he said. 'I'm in my third year. Look . . .' He paused. 'This is difficult. I really didn't know that Baby had sisters. I did ask her, you know, and she said no, that she was an only child.'

'Oh.' Becky momentarily felt mildly hurt by this, but then she nodded. 'That's sort of typical of Baby, I suppose,' she admitted. 'I think she'd have liked to have been the only one.'

'Yes.' He nodded. 'Now let me explain. The boat didn't get in on Sunday night because of the fog. I'd arranged to meet Baby in Sandymount. I've been living there in a flat. My parents live nearby, on Merrion Road,' he added. 'Anyway, the boat didn't dock until the following morning, and I went to Sutherland Square for four thirty that afternoon – that's where Baby and I would regularly meet – and she never turned up.'

'Why didn't you phone?' Becky asked.

'She'd told me not to. She said her parents wouldn't like it.'

More likely that she was afraid you'd find out she has sisters, Becky thought.

'So I went again on Tuesday, and when she didn't turn up I thought maybe she was off sick. I waited for Anne Marie outside St Martin's on Wednesday, but she never appeared, and then yesterday I finally saw a paper from Wednesday and found out that Baby was missing.

I didn't see it until last night,' he said a little defensively, 'and then there was the item on the news about the girl in the bomb . . .'

Becky was about to ask why he hadn't phoned then, but he looked so upset.

'This morning I went to the police, and I was interviewed by a detective this afternoon.'

'What did they say?' she asked.

'Well . . . they went through everything, even making it sound like I needed an alibi . . .'

'Fair enough,' Becky heard herself saying. Her confidence was surprising her. It was as if she were not prepared to leave anything unsaid. 'I mean, you must be the reason she slipped out of the house on Sunday night.'

'I know,' he said. 'Anyway, they've confirmed I was on the boat in the middle of the Irish Sea and so I'm in the clear. My parents were there, and so were hundreds of other passengers.'

'So why did you want to meet me?' Becky asked.

He was silent for a moment.

'Look,' he said. 'First of all I didn't know you existed, and I was shocked. Then there is the fact that I . . . I really like Baby . . . I really do. And if there's anything I can do, I want to do it.'

He met her eyes squarely.

'I really mean that. I have an idea what you're all going through . . .'

Becky noted in an abstract way how he spoke of Baby in the present tense. 'I really like Baby', he had said, not 'liked'. He doesn't give the impression of knowing of anything that might have happened to her, she thought.

'Do you have any ideas?' she asked.

He hesitated.

'Look, I don't want to upset you,' he said. 'I mean, not any more than you already are. But it occurred to me that if she lied about you and your sister, maybe she lied about other things. I tried to talk to Anne Marie, but she just clammed up. The detective, chap called O'Connor, had mentioned you and your sister, and so I asked Anne Marie if she'd introduce us.'

Becky nodded.

'Go on,' she said.

'I was thinking if maybe you could talk to her – to Anne Marie, I mean – she might tell you something. It's just a thought.'

'You are the "H" in the letter, aren't you?' Becky said.

He looked slightly embarrassed.

'The one sent over Christmas?' he asked.

'Referring to plants,' she said, hoping that would clarify matters. He nodded.

'Yes, that's me,' he admitted. This time he didn't meet her eyes, but she could hardly blame him as she thought about what the letter had said.

And he was both kind and chivalrous. He went with her to the bus stop, walking on the road side of the pavement, and he said supportive things, that he was there, that she should feel free to contact him. He gave her his number, and she checked that he had theirs.

'You can phone, you know,' she said to him. 'Really, it's all right. Especially now.'

On the bus she thought how much easier it was when she was talking, when she was with other people, when she felt that the worry was being shared.

It's not that it makes it go away, she thought. Nor that it makes what's happening any smaller. But it does help to talk. It makes you feel not so alone.

She stared out of the bus window at the houses they were passing, and wondered what was going on behind those walls.

Maybe other people with problems, not like our problem, but other ones, maybe ones just as frightening in their own way. This must be what Mr Jones said about talking. When you talk, it's not quite so bad.

Chapter Eleven

I n bed that night Becky lay looking at the ceiling, memories of the day flooding through her. Brona was already in beside her, not having bothered to wait for a nightmare to waken her and bring her to Becky's side.

I wonder what her nightmares are like, Becky wondered. I wonder what Baby's are like. *Are* like? *Were* like? Does she have nightmares? Is she alive? Baby, where are you?

She tried to move away from images of Baby, and directed her mind back to the afternoon. Mr Jones did not appear to have been in school.

But then he is only part-time,' she thought. 'I wonder what else he does. I wonder how old he is. It was always difficult to judge an adult's age. Clearly older than Hugo, because Hugo is still a student . . . but more than that she could not work out.

Later, when she was sitting on his knee and he had undone her tie, she would ask him, 'How old were you when you first came to St Martin's?'

'Twenty-four,' he said.

'I'm surprised the nuns employed you,' she said with a grin.

'Don't be cheeky,' he said. 'Anyway, why wouldn't they? Am I not charming?'

'Well, that's exactly what I was getting at,' Becky said mischievously. 'And I didn't think Mother Immaculata would succumb to those charms,' she added. 'But you can never tell, I suppose.'

'It's a long story,' he said with a smile. 'But basically she employed me on my reputation and a recommendation. You remember I came in just after Christmas? Well, she was desperate to get someone, as one of the nuns was ill, and a cousin of mine did the recommending – my age didn't come into it until she met me . . . oh . . . just a few days before the school reopened. By that point she had virtually agreed to

171

it. She was surprised, I must admit, when she saw how young I was, but I had an excellent CV, on which I had omitted my age. And she needed someone on the first Monday of term.'

'And you fitted the bill,' Becky said.

'Yes. It suited me perfectly – I was trying to keep various options open, and I needed to supplement my orchestral work,' he continued, as he opened the buttons on Becky's school shirt. 'Now, what have we here?' he asked.

But in the dark on that long Friday night Becky's mind moved on to think about Hugo Mombay Humphries, and little by little her thoughts returned to Baby.

Tomorrow I'll go to see Anne Marie, she thought. I'll ask questions, and maybe get answers.

Her mind wandered back to the Christmas holidays and she tried to remember the various nights when Baby went out.

They were always nights out with Anne Marie, and usually staying over at Anne Marie's, weren't they? she asked herself. That first night of the holidays when she didn't come home, and I got into trouble over the key – oh God, if I hadn't given her that lie on a plate, maybe none of this would ever have happened. Maybe she'd have got into a sufficient row that she wouldn't have been allowed out again . . . but then she wouldn't have been allowed out on the night she disappeared . . . I mean, she just went . . .

Becky thought about that and about how she felt responsible. Then she pursued the train of thought about Baby going out. She could recall at least two other evenings when she had gone over to stay with Anne Marie.

And everyone seemed so prepared to lie and to cover up . . . like that chauffeur of the O'Mahonys'. She recalled how he had lied about bringing Baby home on the last night of term. She wondered if she should tell the detective about him.

'What do you think has happened to her?' Anne Marie asked Becky the following day.

Becky had called to the O'Mahonys' house, and Anne Marie, after an initial chilly reception, then seemed to warm up. They were sitting in what appeared to be a library or study. Becky was unsure which.

And I thought our house was quite large, she thought. You live and learn.

172

The O'Mahonys' house was much larger, and although it stood only two storeys high, it had a basement, and it seemed to sprawl back endlessly.

'I don't know,' she replied to Anne Marie's question. 'At first I thought she had run away, but then there was this thing with a window which she had left open, and so she really did mean to return. And Hugo . . . well, she was supposed to be meeting him. So she didn't run away or anything, which is what the police thought . . . at least that's what I think they thought at first. It's all so complicated. Anyway, Baby liked comforts and being comfortable, and that was all there at home.'

'Yes, I know. I know what you mean,' Anne Marie said. 'I think what I really meant is, do you think she's alive?'

Becky sat motionless. It was so frightening when it was put into words. She couldn't bear the thought of answering, and didn't know how to anyway.

'I don't know,' she said after a minute. 'What do you think?'

'I'm scared,' Anne Marie admitted. 'She . . . you know . . . she took risks, I suppose.'

'How do you mean?' Becky asked.

'Oh, I don't know.' Anne Marie seemed vague again. She swung around in the armchair she was sitting in, so that her legs were over one of the arms. 'I don't know,' she repeated.

Looking at her watch, she said, 'I've things to do, so is there anything else you want to know?'

Of course there is, Becky thought, but did not say aloud.

'Well,' Becky said, 'you remember that evening, the day that term ended and Baby spent the night here? She was supposed to be home that night. What happened?'

Anne Marie dropped her head back so that her hair hung down the side of the armchair, and she stared at the ceiling. Becky looked up to see what Anne Marie might be looking at. The ceiling was painted white and was very high. Other than that it was difficult to see what was absorbing Anne Marie's attention.

'You know,' Becky continued carefully, 'if I tell my dad that your chauffeur lied to cover for her, he'll be over here rather smartly . . .'

'I am going to answer you,' Anne Marie said quickly. 'I was just trying to remember which night it was. Oh, yes . . . that night . . . We went to town and got a bit delayed, I suppose.'

'But where?' asked Becky. 'And with whom?'

173

'I think it must have been with Hugo,' Anne Marie said. 'He was Baby's boyfriend, you know.'

'I know that. But I also know that you weren't with Hugo. He told me he left for England that morning.' Becky felt chilled as she heard the past tense used by Anne Marie. And she knew then that Anne Marie thought Baby was dead.

'So who were you with?' she persisted.

'We met a couple of blokes,' Anne Marie said slowly. 'I don't even remember their names. We got back too late and ...' Her voice trailed away.

'Were you drinking?'

'I don't see why I should answer you at all,' Anne Marie snapped.

'You don't have to,' Becky said. 'But she's your best friend, and she's my sister, and I don't know about you, but I can't bear what's happening and I want to find her. Please help me. Please.'

There was silence again from Anne Marie. She swung back on the chair so that she was sitting normally.

'Look, I'll tell you,' she said, 'but you have to promise not to tell your parents. They'll get on to mine, and I'll be in hot water.'

I'm not promising anything, Becky thought, but aloud she said, 'I won't tell them anything they don't need to know.'

Bit by bit she got snippets of information: Baby and Anne Marie dropping into a pub, having a drink, being chatted up by men who didn't know they were only seventeen.

'Just a bit of fun,' Anne Marie said defensively. 'Only the odd drink or two.'

Becky asked her about the marijuana plants and at first she appeared to know nothing about them, but then she admitted she did know about them. Anne Marie said that she thought Baby might have got them from Hugo.

'He didn't have enough light for them, and Baby's room with its panoramic view had very good light,' she said. 'But of course I didn't know what they were,' she added hastily.

Like hell you didn't, Becky thought, but she said nothing, just smiled benignly and listened.

'There was a second letter in her room,' Becky said.

'I know, the police already asked me. I've no idea who it was from. You see, we met loads of different fellas. They wanted me to list every name I could think of, and the only one I could remember was Jasper, and that's because Baby said, "Oh Sir Jasper, do not touch." It was more fun than in a disco. And it meant we never had to pay for a drink – well, hardly ever. I don't know who the other letter was from.'

'And the other times over Christmas when Baby went to your house – did you go out those times?'

Anne Marie hesitated.

'Well, yes,' she admitted. 'But sometimes we'd split up. She ... I don't know how to put this. She always seemed to meet someone, and often I went on home alone and left her. If she was running very late she'd just let herself into our house through the basement, otherwise she just went home.'

Wow, Becky thought. It's like she had a whole second existence going for herself. Gorgeous Baby who played with her Meccano, and was the dutiful eldest daughter, and then there was this other person who picked up men in pubs.

A bit of her wanted to giggle at the thought of Mother Immaculata hearing any of this. But it was more hysteria than amusement.

'I suppose you want to take her clothes home,' Anne Marie said.

'What clothes?' Becky asked her.

'The stuff she kept here – for nights out, you know. Her good stuff.'

Becky tried to think what Anne Marie could mean. She couldn't really remember what might be missing from Baby's wardrobe.

'Can I see?' she asked.

They went upstairs to Anne Marie's room, and Anne Marie showed her the gear in question. Becky tried to keep the amazement from both her face and her voice – but she was truly surprised. There was a small fur coat, a couple of skirts, a few sweaters, suspenders, stockings, expensive lingerie. She fingered some of the items.

'Where in God's name did Baby get the money for this stuff?' she asked Anne Marie.

'How do you mean?' Anne Marie asked her.

'I've never seen any of this before,' Becky said. 'And it's expensive stuff – isn't it?' Quality stuff, like Mummy has, she thought.

'I don't know.' Anne Marie seemed surprised. 'I assumed your parents gave her the money for it.'

Becky thought about that. It didn't seem very likely to her. They did indulge Baby, she admitted to herself. But not like this – not to this extent. They couldn't. They were careful with their money. They didn't give her this. And Baby never babysat, of that Becky was sure. As she thought about it, she realised that for someone who had never babysat or done any odd jobs, Baby always seemed to stretch her pocket money very well. Becky looked again at the clothes. There was no way that even a year of Baby's pocket money would have covered those items.

'Can I leave these things here for the moment?' she asked Anne Marie. She felt it would be one more thing that her mother couldn't deal with.

When Becky had left home that morning to go to Anne Marie's, she had told Brona she was going out for an hour.

'Don't go,' Brona said. 'Please.'

'I won't be long,' she'd replied. 'And I'll come straight back.'

'But where are you going? I don't want you to go out.'

Becky said that she was going to drop in on Anne Marie, just for a chat.

'Can I come too?'

'No,' Becky said gently to her. 'It's better that you're here with Mummy and Dad. And anyway, I don't think Anne Marie will be very forthcoming if we're both there. You mind things here. I won't be long, I promise.'

Though neither mentioned it, they were both conscious of something going on in their parents' bedroom. It sounded as if their father were trying to talk to their mother, his voice sometimes loud, sometimes lower, but her voice could not be heard.

'Just lie low until I get back,' Becky said. 'Have a bath or something. Just keep out of their way.'

She could hear herself and she sounded like a grown-up. It made no sense to her; nothing did.

On the landing, she distinctly heard her father saying, 'Don't be ridiculous.' She had never heard him using that particular tone of voice before. It contained anger and frustration, and possibly despair, but she could not be sure.

Behind the closed door, Elizabeth Dunville lay in bed on her side.

'For goodness' sake,' John said to her. 'Why are you saying these things?'

'I don't know,' she said. 'I only know . . . I am absolutely sure that Baby is dead.'

'But yesterday you said she was alive. You were the one who was adamant that she was not the girl in the bomb.'

'That's what I felt yesterday. Sometime during the night, she died.'

Elizabeth closed her eyes.

'It's over,' she said. 'It's all over now.'

When Becky returned from Anne Marie's, she found Brona and her father in the breakfast room. She knew immediately from their faces that something had happened.

'What is it?' she asked. 'What have you heard?'

John shook his head.

'It's Mummy,' Brona said.

Becky noted the whiteness of her father's face and that Brona had been crying.

'What's happened?'

'Mummy says Baby is dead,' Brona said.

Becky looked to her father. His face said nothing. He looked tired and drained.

'It's not rational,' he said to her. 'It's just your mother feeling that Baby . . . that Baby has died.'

'But why? What makes her so sure?'

'I don't know. She says it's maternal instinct. I don't know.'

'And do you think she's . . . dead?' Becky asked.

She hated the word 'dead'. She hated it coming from her mouth. She hated what it meant – the finality, the termination of everything as they knew it. Dead like an unnamed girl in a car bomb. Like her grandparents. Dead and gone for ever.

'I don't know,' he said. 'I don't feel anything.'

Becky went and phoned Uncle James and told him what was going on.

'We'll be right over,' James Fitzgerald said.

Aunty Nancy, Uncle James and their cousin Eleanor arrived about forty minutes later. By this stage Brona was lying on her bed, crying.

Becky watched with relief as her aunt and uncle took over.

'I don't know how your mum does it,' she said in an aside later to Eleanor.

'She can be quite impressive,' Eleanor said. 'Funnily I'd never really noticed it before. Maybe I was aware of it, but I'd never seen it. Not like now. I know she's a great committee person, a great organiser . . .'

By that stage Aunty Nancy had found out that Rhona Brophy was

Brona's best friend. She had phoned the Brophys, all but interrogated them, decided they were 'acceptable', and had prevailed upon them to take Brona for twenty-four hours with the express purpose of distracting her. This was something Rhona Brophy was well qualified to do, and Becky was even more impressed at how her aunt had worked this out.

A red-eyed Brona was then driven by Uncle James down to Sandymount and brought up to the Brophys' house complete with overnight bag and a teddy bear which he bought for her on the way.

'They struck me as being totally bananas,' said Uncle James to Becky on his return.

Becky, who had never thought of Uncle James other than as her cousin Eleanor's dad, and a bit of an old fuddy-duddy, was finding him very supportive and more entertaining by the day. She giggled at his comment, and agreed wholeheartedly. He had this ability to uplift her from the situation, albeit briefly.

I wish I'd got to know him when we were all happy, she thought. But then, I did know him when we were all happier, and I never saw this side of him. Maybe it takes terrible things to happen to see how people really are.

'Rhona Brophy's father appears to think he's Fred Astaire,' Uncle James continued. 'He was wearing a monkey suit, spats and a top hat. And he was carrying a stick.'

'Ummm,' said Brona Dunville, in the Brophys' house, 'why is your dad dressed like that?'

'Like what?' Rhona asked, an expression of mild puzzlement on her face.

'Well . . .' Brona hesitated. But she had met Mr Brophy often enough to know that this was not his norm. 'Well, you know – like a penguin.'

'Oh, I see,' laughed Rhona. 'We're having a fancy dress party tonight – they're twenty years married. He's been practising since he got home from work yesterday evening. Wait until you see Mummy's red wig.'

This was a distraction all right.

'We'll have to dress you up too,' said Rhona cheerfully.

'I don't have anything with me,' Brona said. 'I could help serve the food or the drinks or something,' she added hopefully.

'Nonsense,' said the Fred Astaire lookalike as he tapped his way into the kitchen to join the girls. 'With a blonde wig on your head, and that teddy bear you're carrying . . . Rhona will sort out some clothes – sure, you're a dead ringer for Shirley Temple.'

And Brona found herself laughing delightedly.

In Elizabeth Dunville's bedroom, Nancy sat beside her on the bed.

'These are just feelings you have,' she said to her sister-in-law.

'They're more than that,' Elizabeth said. 'I know. I can sense it completely. Baby is dead. Now I don't want to talk any more.'

She curled on her side again, her knees pulled up into a foetal position, and lay there pale-faced, sometimes sobbing a little, mostly lying silent. Eventually Nancy pulled the covers up over her shoulders and left her.

'It's like despair,' Nancy said to John and James in the drawing room.

In the dining room, with the folding doors slightly ajar, Becky and Eleanor listened to the adults talk.

'But what sparked it off?' asked James.

'She says that after having felt hope all week, having been sure that Baby was alive but somewhere terrible, in deep trouble, in danger, she now knows that Baby died during the night.'

Eleanor and Becky looked at each other.

'Did she say anything else?' James asked.

'She said, "The sins of the fathers are visited on the children", but what she meant was unclear,' Nancy replied.

'What *could* she mean?' John asked. 'What have I ever done – I mean, I do my best. I work hard, I give them a good home, a good education. I love them. We dote on Baby . . . love them all,' he added, as, unseen by the girls in the dining room, Nancy jerked her head at him towards the partially open doors, warning him of ears other than their own which were listening in.

'Let's go out for a walk,' Eleanor suggested to Becky. 'Down by the Dodder. I like it there.'

They wrapped up in their coats, gloves and scarves and were about to set off up the road towards Ballsbridge when Becky said she wanted to go the other way, down Lansdowne Road and over the railway line, and double back up by Marian College.

'That's the way Baby must have gone to meet Hugo,' she said.

'Who is Hugo?' Eleanor asked.

On the way, Becky told Eleanor all of the bits of information she had gathered.

'Hugo is her boyfriend,' she said. 'And it was he she was going to meet that night. And she left the window open because she was planning on coming back. That's all definite.'

'Have you met Hugo?'

Becky filled her in on her meeting the previous day, in Sutherland Square and Trinity College, and coffee in the Buttery, and the tall, gentle Hugo with his English accent.

'I always forget you're younger than me,' she said to Eleanor after a few minutes. 'I mean, you're really Brona's age, but you and I have always palled up together.'

'It's to do with my being in class with girls up to three years older,' Eleanor replied in her serious way. 'I've learned to adapt to whoever I'm with.'

'Skilfully,' Becky said. 'I'll give you that. I'd hate to be in your class, but you handle it all right.'

Eleanor shrugged. 'You adapt to whatever you have to adapt to,' she said philosophically.

Adapt, Becky thought. That's what we are doing – it's what we have to do, because if we don't, we won't survive. It was a fleeting thought, and she tried to hold on to it because it seemed important. More than important, it seemed vital.

'What did you think of Baby?' she asked Eleanor as they walked down Lansdowne Road.

'We had little to do with each other,' Eleanor said. 'In school she never spoke to me, never acknowledged my existence. And at the odd family thing – well, she ignored me, I suppose.'

'If you had information . . . like, if you knew something . . .' Becky said. 'If . . . oh dear, this is so difficult. If you knew something that might be important, who would you tell it to?'

'About Baby?' Eleanor asked. 'If it were the kind of thing I couldn't tell my parents, I'd choose someone I trusted and tell them. An adult, someone outside, someone who could make judgements, and who could assess what I had to tell. Can you tell me?'

Becky shook her head.

You're too young. You're too close, she thought.

'You're family,' she said aloud. As an afterthought, she said, 'Your parents are being wonderful.'

'Yes, well, just don't go out to dinner with them,' Eleanor said cryptically.

'Why ever not?'

'Don't ask,' Eleanor said with a shudder.

Nancy tried to talk Elizabeth into going to church with her. She cajoled, she pleaded. 'For me – I need to go to church,' she said.

But Elizabeth, lying on her side, said, 'Go away,' and eventually Nancy went back downstairs.

'John's gone into the hospital,' James said when Nancy asked where he was.

They looked at each other, and then he came and embraced her.

'Will they get through this?' Nancy asked.

James didn't answer.

In the Brophys' house, Brona helped to prepare food, and then she and Rhona went to Rhona's bedroom, and they lay, one on the floor, one on the bed, and Rhona said they should try and remember the funniest things that had happened to them both.

'Your first day in St Martin's,' Brona suggested.

'God, that was a day, wasn't it?' Rhona giggled.

'In you came into the classroom – late. Class had started, and Rodriguez looked at you and said, "Who are you?" Do you remember?'

'And I said, "I'm Rhona Brophy",' replied Rhona.

'And I thought, I hate you Rhona Brophy, your name is too like mine.'

'And Rodriguez said, "What kind of a name is that?"'

'And you looked at her and said, "What do you mean?"'

'And she said, "That's not a Christian name."'

'And you said, "Sorry, Sister, my Christian name is Rhona. My surname is Brophy."'

'And she said, "Don't be so cheeky. Rhona is not a name you give to a Christian. It is not a God-given name."'

The two of them grinned.

'And you said, "Well, my dad rushed me to the church and forgot to check with my mum what to baptise me, and as the priest held me over the water font he asked my dad what I was to be called."'

'And Dad looked around in desperation at the Stations of the Cross and he saw Veronica and he said, "Veronica". And Rodriguez said in her deepest, loudest voice, "VERONICA?"'

'And you said, "Well, Sister, he might just as easily have seen Pontius Pilate first, and then I would be Pontius Brophy."'

'I thought Rodriguez was going to have a fit. She went sort of purple and accused me of blasphemy.'

The two of them were now shrieking with laughter.

'Is it true about the Veronica thing?' Brona asked.

'It's a family myth, and I'm sticking to it,' Rhona said. 'And Mummy hated the name Veronica, so she called me Rhona.'

'Rodriguez behaved as if you had been called Rhona just to spite her, remember?'

'And she told me to sit beside you, and you smiled at me.'

'A friendship made in heaven,' Brona said.

'Funny how she always makes us sit apart in her class now.'

'Jealousy on her part,' said Brona. 'Just because she doesn't have a best friend. Imagine if you had been called Pontius, though. That would have been brilliant.'

'Not for me,' said Rhona with a giggle.

James and Nancy took Becky back to their house with Eleanor for the night.

'Are you sure it's all right for me to leave Mummy and Daddy?' Becky asked her aunt before they left.

'I think it'll be good for them,' Aunty Nancy said. 'Time together. Maybe they will talk.'

Becky didn't say anything. She couldn't imagine what they could say. It all seemed so hopeless. Her mother was lying in bed, not speaking. Her father, grey-faced, paced the drawing room when he returned from the hospital.

'The girl in the bomb,' Becky had said to him. 'Do they know who she is yet?'

'There are two families supplying dental records today,' he said. 'More than that I don't know.'

'That means that other people have been going through what we're going through,' she said. 'How awful.'

'Every story is different,' he replied tightly.

She wanted to say, 'Are there people we can talk to? Are there rules for what we should do? I don't know what to feel any more,' but she said nothing.

Her father's pacing, and the amount of cigarettes he was getting through, seemed to say that he didn't have the answers she so badly needed.

They had dinner in the Fitzgeralds' dining room, and during it Nancy talked, as she always did, about all sorts of things.

This is easier, thought Becky. As long as I concentrate on what she's saying, it does act as a distraction.

The only blip occurred when her aunt talked about the following summer.

'You and Brona can come with us on holidays,' she said.

'That will be nice,' Eleanor said quickly, as if she could turn the observation away from what it really implied.

'But ... but,' Becky said. 'That sounds as if you don't think this will be over by then.' She looked at her aunt with fear in her eyes.

'I'm sure it will be long resolved by then,' her uncle interjected. 'And there's plenty of time for looking at it from that angle. But what your aunt meant was that no matter, it would be lovely to have you girls with us on holiday.'

But it was there. It hung in the air. The idea of the long months of winter and spring and the Dunville situation unchanged.

Becky tried to bite back the tears, but slowly her eyes filled up and she felt them overflowing.

Tucked up in bed in one of their many spare bedrooms, she tried to hold the tears back again, while Aunty Nancy sat beside her and stroked her hand.

'I'm so sorry,' her aunt said. 'I didn't mean to make you cry. I'm so so sorry.'

'You didn't make me cry,' Becky sobbed. 'It's everything that's happening that's making me cry.'

And now that I've started, she thought, I just don't seem to know how to stop.

In the Brophys' house the fancy dress party got under way. As Shirley Temple, Brona acquitted herself quite well, tap-dancing her way around the room with Fred Astaire and Ginger Rogers.

'You having fun?' Rhona asked her.

Brona nodded.

'But I hate the way someone keeps putting on "Go Away Little

Girl" every time the record gets changed,' she laughed. 'Everyone points at me!'

'Oh, you can rely on Dad to keep putting on Fred Astaire's stuff,' Rhona said. 'He's in his element.'

'What's going on in the hall?' Brona asked, as through the open door she could clearly see a woman with a long curly blonde wig, dressed in boots and a miniskirt, with a low-cut top out of which her uplifted breasts were bulging. Around her neck was a chain, from which a card hung below her ample cleavage, and written on the card was

MISSING
WOULD YOU LIKE TO FIND ME?

Fred and Ginger were remonstrating with her.

Rhona's eyes widened in amazement, and she gave the door a kick with her foot to close it, but somehow missed.

'Nothing. Some silly cow,' she said, taking Brona by the arm.

'No, but really,' Brona said. 'What on earth is going on?'

Rhona's parents were behaving in a very agitated way, and Brona could see them gesticulating towards the living room.

Rhona kicked the door again, and it shut and she started to dance with Brona, who was still trying to register what she had just witnessed.

'Was that ... was she ... was that woman dressed up as Baby?' she finally asked Rhona.

'Don't mind her,' Rhona said, by way of confirmation. 'She's gone home now. I'm sorry,' Rhona added. 'I really am. No one would have wanted you to see that. She's just some silly friend of my parents, it didn't mean anything.'

Brona nodded. She felt disbelief.

'Bloody tasteless,' she heard Rhona's father mutter as he came back into the room. He glanced at her and could see from her face that she had witnessed the scene in the hall. Coming up to her he said, 'A silly woman – crass – forget it. It meant nothing.'

But it did mean something, Brona realised, though she couldn't quite find the words to identify what it was at that moment.

'We'll go out to lunch tomorrow, to celebrate your birthday,' Aunty Nancy said to Becky in the spare room.

'But Mummy and Daddy ...' Becky said.

'James will phone and ask them along too,' Nancy said.

'You know that tomorrow is Baby's birthday too?' Becky said. 'She will be eighteen,' she added, forcing herself to make it sound as if Baby would somehow be celebrating that fact.

'I know,' Nancy said gently. 'I know that. That may be why your mother isn't handling this weekend too well,' she added as an afterthought.

'It seems wrong to celebrate my birthday,' Becky said.

'Why? Why shouldn't you celebrate it?' Nancy said. 'It's not your fault what has happened. And it is your birthday. Why shouldn't you have a little joy in your life? And anyway, your uncle and I want to take you out.'

'Mummy and Daddy won't come,' Becky said.

'Don't worry about that. They'll do whatever they have to do to get through the day, but we're going to do something nice with you,' her aunt said. 'Now I want you to go to sleep, and starting tomorrow you're going to eat properly.'

Becky didn't say anything.

'I want you to promise me that you'll eat what I tell you to eat,' her aunt persisted.

Becky nodded. It was nice to let go, to let someone else take over and do the organising and the worrying, and to take care of her, even if it was only for a little while.

The bedclothes felt fresh. They smelt of spring, she thought.

'Will I leave the light on?' her aunt asked gently.

Becky could feel her eyes closing, and sleep crept slowly into the darkened room.

Chapter Twelve

Lunch in The Hibernian Hotel turned out to be a somewhat different experience to one Becky might have imagined.

While Uncle James parked the car, she, Nancy and Eleanor walked up the steps into the hotel, and the first person she saw was Mr Jones.

If she were surprised, it was nothing to how Mr Jones felt.

He was sitting on a Louis Quinze chair beside the wall, reading a paper, his long legs crossed, wearing a dark blue tie and a suit. At first Becky noticed his ankles.

What beautiful bones, she thought, and then she looked up and saw who it was.

He looked completely startled, and his eyes went from one girl to the other and then to Becky's aunt. Becky realised that he probably thought Aunty Nancy was her mother, and that Eleanor was her sister. She didn't know if he had yet identified Brona in school as the third Dunville girl.

He stood up when he saw them, and Becky bit her lip trying to contain her pleasure. Mr Jones smiled at her and came over and introduced himself.

'I thought you were Rebecca's mother,' he said, when Nancy said who she was. 'I didn't realise you had a cousin in the school,' he said to Becky, having said hello to Eleanor.

Nancy Fitzgerald gave him the third degree. Her amazement that he was working at St Martin's was evident.

'As a teacher?' she said. 'You're employed as a teacher by the nuns?'

'Yes, indeed.' He smiled at her.

Becky was blushing with embarrassment.

'And you teach my daughter and nieces singing?' she persisted.

'I do indeed,' he responded.

'And are they improving?' she asked.

186

'It's early days,' he replied. 'Eleanor is doing very well, and I can safely say that Rebecca is going in the direction I want her to go in.'

They went into the Lafayette, which was the dining room. James Fitzgerald caught up with them, and as they sat at their table, Aunty Nancy was bubbling over.

'A man, James,' she said.

'But what's wrong with that?' he asked.

'A *young* man,' she said. 'Go out to the foyer and take a look. Tall fellow with fair hair. He's teaching them singing.'

Disbelief and amazement radiated from her.

'For goodness' sake, Nancy,' joked Uncle James. 'I'm not going out to reception to take a peek at a tall young man. What would people say? And at least it's singing he's teaching them, and not biology.'

Becky giggled and so did Eleanor.

'It's not a laughing matter,' Aunty Nancy said, ordering a gin and tonic. 'One cube of ice, and two thin wedges of lemon,' she said to the waiter. 'No pips, and make sure the lemon has been scrubbed.'

In an aside to Becky, she said, 'I always think of dirty Sicilian hands picking my lemon off its tree. I'm sure they don't wash in Greece.'

'Mu-um,' Eleanor said, as Becky tried to hide her grin.

'I think you'll find Sicily is part of Italy,' Uncle James said, picking up his menu.

'Italy? Greece? Who cares?' said Aunty Nancy. 'It's hygiene that is the issue.'

Gawd, thought Becky to herself, in very un-Beckylike language. I can see now why Eleanor isn't too keen on dinners out with her mother.

'Did you get parking close by?' Eleanor asked her father in an effort to change the subject.

'No problem,' he said. 'Just down Dawson Street, no distance for you ladies afterwards, unless you want to go for a walk.'

'A walk?' Becky said. 'Oh, maybe afterwards Eleanor and I could go and walk through Trinity College. I . . .'

Her voice trailed away. Suddenly that walk on Friday with Hugo Mombay Humphries seemed wonderfully nostalgic, almost as though it belonged to another world. Not her usual daily one, nor the nightmare one she had been living in for the last week, but some other one . . . a place where green fields even in winter became a place of safety, where the walls of the college offered security, where the darkness and cosiness of the Buttery offered mystery and romance.

A haven, she thought.

It reminded her of something, but she could not readily bring it to mind, as Aunty Nancy, having checked the menu, returned to the topic of male teachers in a convent.

'He doesn't live in the convent?' she suddenly asked Eleanor, who looked surprised but then said she had no idea.

'Of course he doesn't,' Uncle James said. 'For goodness' sake, Nancy, why would he live in the convent?'

'I was just concerned for the nuns,' she replied. 'I mean to say. They've employed him, which is incredible. And if they're capable of that, who knows what else they might have got themselves inveigled into. A young man like that . . . with one thing on his mind.'

'Nancy,' laughed James agreeably, 'I think there is only one person around here with one thing on her mind.'

And the girls giggled behind their menus.

'She said what?' Mr Jones said later to Becky, as he slipped his hand up under her tunic.

'She said you had only one thing on your mind,' Becky said with a grin.

'Well, she was right about that,' he said, as his fingers reached the top of her thighs.

Becky looked around at the walls, at the paintings of bygone days in their enormous gilt frames. She looked at the face of Lafayette and she wondered if the painter had caught the real man. She was startled from her reverie by the arrival of John Delaware.

'James, Nancy,' he said as he came upon them. 'And Eleanor, good to see you again. And it's Becky, isn't it?'

They all shook hands and James asked him if he'd like to join them.

'But I'm intruding on a family affair,' he said.

'Not at all. We're celebrating our niece's sixteenth birthday.'

'Sixteen?' he said. 'How delightful.'

Becky smiled, not knowing what to say.

'But that means I really am intruding,' he said. 'Your birthday and all.'

Becky shook her head.

'Not at all,' Uncle James said. 'It's a case of the more the merrier.'

'I've been thinking about your family a lot this week,' John Delaware

said to Becky. 'Like everyone else, I suppose. The newspapers . . .
radio . . . television . . . my thoughts . . .' He gestured towards her
and then let James deftly change the subject.

Becky watched him as the adults talked. In a way he reminded her
of her father. Same English accent, same bearing, same manners.

But jollier, she thought. Less . . . She looked for a word that would
fit. The only one she could come up with was 'cold', and it seemed a
bit unfair on her father.

He was dressed in a tweed jacket, grey trousers, white shirt and a
bright red tie.

Just as smart as Daddy, she thought. But completely different.
More . . . The word she was looking for was 'flamboyant', but she
couldn't immediately find it.

He offered around his cigarettes, even to the girls.

'For goodness' sake, John,' Nancy said. 'They're children.'

'Better for them to learn how to say no than to be waiting to sneak
outside for a puff behind the bicycle sheds,' he said jovially. 'Isn't that
right, girls?'

'It's a wonder your wife puts up with you,' Nancy said, with what
sounded remarkably like a snort.

John Delaware winked at Becky.

'She doesn't, actually,' he said with a laugh. 'She left years ago.'

He didn't seem grief-stricken, Becky thought. On the contrary, he
sounded matter of fact and possibly even a little wry.

Suddenly the term 'talking helps' sprung to her mind and she saw
it in a double context – both as talking about what had happened,
and also this kind of talking, which was a total distraction to what
was going on at home in Lansdowne Road.

'Well, girls,' said John Delaware to Becky and Eleanor, 'will we have
a go at the hors d'oeuvres trolley? It looks perfect. Perfect. Perfect.'

'Isn't he nice?' Becky whispered to Eleanor as they returned with
their plates.

'Mummy says he's a bounder,' Eleanor whispered back.

A bounder? Becky thought as she watched him across the table.

At that moment three people who had come in and were being
seated at the end of the restaurant caught her attention.

Unbelievable, she thought, as she identified Hugo Mombay
Humphries. He was with a man and a woman, and she presumed
they were his parents. Does everyone have lunch on Sundays in here?
she wondered.

She could not work out if he had seen her. She rather hoped not. She could imagine what Aunty Nancy would say if he came over to speak to them. Apart from anything else, she'll think I know every man in Dublin, Becky thought, when in fact I don't know any. Well, not really . . .

She would have liked to have pointed him out to her cousin Eleanor, but it was impossible to do so at the table. Maybe later, she thought.

Hugo's father was an older version of himself, just as tall and lanky but with hair greying and thinning. His mother was remarkably chic, in a dress and matching jacket. Becky had already seen her fur coat being removed by the maître d'.

Keeping an eye on Hugo's table, she was aware that there was a lot of conversation, but virtually no smiling, no laughter. She wondered if Hugo were filling his parents in on the events of week. It certainly looked like he might be. Occasionally his mother reached out and patted his arm, but they were too far away for Becky to hear anything they were actually saying.

'Where's your younger sister, Becky?' John Delaware's voice cut across her thoughts.

'Oh, Brona – she's gone to stay with her best friend for the weekend,' she said.

On the Sunday morning, Brona Dunville and Rhona Brophy were helping to clear up after the party.

'You're awfully quiet, Bro,' Rhona said to her pal, as they picked at cold food left over from the previous night.

They were sitting in the kitchen, both dressed in bell bottoms, sweaters and loose open shirts.

'I keep finding myself praying,' Brona said.

'Praying?' Rhona couldn't have been more surprised.

'Yes. Going over and over the prayers we've been taught. I can't bear the silence . . .' Brona looked like she might cry. 'The silence in my head, I mean.'

'That's awful,' Rhona said. 'Next thing you'll have a vocation and then you'll be a novice and then a nun and then . . . God, can you imagine sailing through the convent, sharing a dorm with Sister Rodriguez . . .'

'Oh shut up, Rhona,' Brona said. 'It's only prayers. It's only a way of hoping that this will all get better.'

'I'm sorry, Bro,' Rhona said. 'I didn't mean to upset you. Daddy said I'm to distract you, and I'm not doing a very good job of it if by the time you leave here you've taken to prayer . . .'

Brona didn't say anything. She just suddenly knew that she didn't want to go home, but she didn't know how to say it. She had a feeling that things weren't going to get any better.

'Why does cold food taste nicer than hot food?' Rhona asked.

'Does it?' Brona said, nibbling a piece of rubbery cheese and a dried-out cherry.

'I only said that to distract you, Bro,' Rhona said.

Brona looked bleakly at her.

'Have you always lived in Ireland?' Becky asked John Delaware.

'No,' he said to her. 'I only came over about six weeks ago. I work in London. Well, I'm based there. But I've bought a place over here and I'll be moving into it next month.'

'Where are you staying now?' she asked.

'Right here in The Hibernian,' he said. 'It's wonderfully central,' he added by way of explanation. 'Now link my arms, girls,' he said. 'The ground is still slippy from the frost.'

Becky and Eleanor and he set off down the steps from the hotel on to Dawson Street.

'We'll be back in half an hour,' he had said to James and Nancy with a wink. 'Just enough time for you to have coffee and pick up the tab.'

'This is delightful,' he said to the girls on either side of him. 'Delightful, delightful.' 'I love a cold, crisp day like this,' he added.

'It is awfully cold, isn't it?' Eleanor said. 'Would you mind if I went back to the hotel? I'm going to freeze. Unlike Becky, I didn't come out warmly enough dressed.'

She left them then and returned to the hotel, while Becky and John Delaware continued on down Dawson Street, cutting across Duke Street to Grafton Street.

'It would have been nice for you to have seen the Christmas windows in Switzers,' she said to him. 'But they're already gone. They're done with music and puppets each December. We always come in as a family and look at them.'

This is extraordinary, she thought, all too aware of the anomaly of the situation. There she was, walking down Grafton Street on a winter's afternoon with a man old enough to be her father. She wondered if he were going to talk about Baby's disappearance, but

191

he didn't. He seemed quite content to ask her questions about Dublin, and her normal life.

That was how she saw it now. There was her normal life, which was the one she had lived before Baby's disappearance, and then there was her 'nightmare' life, which was the one she was in the middle of. They went in the front gates of Trinity College, and she breathed deeply.

'I'm going to come here when I'm finished school,' she said to him as they crossed the cobblestones in Front Square, and she realised she had formulated this plan over the previous forty-eight hours.

'Wonderful place,' he said. 'Wonderful, wonderful, wonderful.'

She found herself smiling as she started to gather his speech patterns in her mind, and at the enthusiasm which seemed to emanate from him.

'Do you know the names of the different buildings?' he asked her.

But the only place she knew was the Buttery.

'We'll get you a book that'll have it all, and next time we walk through here you can tell me all the names,' he said to her, patting her hand, which was linked through his arm.

His enthusiasm even surpassed her own and she found that terribly uplifting. And the fact that he supposed there would be another time walking through there gave her an outlet from the mixture of suffocation and the emptiness of her home.

John Delaware told her stories from the war – a time and a place which her doctor father rarely if ever mentioned. They had walked through Trinity College by that stage and were coming back along Nassau Street.

He told her about North Africa, where the food had sand in it, and the heat in the daytime was relentless and the nights were so cold. A place where armies moved and were quartered and then moved again, where young men flew in the dark, where dates grew on trees in oases, and lorries broke down in the sun.

'My plane came down on a night flight,' he said. 'Took a bullet here,' he added, tapping his chest. 'That's when I met up with your father again. Had known him in school. There he was in the hospital in Alexandria. Came home on the same ship with me.'

'Was he out there long?' Becky asked.

'Couple of years,' came the reply. 'We finished school in 'forty-one, and we were out there at the start of 'forty-three. Great days. Great days. Great days.'

'And when did he meet Mum?' she asked.

'Goodness me,' he replied. 'I don't know. Must have been after that. We didn't know a girl between us until then. Could have been a while after that,' he continued. 'He must be a good bit older than she is, isn't he?'

'I don't know,' Becky said. 'It's not the kind of thing that's discussed at home.'

She wanted to ask him about himself, but she found it too difficult. In the world in which she was brought up, one didn't ask personal questions of adults.

They walked back up Dawson Street to The Hibernian. Her uncle and aunt were still at the table with Eleanor.

'Thought you were never coming back,' said Eleanor.

Just as Becky sat back down, having noticed that the Mombay Humphries were still sitting at their corner table, a birthday cake with sixteen candles and accompanied by five waiters appeared at her table and was placed in front of her.

Oh no, she thought with embarrassment. There's no way Hugo hasn't noticed me now. Thank goodness Mr Jones didn't come into the restaurant for lunch.

Glancing up above the candles, she took in her relatives and John Delaware singing 'Happy Birthday', along with some guests at the tables nearby. Looking across, she saw Hugo Mombay Humphries smiling at her and then speaking to his parents.

When the singing stopped and she had blown out the candles, she caught Eleanor's eye and Eleanor grimaced. Becky knew that Eleanor too would have hated such attention being brought to her. Unlike either Baby or Brona, she thought. Both would thrive on it. Especially Baby.

A few moments later a bottle of champagne appeared at the table.

'With the compliments of Sir Hugh ...' said the waiter, gesturing towards the corner table, where the three Mombay Humphries were holding their glasses up to her. 'He would like to wish the young lady a happy birthday.'

Becky smiled and blushed alternately, and Eleanor giggled and said, 'You're redder than the red writing on the cake.'

'Do you know them?' Uncle James asked her in surprise.

She was unsure how to respond, but at that moment Sir Hugh came over to the table, and apologised for intruding. Introductions were made, and Sir Hugh shook hands with everyone at the table before turning to James Fitzgerald.

'My son and your eldest niece are friends,' he said by way of explanation.

Then to Becky, 'Our thoughts are with you.'

'Thank you for the champagne,' she said.

'I hope you're allowed to have some,' he continued, smiling at her.

'Without a doubt,' said Uncle James.

With that Sir Hugh excused himself and returned to his table.

Becky said nothing. She knew Sir Hugh had meant well, but it was as if the ghost of Baby was there at the table, hovering unseen in everyone's mind.

Where are you, Baby? she thought.

Glasses clinked in front of her and she joined in and forced a smile back onto her face.

When they got back to the Dunville house, Becky overheard her aunt reminding her father that it was her birthday. He came and gave her a hug, and said something about a present as soon as was possible. Becky patted her pocket, where a ten-pound note from John Delaware was lodged, and five pounds from her uncle and aunt.

'Include her more in what is happening,' she also heard Aunty Nancy saying to her father. 'She's sixteen now. She's a smart girl – she's certainly impressed us today. She knows all kinds of people, and knows how to comport herself. So include her.'

He doesn't know how, Becky thought to herself. That's not how our relationship works. He probably could have included Baby, but he can't do it with either me or Brona.

'Now,' said Nancy to her brother-in-law, 'how is Elizabeth doing this evening?'

'Dr Moody came earlier,' he replied. 'He sedated her.'

He looked exhausted, Becky thought. As if he hadn't slept at all.

'Can I make you tea, Daddy?' she asked.

He shook his head.

'Any news from the police?' Nancy asked.

'Conor O'Connor dropped in to check up on us. At least that's what it felt like.'

'Is there anything new there?' Becky tried.

194

Again he shook his head. 'There's nothing. One week on, and it is as if Baby fell off the planet,' he said.

It was unending, Becky thought. Unending and unendurable.

Mrs O'Doody had been sent home early by Nancy, who produced sandwiches and tea, and insisted that both father and daughter ate them, while James and Eleanor went to collect Brona.

'Now,' said Nancy firmly, 'I want you two to eat properly. It's a good example to Brona, and you are both going to need your strength to get through this week. Proper eating is the way to start. Three meals a day. And no cutting corners, Becky.'

Becky and her father exchanged a small grin.

'You are formidable, Nancy,' he said to her with a smile. 'We promise to eat, don't we, Becky?'

That night she thought how much she had changed in the previous week. She had been the dreamer and the thinker, the one who had prayed so hard early in the week, whereas now she could not think of a prayer to say. She had been the one who played with words and fiddled with logic. And now all she wanted was continual human company.

Companionship, conversation ... anything so that I don't have to think, she thought. She hoped Brona would come and get into bed beside her.

But their roles had been reversed, and Brona was lying in her bed looking at her ceiling, praying for all she was worth. She did not think of the words of prayer as Becky used to do. She just used prayer as a mantra, moving from one Hail Mary to the next, from Glory Be to The Lord's Prayer, drifting in and out through carols and hymns. The words to her were meaningless, but they had become the only way she could deal with despair, praying to a God who would not answer.

Chapter Thirteen

'What do you mean, a fancy dress party?' Becky asked Brona at the bus stop on the Monday morning.

'Some anniversary – I don't know. They all dressed up. Had guests in. You know,' Brona replied.

'And what did you go as?'

'Shirley Temple.'

'Oh.' Becky looked at her. It seemed difficult to imagine, the way her sister looked now, in her school uniform, with her dark brown hair curling on to her shoulders, and her very pale face. Yet at the same time, under normal circumstances Shirley Temple would have been the ideal character for her.

'Was it fun?' she asked.

'It was okay. What's Pan's People?'

'I don't know,' Becky said. 'Why?'

Brona scuffed her toe along the pavement.

'Don't do that,' Becky said. 'You'll have Mother Immaculata after you for not having cleaned your shoes. Anyway, why do you ask what Pan's People are?'

'Rhona went as one.'

'What did she look like?'

'Sort of like a go-go dancer.'

'Oh.'

Becky thought about this.

'Maybe it's something on the TV.'

'Suppose so. Are you sorry we don't have a telly?' Brona asked.

'I never really thought about it until last week,' Becky said.

'I think we're the only people in the whole of Ireland without one,' Brona said dramatically.

'Doesn't really matter, does it?' Becky asked her.

'No, suppose not. Why did you think about it last week?'

'Because we were on it, silly.'

196

'What? What do you mean?'

'Just that. Remember the cameras outside the house on Wednesday? They were television cameras.'

'How do you know? Why didn't I see them? How come no one told me?'

Becky didn't answer. There were no answers to most questions, she thought.

'Would you have liked to have seen yourself on it?' Brona tried again.

'Not like that. Not under those circumstances. Baby . . .'

It was the first time Baby's name had been mentioned that morning.

In the house, all had been quiet. Their mother hadn't stirred. Mrs O'Doody had come in early and seen the girls off. Their father was already gone to the hospital.

'You going to be okay?' Becky asked her sister.

'Yup, I'm fine,' Brona replied.

It was all very short and concise between them. Becky had the distinct feeling that Brona wasn't telling her whatever was on her mind. But then she, Becky, wasn't telling either. She had decided to just get through the day in school, and not think about what coming home meant. Not think about the feeling in the house, the emptiness, as if Baby's absence had also removed their souls.

And Baby has been away before, she thought.

'You know, Brona,' she said aloud. 'I was thinking . . .'

'Don't know why you bother,' Brona said.

'Come on, Brona. Don't be like that. I was thinking about when Baby went to Irish College and she just wasn't there at home for a month.'

There was a grunt from Brona.

'Well, I was thinking that that is how we should pretend this is. Just think of it in terms of Baby being gone for a month to Irish College, and then if she gets home earlier, then everything will be all right.'

'And if she doesn't come home after the month?' Brona asked.

'Then we'll think about that then,' Becky said firmly.

'I don't think that's how Mum and Dad are seeing it,' Brona said.

'I know. But I think that's how you and I should see it. Let's just see it as time out from Baby, and when she comes back—'

'*If* she comes back,' Brona said.

This is too difficult for me, Becky thought. She can't see what I mean. She can't see that if we start thinking like that, then there is nothing. There is no hope. We have to be like Dad . . .

'Brona, we have to be like Dad,' she tried.

'Whatcha mean?' Brona said sulkily. Her mood seemed to be getting worse by the minute.

Becky glanced up and down the road. There was no one approaching.

'Listen to me.' Becky dropped her bag on the pavement and took Brona by the shoulders. 'Just stop being like that and listen. You could go back inside the house and get into bed and stay there. It won't make any difference except you'll feel like shite. Or you could lift up your chin like you did at Assembly the other day, and be like Dad, who has gone into work and will help his patients, and make people better, and at least he'll feel at the end of today that he's got something right. For God's sake – don't you see it?'

Brona was standing there looking at her with her mouth open.

'What's wrong with you now?' Becky said.

'Did Saint Rebecca Dunville say "shite" or are my ears deceiving me?' asked Brona in a perfect imitation of Mother Immaculata.

Both of them laughed. Becky picked up her bag as the bus pulled in.

So that's how I do it, she thought. That works.

'Can I tell you what happened at the party?' Brona said slowly, and Becky realised that they had somehow reached a level of rapport where Brona felt safe enough to talk freely.

'Go ahead,' Becky said.

So Brona told her about the woman dressed as Baby.

'That is awful,' Becky responded, when Brona was finished. 'Awful.'

'But why is it so awful?' Brona asked her. 'It made me feel sick and frightened, and I don't know why.'

'It is awful because it is as if Baby is already history to some people, and that is frightening,' Becky said to her. She glanced at Brona's face and saw the terror in it. 'Listen to me,' she added, 'there are going to be difficult and horrible things like that – I'm sure more things will happen that are difficult to handle. You can tell me about them,' she said to Brona. 'Don't bottle them all up.'

Brona nodded and mumbled, 'Hmmmmm.' After a moment's pause, she then said, 'Thanks, Becky. I don't know what I'd do without you at the moment.'

They smiled at each other.

There is a good feeling between us, Becky thought, and she knew that that made her stronger. And added to that, Brona sat voluntarily beside her on the bus, even though there were at least six of her classmates in a group upstairs.

They didn't talk as the bus headed towards town, but a couple of times Brona let out a small snigger, and once she elbowed Becky in a half-friendly way, and they looked each other in the eye, and Brona mouthed, 'Shite.'

The bus stopped on Sutherland Square and they dismounted.

'Now,' Becky said firmly to Brona, 'go and join your friends.'

'I want to stay with you,' Brona said.

Becky shook her head firmly.

'No. Do the chin-up bit. Just go and do it. I promise it'll be better.'

'Shite,' said Brona with a laugh.

Shite for me, Becky thought to herself with a grin. But definitely better for Brona.

At Assembly, Mother Immaculata prayed.

Becky took a look at Brona. She could see a little more than just her profile. For a moment she thought how like Baby Brona looked. Dye her hair and curl it, and she would almost pass for her.

Becky thought Brona looked all right now, standing beside terrible Rhona Brophy. At that moment, Rhona turned and looked at Becky and gave her a wink. Becky found that wink somehow comforting, despite the fact that it was remarkably cheeky.

'Pray for our dearly departed,' intoned Mother Immaculata, while Becky tried to decipher the wink. 'For those who have gone before us, for those who are going, and for those who are missing.'

'Amen,' intoned hundreds of girls.

Missing? wondered Becky. How many are missing?

She glanced around at her peers. Many of them were looking at her out of the corner of their eye. Becky directed her gaze forwards. She saw Rhona take one of Brona's hands and squeeze it. She wished there was someone to hold her hand.

'Are you all right?' Mr Jones walked beside her in the corridor.

Becky nodded.

'Do you have a close friend?' he asked. 'You always seem to be alone.'

She shook her head. She felt embarrassed that she didn't have a special friend, or a group to hang around with, but there was no point in lying to him. He had seen her often enough just by herself.

'You need to talk,' he said firmly. 'It will do you good. I'll meet you after school. Around the corner. Say, twenty minutes after school ends. Is that all right?'

That thought kept her going through most of the day.

At lunchtime Brona came sidling up to her in the refectory before the nuns came in for dinner.

'Do you think it would be okay if I went back to Rhona's after school for a bit?' she asked.

'Sure,' Becky said, feeling a momentary flash of envy that Brona had somewhere else to go, but then, remembering her own plans for later, the envy soon died. 'If you phone Daddy and tell him, he'll pick you up on his way home. You'd better phone home too,' she said. 'You don't want Mummy worrying.'

Brona scowled.

'Can't you tell her when you get in? If I phone I'll probably just get her out of bed.'

Becky nodded, but deep in her heart she hoped that today would be different. That today her mother would be up and doing things, that she'd be a bit like Aunty Nancy.

Seeing Eleanor, she went over to her.

Eleanor was sitting with a group of girls from her class and did not see her approach. She was reading something under the table. Four pairs of eyes looked up at Becky, and they halted their conversation. Normally Becky would have steered clear, as she was a bit in awe of Eleanor's friends, but she suddenly didn't care what they said or thought.

'Eleanor,' she said to her cousin.

'Oh, hi, Becky,' Eleanor said, looking up.

'How are things?' one of the girls asked her.

The others said nothing but just looked at her.

Becky shrugged. She didn't know what to say, and she was uneasy in front of this group.

'It'll be all right,' the girl said.

'It had better be okay soon,' said one of the others. 'We pray for that sister of yours morning, noon and night. I for one am going to thump her when she gets back.'

Becky found herself smiling. It was all so normal . . . banter and teasing, and yet not unkind. She had always thought that this group of girls was way too sure of themselves to even notice a lowly fourth year like herself. And yet there seemed to be kindness emanating from them.

One of them, with a long blonde plait and navy-blue eyes, said, 'Baby Dunville is probably sitting sunning herself in the South of France.'

'And wondering should she send the whole school a postcard,' another one added.

'Well, I wish she'd send us one at home,' Becky said.

'It will be okay,' the girl repeated.

Becky felt the pricking of tears behind her eyes.

Looks like I can't handle sympathy, she thought, so she just nodded at them.

'Eleanor,' she said, addressing her cousin again but in a lower voice, 'is your mother going to our house today?'

'Just this morning,' Eleanor said. 'She has something on this afternoon, I think. She told me when she and Daddy dropped me back here last night, but I can't remember what it was. Problem?'

'No,' Becky replied. 'No problem. I just wondered. It's nice when she's there,' she added vaguely, and moved off.

She was aware of the group of girls watching her as she left the room, and knew that they would immediately ask Eleanor what was new. But there was nothing new. Nothing.

It was eight days since Baby had gone, seven days since they had found out, and since then absolutely nothing. A void. No more, no less.

Becky glanced back as she went through the doorway. It all appeared so normal. It was as if in everyone else's life it was just a normal day, and it would have been that for her too had Baby not disappeared. She thought about that as she walked along the corridor.

We got up in the morning, and we went to bed at night, she thought, and we did what we were told – Brona and I, anyway. Though not Baby. And although we did what we were supposed to do, everything is changed. All because of Baby. And yet if Baby had come home that night, then all would be as it was.

She suddenly realised that maybe Baby had sneaked out on other nights, and had returned safely, and no one was any the wiser.

There is nothing we could have done to prevent it, she thought, trying yet again to rid herself of the guilt of having closed the window. And yet she wished she had left the window open, or not come downstairs at all that night, and then she wouldn't have known about the window, and then she would not be carrying that particular sense of culpability. And then she realised that all of the ifs could go back a long way. If only Baby's footstep on the stair had not woken her, if indeed that was what had disturbed her, or if only Brona hadn't destroyed her pink sweater that night, then maybe Baby would have been able to sneak out earlier and would not have ended up disappearing.

And back and back it goes, Becky thought. If only Brona had not decided to dye her hair, or if Mummy and Dad hadn't spoilt Baby the way they did, and that ridiculous thing of her playing with the Meccano – so clearly a ploy for attention, and she didn't really need any more attention anyway.

She shook her head in an effort to stop winding the clock backwards to find out where it all started.

At four o'clock that Monday afternoon, when school was out, Becky tried to hover in the cloakrooms, but it was one of those days when Sister Rodriguez was doing her in-house police work, and Becky found herself out on the street at about three minutes past four. The lower end of Sutherland Street had now been cleared from the bomb blast of the previous week, and so she walked slowly down it in the direction of Sutherland Square. Glancing around at the other departing girls, she noticed that she was the only one of her age wearing her beret. She took it off and stuffed it in her coat pocket.

I'm so prim, she thought. Bit like Mum. She's quite prim.

She thought about the word 'prim' as she headed for the Square to pass the time. I'm going to freeze while I wait for Mr Jones, she thought. Primly frozen in Sutherland Square. Poor headline. Her mind wandered through words and worlds as she contemplated primness and prissiness, and how her mother must once have been like her in another world, postwar – young and full of hope. And now she's lying in despair in her bed, and none of us can reach her.

She wondered whether there was anything they could do to help her – other than finding Baby, which was an impossibility.

Sutherland Square was out of bounds for the girls of St Martin's. But who cares? thought Becky Dunville. Who gives a toss? What does it matter anyway?

She smiled grimly as she thought how ten days earlier she would never have thought of disobeying the rules and going somewhere out of bounds. That day, before Christmas, when Simon Carter had let her out into the lane was the first time ever she had broken a school rule, but that had been different. She realised that she had not thought about Simon Carter since she had met Mr Jones.

We change, she thought. I used to care.

But now she didn't care. The rules seemed ridiculous and pointless, even though she knew they had a purpose, and even though she knew that had Baby obeyed the rules, this crisis would not have occurred.

The frost-covered grass looked crisp and hard, each short blade frozen white and pointing upwards. The pathway was marked with white swirls of ice which had never thawed during the coldness of the day.

A robin, bright red-breasted, the most colourful thing in the Square, came and chirped on the path close to her feet.

'If I were Brona,' Becky said to him, 'I'd have a pocket full of crumbs and you could have them – but I'm me, good little me, and of course my pockets are clean.'

Good, boring little me, she thought.

But then she thought about Mr Jones and his nice long legs and his ankle bones, and his grey-flecked eyes, and she wondered what on earth he wanted to talk to her about. Her watch showed it was already twenty past four, so she got up hurriedly and headed out of the Square and back in the direction of the school. There were no more girls coming out of the school, and the street was already empty.

His car was parked just where it had been the previous time. He was looking the other way over his shoulder so he didn't see her approach. Shyly she tapped on the window and he turned around and smiled at her.

What white, even teeth he has, she thought.

Walking up the drive to her house at five thirty, she wondered again what that had all been about. It was as if he wanted to offer her support, to say that he was there if she needed someone to talk to. He'd brought her to Baggot Street, where they had had coffee.

She had looked around nervously in the café and he had put a hand on her shoulder and said, 'Don't worry. If anyone sees us, I'm your form teacher, and I'm just concerned about you. Somebody ought to be,' he added under his breath.

Sitting at the table, waiting for him to rejoin her with the coffee, she wondered what he meant.

From my point of view, she thought, I rather like the idea of someone being concerned about me. This is the most alone I've ever felt in my life and I need to have contact with people. I need to listen to people talking and to remind myself that there is a normal world out there ... out here ... out wherever. I need to talk and to be talked to.

But she wondered what he meant, what angle he was looking at her from, what made him feel that she was not being minded.

She felt unsure what to say to him when he was talking, but it didn't seem to perturb him. He talked away, and when he asked her questions, she answered them as clearly as she could.

'What's the situation with the police now?' he asked.

'One man – Mr O'Connor,' she said. 'He keeps making contact, phoning, coming around, talking to us. He's awfully nice. But it seems ... well, they're sure that she wasn't kidnapped – not for money anyway. That's what Uncle James said all along. They say she went out of her own volition, and either decided not to come back, or something happened that she couldn't come back.'

She sipped her coffee.

I'm getting quite good at drinking coffee, she thought.

She was aware of him watching her and she wondered again what he wanted.

Is he just being kind? she asked herself.

'I've been thinking,' said Mr Jones. 'What you're going through must be very isolating.'

Becky didn't know what to say. There weren't really words to describe it.

'It's more unreal than anything,' she tried. 'Like you can't quite believe it. You know ... we are, I mean, were ... just an ordinary family, a lucky family really, and suddenly we're not.'

She looked away. Any kindness brought the burn of tears behind her eyes and she could not, would not cry in front of him.

He reached his hand across the table and took one of hers in it and squeezed it gently.

204

'You're not alone,' he said.

She took in his hands, one holding the handle of his cup, the other holding her small hand. His were long, strong hands with slim, supple fingers, perfectly filed and polished nails.

A musician's hands, she thought.

'What do you do when you're not teaching in St Martin's?' she asked. 'I mean, do you teach in another school too?'

'No.' He smiled at her. 'I'm with an orchestra. I'm a conductor.'

'Oh.' She couldn't think of what to say. 'How interesting,' she tried.

She wondered who ironed his shirts. He was always so well turned out.

She liked the way he had removed his tie and left his top button open. She forced herself to look away from his neck, but he must have seen her staring, because he said, 'I take the tie off as soon as I get out of school.'

He was smiling again, and he released her hand. She fiddled self-consciously with her tie, wondering if she should have done the same.

She told him about Hugo Mombay Humphries and her trip to the Buttery the previous week.

'He sent one of the letters to Baby,' she said. 'He was her boy-friend.'

'Then you should steer well clear of him,' Mr Jones said.

Becky thought about that for a little.

'He seemed kind,' she said reflectively.

'I'm sure he is kind,' Mr Jones said. 'But I wouldn't like you getting mixed up with someone who wrote such a letter.'

Becky blushed. She knew what he was alluding to. She thought briefly about the letter – it really was something that made her feel unsettled. The idea that Mr Jones had read it and knew that she had read it was both embarrassing and exciting. She would have liked to have asked him if its contents referred to something which was perfectly normal among adults, but she was too inhibited to ask such a question.

He brought her home and she got out of his car outside their house.

'Are you all right now?' he asked.

She looked back in at his smiling face.

'You're very kind,' she said as she closed the door.

'See you tomorrow.' He waved and pulled away.

Walking slowly up the drive, Becky took in the façade of the house and noticed that there was no smoke coming from the chimneys.

Mrs O'Doody must have gone home early, she thought. That must mean that Mum is up and about.

She rang the bell as she took the key from under the flowerpot, hoping that the ringing would alert her mother to her arrival and that she would not startle her by just walking in.

Hesitating while she waited, hoping that her mother would answer, she shifted from one foot to the other in the porch, but no one came to the door. She slipped the key into the lock and turned it, and then returned it to its place under the pot. Later she would remember this. She would remember the door opening slightly, and how she pushed it further, how she stepped into the hall and closed the door behind her. She called out, 'Hello, I'm home,' as she took off her school coat and hung it up, then, picking up her bag, she headed into the kitchen to see if her mother was there. Passing through the breakfast room, she registered that the fire had been lit, but that its dying embers were all that was left. There was no one in the kitchen.

'Hello,' she called again, her voice echoing through the pantry and the larder.

Back to the hall she went, her feet silent on the thick hall rug over the carpet. At the bottom of the stairs she paused again and looked up the stairwell.

'I'm home,' she called. But there was just silence.

Later she would remember these moments with the same clarity with which she recalled the bomb in school the previous week. She would remember going up the first six stairs and then turning on the half-landing as she started to climb the next set of stairs. She would remember the last light coming in shafts like golden pencils through the windows, and how it reflected on the photographs on the wall. She glanced at the photos and looked into the large eyes of her missing sister, then she climbed the next set of stairs. Pausing on the next turn, she looked again at the evening sky – and it was clear and stark, black with golden strands, as though it were being etched for ever into her consciousness. But of course at that moment she did not know that.

On the windowsill was a toy of Baby's from long ago – a cream-coloured plastic model of Laurel and Hardy, with their hats on and their lips painted red. She picked it up and pressed the bottom so that the two men lifted their hats to her. Replacing it on the sill, she wondered why it was kept there, what relevance this toy from the fifties could have to their lives.

As she reached the landing, she noticed that every door was closed except for her parents'.

'I'm home,' she called again. 'It's me.'

She slung her bag down outside her own door, and going to her parents' room she said, 'Are you there, Mum?'

Chapter Fourteen

That Monday morning, Elizabeth Dunville had moved in her mind from her sedation to a place which was full of demons. She was aware of John getting up and dressing, kissing her lightly on the cheek and then departing. In her fuggy state, which was not fuggy to her, but which had a clarity beyond any clarity she had ever known, she heard her two younger daughters rising and leaving for school. She was aware of the arrival of Mrs O'Doody, who looked in on her. Resolutely she kept her eyes closed.

She lay there in her white satin nightdress, her head resting on a pillow of the softest broderie anglaise.

Her thoughts came in short snaps into her mind.

I would like to have been able to bury you, Baby, she thought.

A while later she reached into her bedside table drawer and took out Baby's sweater and breathed it in.

When they find you, you will rest with me, she thought.

Just before her sister-in-law arrived, she said to herself, God, forgive me.

Nancy Fitzgerald pulled up at about nine thirty. She came in and talked to Mrs O'Doody about the importance of seeing that the girls and John ate properly, and of keeping a particular eye on Becky, who seemed to sometimes forget to eat unless reminded. She'd noticed this while Becky was with her over the weekend.

'And she has a good appetite when she's coaxed to eat,' Nancy said to Mrs O'Doody. 'So just keep after her. Like with a child . . . one more bite for me.'

Mrs O'Doody laughed.

'I remember James saying to our daughter Eleanor when she was tiny, "Now open your mouth and let the boat into the harbour",' Nancy continued. 'Anything to get her to eat.'

'Yes, Mrs Fitzgerald,' said Mrs O'Doody. 'I'll keep after her.'

That sorted, Nancy headed for the stairs and then to Elizabeth's bedroom.

'Good morning, dear,' she said to the recumbent Elizabeth, who murmured something about being sleepy.

'Why don't you get up for a while?' Nancy suggested. 'We could go out and have a short walk. It would help to clear away the cobwebs.'

'I've just taken something to help me sleep more,' Elizabeth said. 'I need to sleep today. Maybe tomorrow . . .'

Nancy looked at her.

'Tomorrow then,' Nancy said. 'Shall I leave you to sleep or would you like to talk?' These were all words which Nancy would go over and over in her head later, trying to see how she could have changed the course of history.

'Just let me sleep, please, Nancy,' whispered Elizabeth, waiting for her sister-in-law to leave.

Back downstairs, Nancy talked again to Mrs O'Doody about food, and then headed out to do the week's shopping. Late morning she returned and stocked up the kitchen. She checked on Elizabeth and asked her again if she would like to come out with her.

'I'm just going to go back to sleep,' Elizabeth said. 'Sleep is the best thing for me,' she reassured her sister-in-law.

'I'll phone you later,' Nancy said. 'Around six or thereabouts, so that I don't disturb you. You'll be up by then for the girls, I suppose.'

She looked at Elizabeth doubtfully as she said this, but then she thought that if Elizabeth slept all day she might well get up for Becky, Brona and John's return.

'And I'll be back in the morning,' she added. 'If you're feeling up to it, we could go out for a bit – a little fresh air, cold and all as it is, might do you good.'

'Tell Mrs O'Doody she might as well finish up and go,' Elizabeth said.

Elizabeth heard the hall door closing and then she got up. At her desk in her bedroom, in front of the window, behind the net curtains, dressed in her nightdress and dressing gown, she took out paper and started to write.

I have sinned, she wrote. *And this sin has reverberated down the years. There were times it did not matter, and times when it did. But I think it has always mattered. I betrayed you, John. I sinned against Baby. And I bore the fruit of that sin into the world. My daughter, Becky, is not your child, John. I think you have always known this. I suspect you have. At times I was sure you knew. At other times I thought maybe not, or maybe it didn't matter.*

But now I feel so sure that Baby's death is the punishment for my sin, and the only way I can atone for it is to join her.

Is this the truth?

Is it that I just can no longer live knowing that Baby is gone and that my sin lives on?

She sat back in the chair and thought about that for a while. It did not seem to matter much any more.

She left her chair. She left her desk. She walked across the room. She looked at the bed where she had lain all the days of her married life beside her husband. She remembered how they had coupled on that bed a thousand times and more, how she had lifted herself to meet him, how he would shave beforehand so that the stubble on his chin would not hurt her face while he kissed her in passion.

Back at her desk, she wrote:

You have been a good man, John. And a good husband, and may God forgive me for what I did a long time ago. I cannot forgive myself. I cannot live with myself.

She took an envelope from her desk. She truly meant to fold the page and put it in the envelope and seal it. But she paused again. With the way her mind was moving, some things made sense, and others none at all. She put the envelope down beside the letter. She meant to fold the page and insert it, but her mind was moving backwards and forwards, and she forgot.

She hung her dressing gown on the bathroom door, and ran the bath water. She took the blade from John's razor and put it on the edge of the bath.

Back in her room, she took Baby's sweater from the bed where it lay beside her pillow and held it up to her face again. She was no longer sure if it smelt of Baby or if by its continual contact with herself, Baby's scent had been overtaken. She took it with her to the bathroom, where she locked the door and put the sweater on the towel rail. Then she turned off the taps and stepped into the bath.

*   *   *

At around this time, Brona Dunville had accepted Rhona Brophy's invitation back to their house in Sandymount.

Good, thought Rhona Brophy.

'We'll try and have a laugh,' she said to Brona.

Sister Rodriguez did a surprise swoop on the girls' desks just after the start of the first afternoon class. With the singular lack of compassion for which she was renowned, she looked in Brona Dunville's desk and with an irate snort bade Rhona to assist Brona in carrying her desk outside the classroom door for Brona to tidy.

'In all my days,' she said to the unfortunate youngest Dunville, 'I have never seen such a sight.'

'Should it be exorcised, Sister?' asked Rhona helpfully.

'I'll ask you, Rhona Brophy, not to meddle in the devil's work,' said Sister Rodriguez.

Rhona stood there looking at her, puzzlement all over her face.

'Sister Rodriguez,' she commenced slowly, as if she were trying very hard to understand, 'do you mean that Brona's desk is the devil's work? 'Cos that's why I suggested exorcism. Mother Immaculata once suggested it before.'

The class sat expectant. Rhona Brophy was renowned for the slow and deliberate but very successful needling of her teachers – most especially Sister Rodriguez. She gave the impression of being dense on occasion, and used this to further her cause.

Sister Rodriguez had been burnt once too often by Rhona Brophy.

'What are you talking about, Veronica Brophy?' she snapped.

'Well, Sister,' said Rhona slowly, 'if Brona's desk *is* the devil's work, I don't think my father would like me to be lifting something belonging to the devil outside the classroom. I mean . . .'

Rhona paused as if she could hardly bear the thoughts in her mind. Her eyes grew very large.

'I don't think that he'd like me having to handle something to do with the devil.'

One minute later both Rhona and Brona were outside the door, with the desk in question.

'What's bitten her?' asked Rhona of Brona, with an innocent expression on her face.

Brona was fighting back the tears of laughter.

'You really got her that time,' she giggled.

211

And I got you too, Rhona thought. Daddy would be very pleased with me. He did tell me to distract you.

'I better clean this out,' Brona said, looking inside her desk. Toffee bars appeared to conjoin certain copybooks in permanent unison. Pencil parings and pieces of broken lead were scattered over the piled-up books. There was a slight smell of something like cider, which turned out to be two rotting and furry apple cores.

At the same time as Brona was cleaning out her desk in the corridor outside her classroom, assisted by Rhona Brophy, who had been ordered by Sister Rodriguez to Mother Immaculata's office but who had decided to postpone that particular trip for a while, John Dunville was sitting behind his desk in the hospital where he worked. Doktor von Vecker was seated on a chair opposite him.

'No news?' asked von Vecker of his colleague.

'No news,' replied John Dunville.

'You have to learn how to vait,' said von Vecker.

John Dunville nodded.

Baby Dunville's sweater hung on the towel rail. The bathroom mirror had fogged up. The bath water started to cool, and Elizabeth Dunville lay in it with her eyes closed. Her wait was over.

It was much later when Becky Dunville dropped her school bag on the landing and entered her parents' bedroom. She saw the unmade bed, took in the indentation on her mother's pillow, and wondered where her mother was. She was about to leave the room when she noticed that the chair was pulled out in front of her mother's desk at the window, and she moved across to it. She looked out of the window through the net curtain and saw that in the few minutes since she had stood on the staircase at the window, night had fallen. Switching on the lamp, she glanced down at the desk and saw the envelope lying by itself, with the sheet of paper open in front of her. She took in her name on the letter, mid sentence, and so she started to read it.

She read it twice as she tried to take in its contents, and then suddenly she ran out on to the landing, calling, 'Mummy, Mummy, Mummy.'

For a moment she thought maybe her mother was up in Baby's room, but the closed bathroom door distracted her and she went and knocked loudly on it, calling her mother. She rattled the handle and realised the door was locked. Her brain was moving fast, trying to hold off the terrifying thoughts which were going through her head. Racing back to her parents' room, she picked up the desk chair and brought it to the landing, where she tried to batter the bathroom door. In so doing, she broke a leg off the chair, but made no impact on the locked door.

She was screaming now. She could hear her voice, yelling for her mother.

She raced down the stairs, unsure whether to head for the neighbours or to use the phone. As she jumped the last few stairs there was a ring on the hall door. She ran to it, and pulled it open quickly. Outside, in the porch, stood John Delaware, tall, smooth, well dressed, holding a parcel in his hand.

As he said to her, 'This is for you,' he took in her white face, and her mouth open in a silent scream, and realised all was not right.

'Upstairs, upstairs,' she said.

He pushed past her and raced up the stairs, with Becky behind him. She was gabbling about her mother, a letter, and the bathroom being locked. He put his foot on the door and exerted all his weight, and the lock gave with a splintering of old wood and the door swung open.

Someone was screaming, 'No, no!'

He did not know if it were he or Becky.

'Phone for an ambulance,' he yelled to Becky. 'Go quickly, and phone,' and he moved to the bath, where the red water was already cold.

Ringing for the ambulance in the hall, frozen to the core of her being, Becky Dunville thought of the last rays of sunlight which had come through the landing window, and she knew . . . deep in her heart, she knew it was too late.

The ambulance arrived, and with it Conor O'Connor, who had been passing on his way home and dithering as to whether he would drop in or not. But seeing the ambulance, he stopped the car and legged it up the path. In the hall he found Becky, standing shaking, looking terrified. He took her in but asked no questions, just headed up the stairs, where one look told him all.

'I'll go in the ambulance,' John Delaware said to him. 'Take Becky with you.'

Becky looked up as they came down the stairs.

'There's a letter,' she said to John. 'On Mummy's desk. There's a letter.'

Or maybe she said it to Conor O'Connor. Later, she was not sure.

Someone was holding her. She did not know whom. But there were arms around her and she could not see the ambulance men and the covered stretcher on the stairs. She did not need to see. She knew it all.

'My fault, my fault,' she would say later, and reassuring voices would say, 'No, dear, no, not your fault. Even if you had come home straight from school – it would have been way too late. Not your fault.' But she would still say and think, 'My fault, *mea culpa, mea maxima culpa.*'

In the hospital she found herself sitting on a chair and someone was trying to get her to drink hot sweet tea and she did not know why. She could see the cup in front of her, but it had no meaning, no bearing on her life.

'Take this, and drink from it,' she thought she heard someone say.

Flesh of my flesh, she thought. Who am I? Where are you, Mummy? She looked up at a sea of faces, faces which came and went and shifted in her focus.

Someone asked, 'Where is your father, dear?'

And she replied in a voice she did not recognize, 'Daddy is collecting Brona from the Brophys' on his way home from the hospital.' The prim, proper and polite voice of someone she used to know what now seemed to be a very long time ago.

'For goodness' sake,' said the Matron. 'This is Dr Dunville's daughter. Someone go and check if he's still here.'

'I don't think I am,' Becky said.

There were too many thoughts in her head, too much had happened. She felt as if she had taken leave of her senses, as Mother Immaculata used regularly to accuse various pupils in St Martin's.

And it was Conor O'Connor who held her arm and said very clearly to her, 'It's all right, Becky. It's going to be all right.'

She tried to keep her eyes focused on his, because nothing really made sense and his eyes were kind. Then she turned and found John Delaware there too, and looking into his brown eyes she got the distinct impression that she was looking into a mirror which reflected her own.

The eyes have it, she thought in this strange hallucinatory state in which she found herself.

Then Doktor von Vecker was there and he made her lie down. And sometime later Aunty Nancy and Uncle James came, and then she started to cry.

The headlines screamed, 'BABY DUNVILLE'S MOTHER DIES'.

The inquest said, 'while of unsound mind'.

The spare bedrooms in the Fitzgeralds' mansion were put to good use, and Becky and Brona slept there in the short term. The days were blanks for them. They did what James and Nancy told them. They ate when they were fed. They moved as ghosts whose spirits had left them. Sometimes they touched each other, but they felt nothing.

Eleanor Fitzgerald was taken from school, and home she came, where she tried to keep them company. Their lives were peopled by both constant and passing visitors. The constants were John Delaware, Conor O'Connor, the Brophy family, the von Veckers, and of course the Fitzgeralds. The passing visitors were courageous people who came and spent a little time.

Mother Immaculata was one. She talked firmly to the girls. She talked of a future where the school would offer stability, where there were places in the dormitories for them, where study would give their days some meaning.

'When they're ready,' she said to Nancy Fitzgerald. 'Maybe next week. Probably the sooner the better.'

Father Monaghan came. He shook his head repeatedly.

'I wish he'd fuck off,' Becky said to Brona and Eleanor.

They both nodded in agreement. It seemed a perfectly reasonable wish. Father Monaghan said that Elizabeth could not be buried in hallowed ground. There was a terrible row going on, with Aunty Nancy, usually the world's strongest Catholic, the ultimate defender of the Faith, saying to Father Monaghan that his attitude was disgraceful.

'Unhelpful,' said Uncle James. It was unclear to whom he might be referring, his wife or the priest.

The Reverend William Piper, of their father's church, said that there was a place for Elizabeth in his churchyard.

Mr Jones came and talked to the girls. 'My thoughts are with you,' he said.

A letter came from the British Embassy. The Mombay Humphries offered their deepest sympathy. Hugo sent a separate letter to Becky. In it he expressed his grief for her and her family, and offered to help in any way he could.

The police went through all the letters, looking for handwriting to match the second letter found under Baby's pillow which had made its journey to Conor O'Connor via Brona and Becky's tunic pockets.

'If Baby were alive,' Brona said at the dinner table, staring at her plate of roast lamb, roast potatoes, carrots and peas. She transferred her gaze to the gravy boat, which she was holding in her right hand. 'She would have come home now. For Mummy.'

No one answered. They all felt that she was right.

The funeral was covered by the media. The girls wore their school uniforms.

'I want to wear a mantilla,' Becky said. 'Not my beret.' She was adamant.

Nancy Fitzgerald bought the girls each a black mantilla for their heads.

The coffin was driven past their home on Lansdowne Road. The girls had not been back to it since Monday. Aunty Nancy collected their clothes for them and Mrs O'Doody helped her. As they passed the house, Becky wondered if the bath was still red. She could see the top of her mother's head in a sea of blood. She told no one what she saw. It would be a long time before she discovered that her mother had not in fact slit her throat, but instead had done a neat job on both wrists.

John Delaware appeared at the cemetery. At first Becky was not aware of him, then she felt someone standing close behind her as she stood with Brona on either side of John Dunville. She felt wobbly looking into the frozen rectangular hole in the ground. Her knees buckled slightly, then she found her arm taken firmly and she looked up into John Delaware's face. He nodded slightly, and she felt certain that he had read the letter.

Later, back at the Fitzgeralds' house, there was a consultation going on in Uncle James' study.

'What's happening?' Brona asked.

'Mr O'Connor is having a talk with Uncle John,' replied Eleanor. 'And Mr Delaware and Daddy are in there too.'

'What's it about?' Brona asked.

'I think Aunt Elizabeth left a letter,' Eleanor said. 'It said so in the newspaper. I think it's about that. I heard Uncle John asking Daddy about it this morning.'

Becky said nothing. She wondered where the letter was, and if her father had read it. She was too afraid to think. She had no idea who she was or how she was supposed to behave.

The days and nights were empty. It was as if there were no wind to blow away what had happened. They were frozen in time, caught in the icicles of a winter's day, and the winter seemed eternal.

Chapter Fifteen

Weeks had passed, and Rebecca and Brona Dunville were now boarders at St Martin's in the Fields. On Friday nights they went to the Fitzgeralds' for the weekends. They thought their father was staying there during the week, but they were unsure. There were questions they did not ask, answers which they feared.

Brona thought that Becky had changed completely, and she could not talk to her.

'I'm afraid,' Brona confided to Rhona Brophy, 'afraid that if there is no one living in our house and Baby comes back, she'll think we're all gone, and then she'll go away and never come back again.'

'Do you think she is still alive, Bro?' Rhona asked.

Brona shook her head. 'I suppose not – not really.'

'Does Becky think she is?' Rhona persisted.

Brona shrugged.

'I don't know what Becky thinks.'

Becky was afraid too. Prayer was gone for her. She could not formulate any of the phrases which were part of her past. No one had spoken to her about the letter. She felt that she had no right to ever go back to Lansdowne Road, because she knew she was not a Dunville. She would have liked someone to talk to her, but she did not know how to tell anyone that. Among her peers she had withdrawn even further into herself. She did what study she needed to do to get by. Sometimes she wondered if she had imagined the letter, if she had fantasised the contents, if in fact she really might be Rebecca Dunville after all. Sometimes she caught her father looking at her. But he had become even more remote, even more austere. His hair had started to go grey. He spent most of the time in the hospital, even at the weekends.

He pecked both girls on the cheek when he saw them on Friday nights. Becky was not sure if he were treating her differently to Brona, but he was certainly treating them both differently to before.

*   *   *

218

It was Friday night. Uncle James had collected the girls from St Martin's, and they were back in the Fitzgerald home.

'James and I were thinking that maybe you two would like to go back to your own home this weekend,' Aunty Nancy said to Becky and Brona.

Neither of her nieces said anything.

'You haven't been there in a while and ... well, you probably should. Maybe there are things you want to bring back here,' suggested their aunt.

And so it was that on the Saturday morning, John Dunville drove them home. They were hesitant on the path. Neither girl looked at the other. There were so many unsaid things, so much self-blame, so much distress.

In the hall they stood a moment and breathed in the air. The place did not feel unlived-in.

'Have you been living here, Daddy?' Brona asked.

'Yes, of course,' he replied, looking surprised. 'From Monday to Friday. Mrs O'Doody still comes in – but only a couple of times a week. I don't need her to cook at the weekends, and, well ... I would let her go, but she's been with us such a long time.'

'Are we going to stay?' Brona asked

'We'll see,' he replied.

Becky stood there in the hall. The ghosts of that afternoon were with her. The light fell differently now, because it was morning and because it was drawing to the end of winter, but she remembered how the last light had looked through the landing window, and how there was no light when she got to her parents' bedroom.

'Are you going up to check on your rooms?' he asked them.

They headed slowly to the staircase.

'Becky,' he said.

She suddenly realised that he had not addressed her by name in weeks, and she wondered why she hadn't been aware of it.

'Yes,' she replied.

'John Delaware brought you a present – a late birthday present – a while ago. He left it here and asked that you'd get it when you finally came back here.'

'Where is it?' she asked him.

'I asked Mrs O'Doody to put it in your room.'

The package was lying on her bed. It was carefully tied, and there was a tiny dried flower looped into the ribbon. Becky unpicked the knot and opened out the ribbon and then the paper. As she was doing this, she recalled that he had been carrying this parcel that afternoon. She could remember opening the hall door and seeing him standing there with it in his hands. Inside the wrapping paper there was tissue paper, and inside that there was a book on Trinity College.

She lifted it out and looked at it. It was full of pictures and history, and she remembered that walk across the cobblestones on John Delaware's arm.

Baby was missing then, she thought. And I thought that was the worst thing that could ever happen.

She put the book on her desk and folded up the paper. The ribbon and the flower she put into her desk drawer.

Does he know I'm not a Dunville? She was no longer sure if he had seen the letter that afternoon. She wished there were someone to talk to.

I want to belong, she thought. I used to think I belonged, but I didn't really and I never really knew it. And now . . . now my name is not even my name.

She sat awkwardly on her bed.

My bedspread, she thought, running her fingers over the candlewick. I chose it with Mum. She was my mother too. They can't change that.

Opening her wardrobe, she looked at her clothes. Then she remembered the clothes which Anne Marie had showed her, and she wondered where they had come from. She wondered if her parents had given Baby the money for them after all.

If they loved her more, she thought, maybe buying her expensive clothes was a part of that. And why wouldn't they love her more? After all, she was theirs.

Sitting on her bed she thought about that, and suddenly wondered if they had bought Brona extra things too and maybe she was not aware of it.

She got up and went to look in her wardrobe, and seeing her clothes hanging neatly and recalling Baby's fancy garments in Anne Marie's room, Becky scowled.

I have too many things in my head which I can't deal with, she thought.

She thought about Mr Jones.

Mr Jones had said to her after she started to board that he would like to take her out for coffee but that he felt expulsion would be the last thing she needed at the moment. He had said this with a gentle smile.

'I wouldn't mind,' she said to him.

'Well I would,' he said. 'But I want you to know that if you need to talk, I'm here.'

She thought about that sometimes. But she was so upset inside that during the day she couldn't talk, and it was only when the lights went out in the dorm at night that she would regularly think about unburdening some of her problems, and it was often his face which came to mind.

Remembering her diary, she took it from her desk drawer, and reaching up the chimney, she took the little key and unlocked it.

I've hardly written in it, she thought. It seems so long ago ...

She turned the pages, glancing at but not reading the words she'd written early in January. Then she started to write.

Dear Diary,

It's been a long time and so much has happened. I'm a boarder in school and Mummy is dead, and Baby disappeared and never came back. Now there is just Brona and me and

She wrote no more.

I can't call him Dad, can I? She stared at the blank page for ages, and then she locked the book and put it away.

'Becky.' It was her father calling her.

She went out on to the landing and looked at him.

'You called?' she asked. She could hear herself. Her voice sounded disinterested ... rude even. She never used to sound like this.

What's wrong with me? she asked herself. Why can't I just be nice again?

'I just wondered,' he said, looking at her pale face. 'I wondered ...'

She would have liked to prompt him or to help him in some way, but she had no idea what it was that he was wondering.

She tried to smile, and raised her eyebrows encouragingly.

'I was just thinking,' he said slowly. 'If I get clean towels from the airing cupboard, would you put them in the bathroom?'

Her eyes went sideways towards the bathroom door, and she realised that it was a full door, complete, no broken wood or hanging lock or ripped-out hinges, which was the way it was the last time she saw it.

She swallowed and looked at the door properly, and for a moment she thought that maybe nothing had happened, that maybe this was back before ... before ... before that day which had no name and which she could not mention. Then, looking closer, she saw that it was a new door, recently painted.

'Yes, Dad,' she said.

At the airing cupboard, he handed her fresh towels, and he hovered in the small room, giving her time to bring them to the bathroom.

'Check if we need any more in there, will you?' he asked.

She turned the handle on the door, and it clicked open easily – much more easily than the old door ever had. Pushing it open, she stood and looked in, taking in a new carpet, and the fact that the walls had been newly painted. The bath was clean and white, and there was a new plastic curtain on the window.

She hung the towels on the heated towel rail. She stood for another moment, unsure whether to let the memories come in or to hold them at bay, then she heard her father on the landing.

'Would you like to go out for lunch, Becky?' he asked her as she left the bathroom.

She nodded.

She would have liked it if he'd come and hugged her or held her, but he didn't.

He just said, 'Call Brona, and get your coats.'

They stayed in their own home that night, and Becky took her book on Trinity back to school with her on Sunday night. She still had not looked at it properly, but every so often she would open it and glance at a photograph. And then she would remember those strong feelings she had had about wanting to go there to study, and what it felt like crossing Front Square, or walking down by the playing fields.

That was your dream, she thought to herself. When Baby disappeared and she went there with Hugo, that was the only positive thing that week. It had been like the emergence of a possibility and something she had never considered before. But for the last month or so she had not thought of it at all. She was so despondent that there seemed to be no way out of the misery she felt. She turned the pages of the book again, before closing it and putting it in her locker.

Two more years of school after this one, she thought. It seemed for ever, but for a moment she saw it clearly. She saw that all she had to do was to hang in there, keeping her head down and steering clear of trouble.

'Rebecca Dunville,' said Mr Jones at first break on the Monday after she and Brona had been home to their house on Lansdowne Road. She stopped and waited for him. She had been on her way out to the gardens.

'Come in here a moment,' he said to her, guiding her into a free classroom. 'Sit down,' he said, nodding towards a desk.

She sat down and waited. At times she had a little stamina, but most of the time all she felt was lethargy, and the desire to lie on her bed and to sleep if that were possible.

'Rebecca,' he said, 'look, I don't want to interfere, you've been through an awful lot and the last thing I want to do is to stir things up on you. But has anyone talked with you?'

She shook her head.

'Do you talk to a priest?' he persisted.

'No. I don't like them. They wouldn't bury Mum in a Catholic place.'

'I know,' he said. His voice was very neutral. 'You go home at the weekends, don't you?'

She nodded.

'Would you like to meet then – for coffee? And we can talk. *You* can talk. I'll listen.'

'Yes,' she said, thinking that she had nothing to lose. I can't be any worse off than before, can I? she thought.

'There's the Venetian Café in Ballsbridge,' she said, afraid that he might leave the suggestion vague and not follow up on it.

'Okay,' he said. 'But it might be better to keep this to yourself. And when we meet there, we'll make it appear by accident.'

She nodded.

She was continually surprised at the way he seemed willing to go out on a limb for her.

I wonder why he bothers, she thought. She saw herself now as being dull, tired, drained – almost lifeless. She could see no reason why anyone, let alone someone as attractive as Mr Jones, would want to spend two minutes with her.

She kept her usual low profile that week. Now and again she was conscious of the fact that she was not really aware of Brona's presence. It was as if Brona had subsided in some way. But then, she reasoned, she wasn't really aware of anyone's presence. Most people seemed to her to be irritants. She only had to look at Sister Rodriguez and she wanted to hit her. And Father Monaghan she now despised. Mother Immaculata she avoided as much as she could. She was aware that the head nun had indeed pulled out all the stops she could at the time of her mother's death. That visit by her to the Fitzgeralds' house had in fact offered a tiny flicker of hope. But it was intangible, and Becky felt fury that none of the nuns had attended the funeral.

'I don't know why they didn't come,' she said to Mr Jones on Saturday in the Venetian Café. 'I don't know if it was because the service was not in the one true holy and apostolic church, or if it was because of what Mum did ... you know ... I mean, it's a sin.'

'They may not have been able to come,' he said. 'For whatever reason. I don't want to hear you becoming bitter, Rebecca.'

'I feel ... I don't know ... angry with them. With everyone.'

'But what your mother did wasn't a sin. Or do you see it that way?'

'I don't know what way to see it,' Becky said. 'We're brought up to think that suicide is a sin.'

'Look,' said Mr Jones gently to her, 'it said in the newspaper "while of unsound mind". That's what the inquest said. It was no sin. She was grief-stricken.'

'But where is their compassion? Where is their Christianity? How come my mum gets excluded from their cemeteries?'

'I know,' he said. 'I'm sorry. It makes no sense. If I were you I'd just be glad that she *isn't* in one of those cemeteries. That she's in one where she's welcome.'

'Glad?' Becky said. 'Welcome?'

'Bad choice of words,' said Mr Jones. 'Of course I don't mean glad. I don't mean that at all. Nor welcome. Bad choice of words,' he repeated.

Becky rubbed tears from her eyes with the back of her hand.

'Look,' said Mr Jones. 'Let's go for a walk in Herbert Park. We can get more coffee later, if you like.'

It's like walking into a tunnel, Becky thought as she looked at the avenue of trees on Herbert Park Road.

'Did you see the letter your mother left?' Mr Jones' voice interrupted her thoughts.

Becky looked as if she had been jolted back to reality.

'Yes,' she mumbled. 'How do you know about it?'

'It was in the papers,' he said. 'Not what it said, just that there was a letter.'

Her head was hanging now, and she couldn't stop the tears. He took her arm and brought her off the beaten path to the benches beyond the duck pond.

He produced a handkerchief from his pocket and he tried to dry her eyes, but the tears were coming too fast.

'Tell me,' he said. 'Just tell me, you poor girl. You've got to talk.'

The sympathy made it worse, because Becky just cried more. But in between the sobs she told him about the contents of the letter.

'I'm not my dad's daughter,' she sobbed. 'That's why she did it. She said in it that *I* was a sin, and that that was why Baby died, and that she couldn't live because her sin was living.'

Mr Jones listened in amazement.

'I don't follow,' he said, when she'd finished.

'Don't you see,' Becky said. 'Mum thought that Baby died because she, Mum, had committed this sin. And that I was the result of that sin . . .'

'But this is nonsense,' Mr Jones said. 'Becky, this is the "unsound mind" . . . this is the verdict at the inquest. This is the proof of her unsound mind.'

'How do you mean?' Becky asked.

'Because it is not logical thinking,' he said. 'It's not rational – it's not sane. It's . . . it's unsound.'

'Are you talking about me not being Dad's daughter?' she asked.

'No. No, I'm not. I know nothing about that. Whether that is true or not is not relevant. I mean, it is relevant, but in a different way. You're not a sin,' he said, drying her eyes again. 'Now blow your nose,' he added, handing her the handkerchief.

'What your mother did has *nothing* to do with you. Nothing. And what happened to Baby has nothing to do with you either. These are separate to you. They are outside you. You're unfortunate in that you're caught by circumstances, but the actual events that took place are nothing to do with you. They're not a reflection on you. They didn't happen because of you. Of course they affect you, but you are in no way the cause or the reason for them. Don't you see that?'

She looked hopefully at him, but she shook her head.

'Look,' he said. 'Baby disappeared. She left the house of her own volition that night. She is responsible for leaving the house, for going out to whatever happened to her. And what your mum did ... *she* did that because she was so distressed over Baby being gone. Not because of something she felt guilty about, and which she dug up in a typical Catholic guilt-stricken way. This is nothing to do with you.'

Becky sat silently.

Mr Jones put his arms around her and she leaned in close to him. It was the most comforting feeling she'd had since Christmas. All she wanted was to stay there against his chest. His coat was open and her cheek rested on the lapel of his jacket, and he smelt nice. She lifted her face up to him to thank him, but somehow her lips opened and he, leaning down to her, moved immeasurably by her vulnerability, brought his lips to hers.

It was a gentle kiss, but her arms slipped around him and then it became a stronger kiss.

'This is not a good idea,' he said to her. 'This is not a good idea at all.'

He stroked her hair and let her lean in against him again so that she could hear his heartbeat.

It seemed an awfully good idea to her, though.

'Will you kiss me again?' she asked him.

They were sitting side by side in the Coffee Dock in Jury's.

'Certainly not in here,' he said.

She moved herself closer to him so that her knee was against his.

'I didn't mean in here,' she said. 'I just meant ...'

She didn't quite know what she meant, except that she wanted him to kiss her again. She wanted to feel her heart tumbling over and over and those excited shivers in her blood, and how her mouth seemed to dissolve ... and how all the pain just slipped away.

'Drink your coffee, Rebecca Dunville,' he cajoled her in a put-on stern voice. 'We'll have none of that nonsense.'

Becky giggled.

'Well,' he said. 'So you haven't forgotten how to laugh.'

And that made her laugh again.

She was in better form when she went home, even though she had no idea what he was thinking or whether he would kiss her again. But it certainly gave her other things to think about and it was with a lighter heart that she took the key from under the flowerpot and let herself back into the house.

'Where were you?' Brona snapped at her.

'Went for a walk,' Becky said obliquely. 'Why? Am I not allowed to do that?'

Brona looked sulky. 'I just wondered,' she said. 'That's all.'

'Afraid I'd run off like Baby?' Becky asked her, her eyes narrowing.

Brona didn't answer.

'Don't talk like that,' John Dunville said, looking up from his newspaper.

They were sitting in the breakfast room. 'Be a bit kinder to your sister,' he added.

Half-sister, Becky thought to herself. Goddamn half-sister. And you know it. You're not even my father anyway, she thought, but she said nothing.

'Do we have to stay on as boarders in St Martin's?' she asked him instead.

He lowered the paper and looked at her.

'I think it would be best until the end of summer term at least, and then we'll talk about it.'

'But why?' There was a whinge in her voice, which she could hear, and she wished it weren't there.

He sighed as he put the paper down.

'Because it offers you stability. It means I don't have to worry all week about you. It means you're both safe.'

'I hate it,' Becky said.

'Me too,' chimed in Brona. 'Don't you miss us, Daddy?'

'Look,' he said, 'I leave at a quarter to eight in the morning, and I'm gone for twelve hours most days. Let's leave it at that for now.'

Then he suggested to them that they could accompany him to buy a television that afternoon.

Both girls lit up with excitement.

'Really?' Brona said.

The trial of Lieutenant Calley was on, and Becky, deprived of a newspaper in school, watched a documentary about him on the Dunvilles' new television.

'Can't we look at something more interesting?' Brona whinged.

'This *is* interesting,' Becky replied. 'Last Christmas – before Christmas – I was babysitting for the Robinsons, and there was something on the news about him. I really want to see this.'

'It's bloody boring,' Brona said, getting up to go to her room.

'I get to choose the next programme,' she called as she went out the door.

Becky tuned back in, and was startled to hear Lieutenant Calley saying that he would always be proud if My Lai showed the world what war was really like.

It's to do with responsibility, she thought. She remembered Mr Jones saying to her that people were responsible for their own actions. The problem was that people get caught in the crossfire of other people's actions. The meaning of Mr Jones' words started to make sense to her. The jury was still out and she wondered if Lieutenant Calley would be found guilty.

All day, that Monday back in school, Becky thought about Lieutenant Calley. The whole episode made her think about that evening in the Robinsons' house, which was the last time she had babysat for them.

What was it that Baby called Mr Robinson? she wondered. It was something funny. But she couldn't remember now. It all seemed to belong to another world. But it's all connected, she thought. Lieutenant Calley was in trouble back then, and he's now about to face the consequences, and his life has continued in a flow between then and now. And in a way our lives must have too – but because of the things which have happened I can only see my life in small segments. Like the fifteen years up until the night Baby disappeared. Then it's as if I stepped into this other place where I had a week of living – if you can call it that – in this family which had had its core shattered. And I was no longer just Becky, just as Brona was no longer just Brona. We became these other two people, the sisters of someone who was deeply loved and who had disappeared. And then suddenly that week was over and we became children who had no mother, only I became an orphan.

She was aware that she was being dramatic, but she had no idea how to sort it in her head. She thought how much she would like to talk to Mr Jones again.

And to have him kiss me, she thought.

Her mind moved to the milkman whom she'd seen in the film at the Robinsons'. At that moment, through the open door into the corridor outside the classroom, she saw Mr Jones, and she blushed bright red and prayed he wouldn't know what impure thoughts had been going through her head.

'Good morning, girls,' he said as he entered the classroom, and those who were outside trooped in after him.

Becky played the chords for the singing class, but there were no overt signs from Mr Jones that he either remembered what had happened between them on the Saturday or indeed would like it to happen again.

But later that day she came back to the question of Lieutenant Calley.

The radio in their common room had been confiscated because of something to do with Sister Rodriguez and the song 'Je t'aime', which meant that Becky couldn't get the news. Radio Luxembourg, now that the nuns had discovered it existed, had been banned. Newspapers were not encouraged in the school, so she decided to try and get out to find out if the jury had brought in a verdict.

Becky left the building when classes were over, reasoning that it was the time she would be least likely to be missed. She headed down Sutherland Street and cut through the Square to the furthest corner, where she knew a newspaper man sold the *Evening Herald* and the *Evening Press*. He always had white cardboard signs with the headlines attached to the railings and she thought that these signs might tell her what was happening in the court case.

She had got it wrong, because when she got there there was no mention of Lieutenant Calley, and so, dejected, she headed back to school, only to be caught by Sister Rodriguez in the entrance hall.

'All I wanted to know was what sentence he got,' she said to the nun.

'It's none of your business,' said Sister Rodriguez.

'But I just wanted to know was he being held responsible,' Becky persisted. 'I didn't do anything criminal. I can't get the news because the radio is gone.'

'I'll tell you something, my girl,' said Sister Rodriguez. 'If there is any justice in this world he will be found not guilty. He was only obeying orders. So take it from me, he is innocent.'

Becky looked at the nun with disdain and dislike. Her eyes narrowed and she opened her mouth to tell Sister Rodriguez that that was the most irresponsible thing she had ever heard.

Fortunately for Becky, Mr Jones took that moment to appear in the entrance hall, and taking in the sight of Sister Rodriguez with a pious look on her face, and the way Becky was standing with her hands on her hips, he interrupted smoothly.

'Rebecca Dunville,' he said, 'I wanted to check if you need new music for the songs for next week.'

'I,' interrupted Sister Rodriguez, 'have caught this girl red-handed. She left the school without permission to buy a . . . a . . . newspaper.' She spat the word out.

'Oh dear me,' said Mr Jones, cutting short a protestation from Becky. 'You mustn't go out without permission, Rebecca. As your form teacher I have to be adamant on this. Now, because of the difficult time you have been through, I'm sure Sister Rodriguez and I can find it in ourselves to overlook this, this one time. But it mustn't happen again.'

Before Sister Rodriguez knew what had happened, he had whisked Becky down the corridor, talking loudly and clearly about sheet music and saying that he had left it in their classroom.

'You owe me a thank you,' he said to Becky.

'I hate her,' Becky replied.

He shook his head firmly. 'You're stuck here. You want to get your exams. You want to get out. You know this is the only way to get what you want in life. So don't pull a silly stunt like that again. You can't address a nun the way I suspect you were about to.'

'I hate her,' Becky repeated. 'She said that Lieutenant Calley was not responsible for his actions at My Lai.'

'What?' He seemed truly perplexed.

'All I wanted was to get a newspaper and see what happened to Lieutenant Calley.'

'Oh, I see. Well I got that one wrong. I thought Sister Rodriguez was alluding to some sort of pornography.'

Becky looked sulkily at the ground.

'Listen to me, Rebecca,' he addressed her again. 'Just listen. If you can't do it for yourself, do it for me. Keep out of trouble. You've had enough trouble to last you for a long time. Now steer clear of it here. You'll end up being expelled.'

'I don't care,' Becky said. 'I want to be expelled.'

'I mean it,' he repeated. 'If you can't do it for you, then do it for me. How do you think I'd like teaching here if you weren't one of my pupils?'

That pulled Becky up short, and she found herself smiling with pleasure.

That puts a new face on the situation, she thought that night in bed. I mean, even if he only said it to make me behave, it's still a nice thought. And he must at least have thought it, to have said it. And he did say it.

That gave her a warm feeling, and she thought about his hand stroking her hair, 'like a father', she thought sleepily, 'and like a lover . . .'

Brona, in her bed in the long third-year dormitory, lay on her back with her eyes closed. *Hail Holy Queen*, she prayed, *Mother of Mercy, hail our life, our sweetness and our hope.* The words were meaningless. She knew on some deep unconscious level that there was no hope. She knew there was nothing except the sterility of the white dormitory, and the darkness of the night, but still her mind sought words to carry her through until morning, until Rhona would come into school and stand beside her at Assembly, until Rhona's fingers would accidentally touch hers as they stood there silently. She longed for her mother and a return to Christmas time. *Away in a manager*, she prayed. *Hail mother most pure . . . through you may we come to the haven of rest . . . O hope of the guilty, O light of the grave.*

An image of the open grave came to her mind, and she forced it away with further prayers. *Good King Wenceslas . . .* She tried to bring the music to mind, but there was nothing – just broken sentences, and the endlessness of the night.

Chapter Sixteen

'You said that I owed you,' Becky said to Mr Jones the following day when he appeared with a newspaper for her. 'Now I owe you even more,' she added, taking it from him.

'Next time you decide to sneak out to get the papers to pick up news from the States, remember they are at least five hours behind us!' he said teasingly.

'Ooops,' she said. 'I never thought of that.'

She took the paper from him and examined the front page.

'Satisfied?' he asked her.

'Yes,' she said. 'Yes. Guilty. Guilty on the first two charges. Guilty of murdering twenty Vietnamese.' Her eye ran on down the column. 'The fourth charge reduced to assault with intent to kill ... either death sentence or life imprisonment ... two of his juniors acquitted ... charges against nineteen others have been dropped.'

She looked up at Mr Jones.

'What do you think?'

'Why is it so important?' he asked her, puzzled.

'I don't know,' she said. 'I'm not sure. It just seems important to me.'

'Is it because of responsibility?' he enquired.

'Yes, I think that is what interests me,' she replied. 'I mean ... we are responsible for our actions ... you said that too.'

'Yes, I know I did,' he replied. 'I did say that, and I did mean it.'

'Easter holidays at the end of the week,' Becky said, looking up hopefully at him.

'And?' he said.

'Nothing,' she said sulkily. 'I just thought ...'

'How about a walk?' he suggested.

'Herbert Park?' she asked.

He smiled.

*   *   *

That weekend when she got home she took out her diary again, and she started to scribble down words that had come to her during the week, words connected with Mr Jones and the things he said. It took her a while to get them all down, and then to re-format them.

Not a poem, she thought. A song. Our song.

She read it through.

Thinking of the future
And plans we've got to make
Looking at the past
The fun times we have had

We've got to talk
We've got to talk

Fill the kettle
Clear the decks
I want to hear you now

We've got to talk

Forget the time
We'll talk until the day is done
And then
We'll talk until the morning sun

I want to talk

I'll hear the things
Which make you tick
The teasing childhood games

Of high days
And down time
Love and less
Some distress

We've got to talk

Of things that really count

We've got to talk

We've got to talk

233

Of mice and men
And sundry things
That make us laugh

We've got to talk

Of life and love
And Lord God above
I want to hear
Everything
And then some more

We've got to talk

We've got to talk

We'll walk in the park
And dance in the dark
But I really want to know

That's why we'll talk.

Underneath she wrote neatly, *Rebecca Dunville, April 1971.*

I wonder would Mr Jones put it to music, she thought. If he wrote the score, I could sing it.

After she had put her diary away, she kept going back to it, and taking it out and reading it over again, wondering whether she should change more bits of it.

I'll ask Mr Jones later, she thought. He'll know.

At dinner, John Dunville asked her if she wanted to invite someone to dinner the following evening.

'I'm having Rhona over,' said Brona.

'No, I don't want anyone,' Becky said.

Although I'd quite like Mr Jones over, she thought to herself.

'Why don't you invite Gabriela?' John asked.

'Because I can't stand her,' Becky said.

Brona and he exchanged a glance, but neither said anything. Becky saw the look, and knew that she must have sounded horrible, but she didn't care.

I don't like any of them, she thought. I don't see why I should have to ask people over who bore me rigid.

Back in her room, she threw herself on her bed.

It's all a farce, she thought. Every last bit of it. The whole thing. A sham. We sit at the dinner table and behave like perfect people and it's all a goddamn sham. The perfect family – Baby ran off, and then Mum went off her head. No wonder. And I'm not even one of them, and no one will talk about it.

'Maybe they don't know that you've read the letter,' said Mr Jones the following day in Herbert Park.

'Of course they know,' Becky said.

'No, steady on. Maybe they really don't know. Or maybe they do know and they think that you don't want to talk about it, that you're not ready to talk about it, or that you didn't take in what you read.'

'Well, what do I do?' she asked him.

'I think you have to let them know that you want to talk about it.'

'But maybe I don't want to talk about it,' she said.

'I don't think you know what you want,' he said to her.

'Oh yes I do,' she said, looking at his mouth.

'Well, I suppose I can kiss you now,' he said with a smile.

She looked puzzled. There was something in his voice that made it clear that things had changed.

'What's happened?' Becky said. She suddenly felt panicky. 'What's changed?'

He took her hand in his and held it while he talked.

'I can kiss you because I'm not your teacher any more,' he said.

'What?' She jumped up, panic all over her face. 'What do you mean?'

'It's all right,' he said. 'Sit down and I'll tell you.'

Becky sat on the edge of the bench. She was shaking.

'I'm not going back after Easter,' he said.

'But you have to,' she said. 'You have to. I couldn't bear it.'

'If I went back, then I couldn't kiss you,' he said. 'And anyway, I'm not going very far away.'

Becky felt a cold fear envelop her. All she could take in was that he was leaving St Martin's, and she saw that as abandonment of her.

'You're leaving me,' she said. It was more like a wail.

'No I'm not, silly,' he said. 'The exact opposite. I'm not leaving *you*, I'm leaving St Martin's so that I can stay with you.'

'I don't understand,' she said.

'Come here.' He drew her in close to him. 'I'm going to teach part time in another school. I'm moving flats. I'll be closer to you. I promise I am not going to leave you.'

'I don't want you to leave me,' she said.

'I am *not* going to leave you,' he repeated. 'Things are going to change . . .'

'I don't like change,' she said sadly.

'I know that. I know. But this is going to be a change for the better. I promise. It means we can spend time together.'

'I don't want to go back there if you're not there.'

It took him ten minutes to calm her down.

'Your problem is that you don't talk,' he said.

'I do talk. I talk to you.'

'Oh dear, oh dear,' he said with his arm around her shoulder, and pulling her in close to him.

She was thinking about her song as he continued.

'You have to find the right person to ask about the letter your mother left,' he said. 'And you've got to talk.'

'Where have you moved to?' Becky asked him, trying to change the subject. 'And where have you moved from?'

'To a basement flat in Sutherland Square. From Sandymount.'

'Sandymount?' she said. 'You mean you lived that close to me, and I never knew? When can I visit your new place?'

'Not until you've done some talking,' he said. 'I really mean it. You've got your Intermediate exams in about eight weeks' time, and you're going to study and do well, and you're going to sort out this other matter.'

They walked around the pond.

'Can I hold your hand?' she asked.

'No, we're going to keep our relationship a secret. My flat is going to be a safe place for you to come to while you're dealing with everything else.'

He's so assured, she thought to herself. I wonder will I ever be like that. It's like the difference between an adult and being me.

She thought of the term 'child-woman' which she had recently come across, and that was what she felt like.

Neither one nor the other, she thought. And yet I want confidence, like the girls in fifth and sixth year. Even Eleanor – she gives off more confidence than I do.

Later, when she was back in her room, she thought about this again, and then she wrote in her diary:

Maybe it's because I feel I've lost my identity. It's like floating between different worlds and not knowing if I belong anywhere. I used to be the middle sister, and now I'm not. I used to think I was a Dunville, and now I know I'm not. And I used to be a child and feel protected . . .

Nothing is safe, nothing is constant, she thought. Each phase of my life is for passing through, for learning from, for taking the best of it with me when I move on to the next phase.

But what can I take with me? she wondered, as she took out her Latin books. I did what I was told. I was a good girl, and look where that got me.

Then she thought of Mr Jones telling her to study and to get that out of the way, so she settled down to her work. For the first time since her world had fallen apart, she found that old satisfaction but she saw it in a new light. She worked solidly for a couple of hours, and was surprised when she saw what time it was.

Is this how I do it? she wondered. Is this the way forward for someone like me? To put my head down? To read and learn? To fill my mind with other things? To find my way to Trinity?

It seemed to make sense. She wondered briefly about Brona, and how Brona was coping, but she felt that she couldn't handle that then, couldn't handle Brona's obvious neediness and Brona's loss.

It was later, much later that she saw that Brona's loss was almost the same as hers, and that of course Brona didn't know then about the letter and its contents, that all Brona felt was an even stronger sense of rejection, because Becky had withdrawn from her and she did not know why.

But then, at that point in time during the Easter holidays of 1971, Becky started to work again. She worked like she had never worked before. Sometimes it went well and sometimes she had poor concentration. She walked by herself in Herbert Park and thought about Mr Jones. She wanted to be with him, but he had said that he would act as her mentor until she got through her exams, and that she must settle for the odd kiss.

Odd? she thought. If these kisses are odd, then give me odd.

'I like odd,' she said to him, smilingly, lifting her mouth to his.

'There is plenty of time,' he pacified her.

She longed for the times they were together, but he was the epitome of restraint.

Brona meantime was spending most of her time in the Brophys' house. Rhona's parents seemed happy to have her there.

'Sure, there's always a place laid at the table for you, Brona, pet,' said Rhona's mother.

'And a bed for you to sleep in,' said her father.

Brona looked from one face to the other. She knew that the welcome was real; after all, Rhona said it to her often enough. 'My parents like having you over. Really they do. They say you're an influence of sorts on me.'

'What does that mean?' Brona asked.

'Dunno,' said Rhona. 'But I think it's good,' she added doubtfully.

But while Brona craved family surroundings, and appreciated what they were offering her, it was her own family she wanted – a mother who was there when she got in from school, who smelt of expensive perfume and whose pearls sat perfectly around her slender alabaster neck, who sat with her father in the drawing room in front of the fire, drinking sherry or a gin and tonic, and who smiled when Brona came into the room. The drawing room fire was seldom lit now. Even now, during the Easter holidays, her father came home so late that he was tired and headed to bed after a few brief words with Becky and herself. And Becky seemed engrossed in studying or something. Brona wondered what Becky was thinking, as it was impossible to read her any more. She was either totally impassive or giving off a very negative attitude to their home life. Brona searched for the diary's spare key, but it had disappeared in the mess in her room and she could not find it.

'Oh, Rhona,' she sighed. 'Life's a bitch.'

'And then you die,' Rhona said.

They looked at each other, horror on Rhona's face.

'I didn't mean that,' she said. 'I really didn't.'

'I know,' Brona said. 'It's just an expression, isn't it?' She thought of the Reverend William Piper. 'Dust to dust,' he had said, and then the gaping rectangular hole in the ground had been filled in. And her bed in the long white dormitory seemed like a coffin to her. *In the beginning was the Word*, she thought. *And the word was with God . . .*

*   *   *

'So, have you given any thought to talking to someone about the letter?' Mr Jones asked Becky.

It was towards the end of the Easter holidays and he was bringing her to his flat for the first time.

She shrugged.

'I have thought about it, on and off,' she answered.

'And who will you talk to?' he persisted.

'The only possibilities are Dad ...' She paused there. It was impossible not to call him Dad, and yet she had a problem with it. 'And Aunty Nancy ... Uncle James, I suppose – there really isn't anyone else. I mean, you know Mr O'Connor, the detective – well, he knows about the letter, he's read it, but he won't know who my real father is. Mr Jones,' she said suddenly, voicing a thought which kept coming into her mind. 'What if they don't know who my father is?'

'They may not know. I realise that. I thought that some time ago. They may not have a clue. But you're still missing the point.'

'What point?' She was puzzled.

'The point is that you've got to talk. That's what this is all about. That's how people get on together, how they cope, how they deal with things – even things like this. The more you talk, the better chance you have.'

'Chance for what?'

'For an even keel, for equilibrium, for connection.'

When they got to his flat, he swung open the gate which led off the street and down to the basement. They went down the steps to his front door. The tiny hallway was tiled, with a rattan mat on it. He took her coat and hung it on one of the hooks on the wall. Her heart pounded with excitement as he swung the door open and they went into the living room.

'Oh, it's so lovely,' she said, taking in the cosiness of the room, the coal fire lighting in the grate, the armchairs on either side of it, the old sagging sofa, a table at the window with two upright chairs at it.

He showed her the rest of the place – the bedroom with its double bed, wardrobe and dressing table. She blushed when she saw the bed, and afterwards when she was walking home, she thought of the bed, how large it seemed in the small room, how she'd wanted to say something about it, to comment on it, but how she couldn't.

Oh God, she thought. Imagine ...

But she said nothing.

The small bathroom made her feel embarrassed too, but it didn't seem to unnerve him at all. He just pointed the odd thing out to her, like the ducks on some of the tiles, and how the heater was high on the wall. And then, taking her hand, brought her back to the sitting room, where he kissed her again.

'Can I come here?' she asked. 'I mean – during school, you know.'

'Of course you can't,' he said. 'You're boarding. You get caught slipping out and you know what they'll do to you. This is somewhere you can come at the weekends. Later, we'll see.'

He kissed her in front of the fire. He tilted her chin up and looked into her eyes and he smiled gently as he brought his face down to hers. Her heart wouldn't stop pounding. It was more exciting than his first kiss in Herbert Park, when she had thought that she would die of excitement.

Back home, she enlisted Brona's help. It was totally for egotistic reasons, but Brona walked straight into it.

'Hey, Brona.' She tapped on Brona's door.

'Whatcha want?' came a dull voice from inside.

'Wanted to ask you something.'

'Come in.'

Becky opened the door. She was always uneasy opening doors now, not being sure of what she'd find behind them.

'I thought Rhona was coming over,' she said. 'Is she not here yet?'

'Nope,' said Brona, eyeing her from where she was lying on her bed.

'Want a hand to clean up in here?' Becky asked.

'What's wrong with it?' Brona said, looking surprised.

'Ummm, nothing,' Becky replied, looking at the floor, where clothes were strewn, and books, and to her surprise, she saw Baby's Meccano.

She almost commented on the Meccano, but then changed her mind.

'I was thinking . . .' she said slowly.

'Hope it didn't hurt,' Brona said.

Becky ignored this. In a way she couldn't blame Brona for being so hostile. After all, I have hardly given her an inch since . . . Becky still hadn't found a word to describe what had happened.

'Brona, you know the way you're not too keen on being a boarder,' Becky tried.

240

'Yes.' Brona sounded a little more alert.

'Well, I was thinking that if we could put a good plan to Dad, maybe we could convince him that we'd be better as day girls.'

'But he said no,' Brona said.

'I know he did. But if we approach it differently. Not like a whinge, but more like, how much more sense it would make. That we could be good company for each other. Don't forget, he's not mad on the nuns, so if we laid it on a bit . . .'

'Go on,' Brona said, brightening somewhat more.

'Dad,' said Brona that Saturday evening at dinner, after Mrs O'Doody, who was re-ensconced at weekends at the Dunvilles', had cleared the starters. 'I can't bear the idea of going back to board tomorrow night.'

'Don't start,' said John Dunville.

'No, but really,' Brona said. 'I'm so lonely for you and Becky. The nuns don't allow us to talk to each other.'

'At all,' Becky interjected.

'And I need family at the moment.'

'Isn't the convent like one big family?' he asked his beseeching daughter.

'You know the school motto,' said Rhona Brophy, who had been roped in to assist.

'*Humanitas et Virtus*,' said Becky helpfully, wondering what Rhona was about to come out with.

'"Divide and rule", that's what it means,' said Rhona.

Becky and her father shared a smile.

'No, but seriously, Dad,' said Becky. 'We are becoming isolated from each other . . .'

'Well, during these holidays, it struck me that you didn't have much time for Brona,' John said, with a raised eyebrow.

'It's because I'd got used to not talking to her, or spending time with her,' Becky said. 'It's not healthy,' she added, hoping that would ring true with her doctor father. 'And I work better here,' she continued. 'You know, exams in a few weeks . . .'

'And we'd be here when you came home in the evening,' Brona said. 'Like a real family,' she added.

'But you often get out of school at different times,' John said. 'And I don't like the idea of Brona being here alone until you get home, Becky.'

'But,' said Rhona, as politely as she knew how, 'those days, Brona could come back to my house. My parents would be so pleased. They're always saying how we should be doing more for Bro. Really. It would be terribly nice. And she has spent most of the Easter holidays in my house because Becky has been studying. And my parents said that she's always welcome.'

'I'll think about it,' John said.

'You're not saying no?' Brona asked.

'He's saying yes,' Becky said afterwards to Brona. 'We've just got to put on a good show – let him see that we can be responsible, and that it is a better option.'

In her room, Becky thought of the Meccano strewn on Brona's floor, and suddenly she knew why it was there. It made her want to cry.

It's Brona's way of trying to connect. She feels that if she can play with the Meccano she might be able to replace Baby for Dad, and that she might somehow manage to recreate the past, she thought.

After Rhona had gone home, she knocked on Brona's door again.

'May I come in?'

'Yup,' came from inside.

'Shall I help you tidy up now?' she asked Brona, who was sitting on the floor, looking at the mess.

Brona didn't answer, and Becky could see that she had been crying.

Brona sat there as Becky started to pick up the pieces strewn among the clothing, and put them in their box.

'You know, Bro,' she said, for the first time using Rhona's name for her sister. 'You don't have to try to make things with this stuff.'

'I thought . . .' Brona started, but couldn't finish.

'I know what you thought. But you're not Baby. Thank goodness. And you don't have to be like her – not now, not ever.'

'What do you mean?' asked Brona in a broken voice.

'I dunno,' Becky said, hesitantly. 'It seems so – cruel, I think, saying this. But I don't think Baby was terribly nice. And all I'm saying is that you don't have to be like her.'

'Why don't you think she was nice?' Brona asked.

'I haven't worked it out,' Becky said. 'It's just a feeling.'

And the image of Baby gleefully holding the money she'd got off Mr Robinson months earlier flashed through her mind.

'I wouldn't say it to anyone else, mind,' she said quickly to

Brona. 'But it's okay with you. Because you and I are in the same boat.'

'We are, aren't we?' Brona said. 'In the same boat, I mean.'

Becky felt it was pitiful the way Brona seemed to hang on to everything, to every crumb of reassurance which was offered.

And yet it's not much, she thought. All I'm saying is that she's not alone in this mess we're in. And that seems to offer her reassurance. I wonder what she'll think when she finds out that we're only half-sisters.

As Becky tidied the floor, putting all the Meccano in its box, she was aware of Brona just watching her. She took in her pale face and her dark hair hanging like a weight around it, and she saw the shadows under her eyes for the first time.

'Come and look in the mirror with me,' she said to Brona.

'Whatcha mean?' Brona asked.

'No, come, really. Let's look in the mirror together.'

Brona got up off the floor slowly and the two of them stood in front of her dressing table. Becky turned on the little lights which surrounded the mirror, and they stood and looked into it together.

'You and I,' Becky said, tentatively at first, and then gradually more firmly, with confidence coming into her voice, 'you and I are going to revamp ourselves. Look at the pair of us. We're washed-out-looking.'

Brona said nothing, just stared into the looking glass.

'In the summer,' Becky said, 'we're going to get lots of sunshine. And we're going to sleep and eat well. And we're going to come out of this stronger.'

She wondered where this was coming from. She knew that what she wanted was to be in Mr Jones' flat, with her chin tilted while he kissed her. But she could vaguely hear his voice saying to her, 'I'll help you, and you'll help Brona.'

Why does he care? she wondered silently, before bringing herself back to the mirror and Brona's pale face.

'We'll get your hair layered again, and if we do go away with the Fitzgeralds, we'll get a tan like you've never seen before, and we'll lie on beaches and laugh.'

'We look awful,' Brona said suddenly, as if she had only just taken in the circles around their eyes.

'Like pandas,' Becky said.

'I like pandas,' Brona said.

'Yes, but not to look like. We need to get ourselves together. Come on, we're not bad looking. We've just been through shit.'

'We're still in the middle of shit,' Brona said.

'I know,' Becky said. 'I know. But look, if we're not boarders, at least we don't have to deal with the cabbage – not in the evenings anyway. And if we eat better, that'll be a start. We won't look so pasty and tired.'

'Do you think?' There was a flicker of hope in Brona's voice.

'Yes, I do think,' Becky said firmly. 'And you're going to keep your room tidy – that'll make you feel better. You'll feel like you're in charge of your life.'

'We don't really look alike, do we?' Brona said, peering into the mirror.

'You look more like Baby,' Becky said. 'Which is lucky for you.'

'She was really beautiful, wasn't she?' Brona said.

'You're nicer looking. When you smile and laugh your face lights up,' Becky responded.

'She looked lovely when she smiled,' Brona said.

'You look better. You don't look like you're laughing at people, you look like you're laughing *with* them. It's nicer . . . more endearing. Trust me.'

Brona smiled.

'Really?'

'Yes, goddamn really,' Becky said.

'Your language has gone to the dogs,' Brona said in Mother Immaculata tones. 'Rebecca Dunville, you belong in a kennel.'

They both laughed.

She's still the little sister, Becky thought later. That hasn't changed. It's just that she doesn't have as many sisters as she used to have.

And she doesn't have a mother, she added as an afterthought. But we won't think about that now. And in fact she doesn't have any real sisters at all, but we won't think about that now either.

These were thoughts which she had put on hold.

'A day at a time,' Mr Jones had said. 'And when that comes easier, then a week at a time.'

I could hardly do an hour at a time back then, Becky thought. I couldn't see further than the moment I was caught in. *I kept my nerves at strain, dried my eyes and laughed at a fall, and, baffled, got up and began again.*

I wonder what that's from? she mused.

She thought about how she used to know so many quotes, how she'd almost lived off them and by them, and now she didn't seem able to connect properly.

A person at a time, she thought. Like connecting with Brona earlier. That was good. It was positive, and I felt better afterwards.

She knew that at the time they were talking, she could believe what she was saying, but she found that she kept losing touch with her feelings and with the beliefs she had articulated.

If we just hang on to certain things, and work from there.

But then the uncertainties seemed so great, and the wave of optimism from earlier seemed suddenly swamped, as she got ready for bed.

She dreamed that night of Salome, a golden-haired Salome, a dream she didn't understand for a long time. It would come to her in snippets over the following week – the dancing Salome in beautiful if scanty clothing, twirling in front of a Christmas tree, with the little lights frosted and shimmering, lighting up the golden curls on her head. And in the dream – if such is the word that could be used – instead of a turkey being lifted from the oven on to its dish, there was a head in a pool of blood.

Then the dream changed, and the setting was beside the Red Sea, where armies were gathering. On one side was a battalion of nuns, and in their right hands they carried crosses. On the other there were people she felt she should know, but whose faces she could not see. And suddenly she was terrified and she did not know where the fear was coming from. There was danger and she could feel it creep up on her until it was in her very bones. She reached back a hand to grasp Brona's, and one of the nuns started a chant.

'Divide and rule,' the nuns shouted in unison, over and over. Then the Red Sea parted, and the waves rolled back to reveal a path down the centre. And she and Brona were running as fast as they could through the sea. And the further they ran, the slower their racing feet moved, and there was no shore in sight, and she knew with certainty that at any moment the waves would reverse and come crashing in on them.

'God help us!' Brona screamed.

And Becky's increasingly sluggish feet stopped moving and she heard someone shouting, 'There is no God.'

When she woke, there was silence in the house. Her heart was pounding. It was as loud as the shout which had woken her. She slipped on silent feet out of her bed and went out on to the landing, where she stood listening. She wondered if someone moving on the top floor had woken her, and she started up the stairs to Baby's bedroom.

ENTER AND DIE greeted her on the upper landing, but her eyes were so bleary from sleep, she could not read the words properly. She opened the door with a nervous hand, turning the handle and stepping back as it swung open. There was silence. Her breathing was coming in short and painful gasps.

'Is there someone there?' she called.

She pushed the door further with her foot, and switching on the light she stepped into the room, and suddenly she was awash with blood, as if the Red Sea was pounding in on top of her. She opened her mouth to scream, but the words were choked in blood.

Drowning, drowning, she thought.

And then she woke, this time for real, and she was lying sweating in her bed, the sheets awash with blood, as her period had come on suddenly and unexpectedly. Terrifying images clawed at her mind as she struggled from the bed and went to the wash basin in her room, and started to run the taps.

Chapter Seventeen

On the Monday after the Easter holidays, Becky and Brona came home together from school. Becky had wanted to go to the flat on Sutherland Square to tell Mr Jones that their father had phoned the school on Sunday and changed their boarding arrangements for the coming term. But she couldn't abandon Brona and she couldn't bring her with her, so she had to leave it until the next day.

They got the bus home, and Becky reminded her sister that they needed to put on a good show when their father got home, as he had said he needed to be convinced that being day girls was the right way forward.

They jostled each other good-naturedly when they dismounted from the bus.

'No dripping and gruel this evening,' Becky said.

'Not for us anyway,' Brona replied with a laugh.

'Apart from anything else, I prefer having dinner in the evening,' Becky said. 'I hated school dinners at one. Hated them.'

'Me too,' said Brona. 'I much prefer bringing in sandwiches for lunch.'

'We just have to get up early enough to make them,' Becky said.

'And we'll take it in turns,' Brona checked. 'Won't we?'

'Yes,' said Becky with her new and spasmodic determination. 'And we'll make a good shopping list once a week, so that we have everything we need.'

'Mummy used to do that,' Brona said.

'Yes, she did. And now we're going to do it.'

And so they headed into this new week. Christ had risen. Christ had died. Christ was born again. Easter was over. Becky hadn't wanted to go to Mass on the Sunday before term restarted. John had said on the Saturday evening, 'What time Mass in the morning, girls?' Becky just said vaguely, 'I don't really feel like it,' and no one said anything.

But then she felt that in the spirit of support and magnanimity between herself and Brona which she was trying to portray to their father she ought to make an effort.

'What time do you want to go at, Bro?' she asked.

Brona looked pleased.

'How about twelve o'clock in Westland Row?' she asked. 'And we could get the bus so Daddy doesn't have to bring us.'

Becky wondered if Brona would have gone without her, but it wasn't worth pushing it to find out.

All I have to do is be nice, she thought. And she had to admit that when she was nice it was easier and she felt better. But even acknowledging that did not change the fact that it was a difficult thing to do.

The following day Brona went home with Rhona, and Becky hovered until they were well gone before heading the long way around to Sutherland Square, as she was afraid of being seen by her schoolmates. She suddenly realised there was no guarantee that Mr Jones would be in his apartment. Flickers of panic went through her mind.

What'll I do if he's not there? she wondered. And then the equally disturbing thought, What'll I do if he's there and there is someone with him? as it started to occur to her for the first time that he presumably had a life of his own that he lived when she wasn't around. This was a bit difficult to imagine, as he was so much to the fore in her thoughts, but it still had to be taken into account.

When she got there, she could see there was a light on in his sitting room. She stood outside the railings, looking down and feeling her heart pounding.

I'll knock on the door, and if there is someone else there I'll just say that I was looking for number seventy-eight, she thought.

But he was alone, as she discovered when she rang the bell.

'What are you doing here?' he said, taking her by the arm and pulling her into the hallway. 'If the nuns see you . . .'

'I checked that there was no one on the street before I came down,' she said quickly. 'Honestly, no one saw me. And I'm not a boarder now.'

Inside his flat, he made them coffee while he listened to how she had talked John into letting them return to being day girls.

'How did Mother Immaculata take that?' he asked.

'Daddy phoned her on Sunday,' Becky said. 'I think it went all right.

He didn't really say. He phoned, then he went in to see her, and when he came home he just said, 'Sorted.' So I think it was all right.'

Drinking coffee, sitting in front of his fire watching the flames flicker and little puffs of smoke emanate from the coals, she felt an incredible sense of security.

'I wish I could stay here,' she said.

'Steady on,' he laughed. 'You've got yourself out of boarding, now take it easy.'

'No, but really, it's such a lovely place. A haven. Like I felt when I was in Trinity – remember I told you about that coffee with Hugo, Baby's boyfriend. That was like this. A safe place. *I have desired to go where springs not fail* . . . I love that poem,' she added.

She quoted on from Gerard Manley Hopkins. 'Such a peaceful place.'

'Now why did I think the poet was talking about a convent and not a basement flat?' said Mr Jones, with a trace of irony in his voice.

'Maybe because of the title of the poem, "Thoughts on a nun taking the veil",' Becky replied, her voice serious. She had totally missed his humour. 'But I don't think he was talking about a convent. I think he meant a state of mind.'

They talked on, and she sprinkled her conversation with lines from the poem.

'It's what Mum needed at the end,' she said. '*To be out of the hail.*'

Mr Jones got up and went to the mantelpiece.

'I have something for you,' he said. 'I'd been going to give it to you next Saturday in Herbert Park, but I'm going to give it to you now, instead.'

He sat back in his armchair and placed a key on the arm of the chair.

'But we have to make a deal,' he added.

She said nothing, just looked at the key and then at him.

'And the deal is,' he continued, 'that you only use it on days when Brona is going to Rhona's, and that it's our secret.'

She smiled.

'I can talk Brona into going to Rhona's every day,' she said with a laugh.

'No,' he said. 'That won't do. This is going to be your haven, but you have to use it both wisely and carefully. It had been meant for you at the weekends, but you may use it a little more often.'

'But I want to be here all the time.'

He shook his head.

'Listen to me. You come here all the time, and it won't be special. Also, you're likely to be seen. Now how would that look? And obviously, some of the time I'm not here . . .'

'Okay,' she said. 'But if I did come and you weren't here, could I do my homework?'

'Yes,' he replied. 'Now come over here and get your key.'

So Becky learned how to smile again, and she learned other things too. There were days when she sat at the table under the window and worked away busily while he wasn't there. Then there were the days when she went home with Brona and was kind to her. And on other days, when Mr Jones *was* there, she sat on his knee and button by button he opened her blouse. He searched her body, turning it from a tomb of pain to a temple of fire and joy. He was slow and methodical, taking her slowly from the gentlest of caresses and teasing touches to the point where she was ready – more than ready – to lie on her back and spread her legs for him. He brought her back to life. While she did these things, she avoided thinking about the void in her life. Then summer came, and she did her exams, head down, filling in page after page of writing, line after line of mathematics.

'Finished,' she said to Mr Jones as she let herself into his apartment. 'It's done.'

'And now what?' said Mr Jones as he touched her knee with light fingers, circling round and round.

She got up on his lap and leaned in against him. 'I've been putting off telling you this,' she said. 'You see, Uncle James and Aunty Nancy are taking Eleanor, Brona and me to Italy at the end of the month.'

'And why didn't you tell me?' he asked her as he kissed her neck.

'I don't know . . .' she said. 'You see, I kept putting the whole thing off in my head. I couldn't think of it and exams and you and everything – so I just didn't think about it.'

'Are you looking forward to it?' he asked.

'Sort of,' she said. 'I don't like leaving you. I find the idea of that really difficult. I like coming here and being with you, and talking to you, and doing the things we do . . .' she said, as he slipped her blouse off.

'I won't be here either for most of the summer,' he said. 'So isn't it as well you're going away?'

'Where are you going?' She was taken aback. She had imagined him there in the flat, waiting hopefully for her return from Italy.

'I'm going to England, doing a bit of orchestral work there – it ties in nicely with the school holidays.'

'Were you going to tell me?' she asked. She felt slightly hurt and also a little disbelieving. From the way he was talking, it must have all been planned, but he had not even hinted at it.

'Of course I was,' he said. 'But like you, I was waiting for exams to be over. I didn't want to say anything that would cause you any upset while you were doing them. It's not a big deal – you'll be away, and I'll be away, and the summer will pass quickly enough. We've plenty of time – I'll be back shortly after you.'

Becky said nothing.

She knew there was no point in sitting in Dublin waiting for him, and she wanted to go away, wanted the sun, wanted to fulfil the promises she had made to Brona.

'And there is something else you've got to do,' he said.

'Do you mean *this*?' she asked, as she kissed his throat.

'No, I don't. And you know it,' he replied. 'But for the moment you can go on doing that.'

'Mmm, what's the other thing I've to do?' Becky asked him, slipping a hand between the buttons on his shirt and running her fingers across his chest.

'You've to talk to someone about that letter,' he said. 'That's to be your project for the summer.'

She grimaced and pulled her hand out quickly, and a button popped off his shirt.

'Now see what you made me do,' she said.

'Oh, I made you do that, did I?' he said. 'What happened to being responsible for our own actions?'

Uncle James, Aunty Nancy, Eleanor Fitzgerald and the remaining Dunville girls went to Florence for a week, and then spent a week at the sea south of Livorno.

'Too many paintings,' was Brona's verdict on Florence. 'If I see another crucifixion I'll die,' she said.

Eleanor, Becky and Brona lay on the sand, slathered in sun-tan oil, their hair tied up. Eleanor wore a hat because her skin was so fair, and she kept creeping in under the sun umbrella. 'Like a hermit crab into its shell,' Brona teased her.

'Better an uncooked hermit crab capable of such a manoeuvre,' Eleanor replied with a laugh.

They ate fish, and tomatoes, and endless pizza, and the days slipped past.

'It's like being in a dream,' Becky said one evening. 'It's so far away from . . . you know.'

And the others did know.

This is wonderful, Becky thought, showering off the sand from between her toes.

'You nearly finished?' Eleanor called through the bathroom door to her. 'I'm so sticky from sun cream and salt water – I can't wait for my shower.'

The three girls were sharing a room in the hotel. Brona, already showered, lay naked on her bed with just a towel partially covering her.

Becky came into the room with one towel around her waist, patting dry her wet hair with another one.

'At last,' Eleanor said. 'I swear I'm going to come up early tomorrow so that I get the first shower.'

'This is brilliant, isn't it, Becky?' Brona said when the bathroom door closed behind their cousin.

'It's the best,' Becky agreed. She felt cleansed in some way. 'We're really lucky,' she said as an afterthought. 'Well, not lucky really, I suppose – but being here is lucky.'

'It's so remote, isn't it?' Brona said.

'Remote?'

'Like in a different world. I sometimes think, oh, I'd love to show Mum this or that – but for a lot of the time, most of the time really, I don't think about her or Baby. Do you?'

'I don't know,' Becky said. 'They're sort of there all the time, but because we're not at home it's somehow different. Maybe that's what you meant about it being remote, is it?'

Brona nodded. 'I just feel full of sun and sea, and all the different sounds. I think I feel guilty because I'm having a good time . . .'

'Don't feel guilty,' Becky said. 'We're going home next week and everything is going to be like it was, so just enjoy now. And for goodness' sake, don't feel guilty.'

They had got closer again, more like it had been just after Baby disappeared and before their mother had died. Brona eyed Becky from her bed.

'Can I tell you something?' she said.

Becky sat on a chair and started combing her hair out.

'Yes. Tell.'

'After Baby disappeared – I don't know when it was – it must have been after Uncle James and Aunty Nancy suggested our coming with them on holidays, I got this idea into my head that maybe . . . oh, I don't know.' Brona stopped and stared up at the ceiling.

'No, go on,' Becky encouraged her. 'Please tell me.'

'I sort of would imagine that Baby was somewhere warm – you know how she liked to be warm and comfortable, and the winter was so cold, and I got the idea that maybe when we came here to Italy, just maybe I'd look up and see her at the water's edge. And I'd imagine running up to her . . . and then I'd get scared. I'd imagine this terrible nothingness like there is at home all the time. You know – the idea of her turning around and just looking at us and that would be that.'

'How do you mean?'

Brona made a face. She was having difficulty in expressing even to herself what the fear was.

'It's hard to explain. It's to do with the fact that if I did see her at the water's edge and went up to her, and she was there – it would mean that she didn't want to be with us, that she'd finished with the family thing, that she'd just gone away. And I found that so awfully frightening.'

Becky listened. She could see what Brona was getting at – that if Baby were there, it would be because she had chosen to be, and their seeing her would be a chance thing, something Baby would not have wanted.

'Yes, I understand,' Becky said.

The following day, lying on her towel on the sand, Becky watched Brona and Eleanor going out on a pedalo. Both girls were laughing as they pedalled the boat outwards. They had asked her to go with them, but Becky said with a laugh, 'It looks too much like hard work for me.'

She dropped her head down so that she was lying flat and thought about what Brona had said the previous evening. There were things there that she could so clearly identify with, and Brona referring to the *nothingness* had shaken her. She knew that nothingness so clearly. It just had not occurred to her that Brona was feeling exactly the same thing.

Propping herself up on her elbows, she searched the water for her sister and cousin, but there were so many pedalos now out on the sea that she could not identify which was theirs.

'Where's Uncle James?' she asked her aunt, who was reading on a sunbed beside her.

'Gone to get ice cream, I think,' her aunt said, 'though it will have melted by the time he brings it back.' She returned to her book.

Becky gazed down the beach at the water, and then she saw a girl, tall, with a stunning body, and long blonde curls, dressed in a skimpy lime-green bikini. She stared in amazement and then pulled herself up on her knees as she tried to take in what she was seeing.

She suddenly realised that if she didn't do something fast, the girl would walk away and be gone. Getting to her feet, she started to run down the sand to the edge, shouting, 'Baby, Baby . . .'

The girl in the lime-green bikini just stood there with her legs apart as the water lapped around her ankles, staring out to sea.

Becky splashed in beside her. 'Baby,' she said, and the girl turned to see what was happening.

Becky stood in shock. From the rear she had had no doubt that it was Baby, but standing beside her, looking into her face, there was no longer any similarity at all. The girl's face was broader, flatter in some way, and she had brown eyes.

Becky stood there staring at her for a moment and then turned, mumbling, 'Sorry, I'm sorry,' as she headed back up the sand to her towel.

Aunty Nancy was standing by her sunbed, waiting for her. She took one look at Becky and said nothing for a moment.

'I thought . . .' Becky said.

'I did too,' Nancy replied. 'I thought the same.'

Becky shook her head. She was too shaken to speak.

'I thought it was too,' Nancy said again. 'When I heard you calling I looked, and I thought it was too . . .'

Becky couldn't swallow. She sat down heavily on her towel and her shoulders shook as a sob wrenched through her.

Nancy crouched beside her and put her arm around her and waited until Becky found her voice.

'I was sure,' she said. She tried to swallow and found there was a lump in her throat.

'It's appallingly difficult,' Nancy said. 'I know. I know what it's like for me and James, and so it has to be a thousand times worse for you and Brona.'

'It's all the unanswered questions,' Becky said. 'All the things that don't make sense ...'

'Tell me what they are,' Nancy said. 'If I have answers I'll certainly try to help.'

'The letter.' It blurted out of her. 'You know, Mum's letter ...'

With that, the pedalo returned to the beach, and their conversation was brought to a halt by the arrival of Brona and Eleanor.

'She's way too strong,' Eleanor complained.

'You're way too weak,' Brona laughed.

'We ended up going around in circles, because she paddled so hard.'

Uncle James arrived back with an assortment of ice-pops and Becky was drawn into more ordinary conversation.

But later in the day, after their siesta, when Eleanor, Brona and Uncle James went to the pool at the hotel, Aunty Nancy took Becky out shopping. They ended up in a bar not far from the hotel.

'Espresso, two,' shouted Aunty Nancy at the barman, holding up two fingers to clarify the situation.

'Why they can't speak English, I just don't know,' she said to Becky.

It had been her one gripe during the holiday. Becky suppressed a grin and nodded at the barman, who was trying to look genial.

'Now,' said Nancy with a definite note of resolution in her voice. 'You were saying ... ?'

Becky tried to look puzzled, but she knew full well to what her aunt was referring.

'Your mother's letter,' prompted Nancy.

'Oh, yes ... that ...' said Becky.

'Yes, that letter,' Nancy said firmly.

And suddenly that was it. In a bar in Livorno, on the west coast of Italy, Becky knew that she was going to get an answer. And she was scared. Suddenly she didn't know what to say. She didn't know the questions to ask. Suddenly she was a very vulnerable sixteen-year-old playing at being a grown-up, with an espresso on the table in front of her and with a lover who had a flat in Sutherland Square.

And that's all of me that's grown up, she thought.

Nancy, watching her face, knew that there were a thousand emotions and thoughts working underneath, and so she said gently, 'Shall we talk about that letter?'

'I don't know what to say,' Becky said.

'Well, let's start by my asking you, did you read it?'

Becky nodded.

'All of it?'

Again Becky nodded.

'Do you remember what it said?'

'Of course I do,' Becky said. 'How could I ever forget what it said?'

'We thought that you didn't remember. We thought that you either didn't read it properly, or couldn't take it in, or that you blotted it out because of what happened just after you read it,' Nancy said carefully.

'No, I read it. It was a suicide note from my mother, and in it she . . . she sort of blamed me,' Becky said.

'No,' Nancy said. 'I don't think she blamed you at all. I think she blamed herself.'

'She saw me as a sin,' Becky said.

'No, she saw you as a love child, the result of something she shouldn't have done,' Nancy said.

This sounded to Becky like well-rehearsed answers, and it occurred to her that her aunt had been waiting for this conversation.

'So, I'm not Dad's daughter?' Becky asked.

And as she asked it, she realised that she must have been hoping on one level all along that there had been some terrible mistake. She didn't look up. She kept her eyes on her cup, and the thick black coffee with its tiny bit of yellow foam around the edge.

'She loved you, Becky,' Nancy said. 'She loved you all. And when Baby disappeared, I think all the fears a mother could have just came crashing in around her, and that was it . . .'

'And do you know who my father really is?' Becky asked.

'Yes,' Nancy replied. 'I do. And before we go on with this, I want you to know from him that he's been waiting for you to ask, waiting for you to be ready . . .'

'He knows? And Dad, does he know?'

'They both know.'

Brona, lying by the pool with Eleanor, looked over at her cousin.

'Did Becky seem a bit odd to you this afternoon?'

'Odd?'

'Oh, I don't know. Distracted, introverted . . . something like that?' Brona was worried. She liked the closeness with Becky, a closeness that seemed to come and go but which she seemed to need more than Becky did.

256

'I didn't really notice,' Eleanor said. 'I think I was just so engrossed in this.' She indicated the history book she was reading. 'I'm getting more and more sure that I want to study history when I leave school next year,' she added. 'I think that's the best thing that's happened to me this summer. Knowing what I want, I mean. Do you know what you want to do?'

Brona shook her head.

'Well, at least you've got three more years,' Eleanor said. 'Plenty of time to be making decisions.'

That wasn't how Brona saw it. She didn't want to make decisions. In fact she didn't want to think at all. The best thing for her on the holiday was the constant companionship, the laughter in the sea, the meals in the warm air, the chatter in their bedroom, the distance from the silence of their home in Dublin. But despite that, she was homesick when she let herself think, so she tried not to think at all.

'Have you no ideas at all yet?' Eleanor persisted.

'I think I just want to get married and have children,' Brona answered.

'I don't think children are on my agenda,' Eleanor said.

There was silence as they each thought about that.

'I wish . . .' Brona said. But the words would not come. To find the words meant to think the thoughts, and she did not want to think about all the lost things which she wished for.

Uncle James, reading the *Herald Tribune* in a deckchair behind them, turned the pages, giving the impression that he was engrossed in their subject matter while he listened to the girls talk.

'I wonder what Becky is planning on doing when she's finished?' Eleanor asked. 'She's such an all-rounder that it's difficult to work out what direction she'll go in.'

'I don't know,' Brona said. 'We never seem to talk about the future.' And as she said the word 'future', it gaped in front of her and she shivered.

Tumultuous feelings poured through Becky. She could not concentrate over dinner. She excused herself and walked alone by the sea, in view of where they were sitting in the outside restaurant.

Now what? she wondered. It's as if we think we weave our own dreams, but we don't ultimately have a say in them. There is someone else who weaves our destiny, and we can only hope. Could I have hoped for better than this? Of course I could. Better than this would

.have been Mum and Dad and Baby and Brona and me. And next best, taking it that Baby is gone, and Mum died, then being Dad's daughter and Brona's real sister, that would have been next best. But someone out there has woven this – a tapestry of deceit and lies, full of the hurts which happen in life, so nothing is perfect. And what do we do?

She looked at the tiny waves lapping on the shore, eternally lapping and overlapping.

We make the best of it, she answered herself. That's what Aunty Nancy says. You're drawn a lot, and you make the best of it. And my real father could have been someone awful, someone I could never have liked – and instead it's someone I do like. So that's all right. Isn't it?

Phone calls were made from Italy. James talked to John Dunville. John Dunville made his own phone calls, and Becky's return flight was changed. When the others flew to London and on home to Dublin, she would stay on in London and do some catching up.

'You'll tell Brona, won't you?' she asked Aunty Nancy. 'You'll tell her after you go on to Dublin. Please?'

'John will tell her,' Nancy said.

'Someone needs to explain to her, and I can't do it – not yet anyway. Not until I've sorted this out for myself.'

'You're not to worry,' Nancy said. 'John will tell her.'

'Is he upset?' Becky asked.

'No,' James told her. 'He's not. He's concerned for you. You're the most important person at the moment.'

'But Uncle James, did he know? Has he always known?'

'These are matters you will have to talk to him about,' her uncle told her. 'Only he can tell you these things.'

'But why is Becky staying in London?' Brona asked, her eyes wide in disbelief when she was told about the change in plans.

'She could do with a week or so,' Aunty Nancy said to her.

'But I don't want to go home alone,' Brona wailed.

'You won't be alone,' she was told. 'We're all with you. And you can come and stay with us when we get back to Dublin if you like.'

'I don't understand,' Brona said. The thought of the house on Lansdowne Road with just herself and her father in it was more than she could countenance.

'It's only for a few days,' Becky said to her. But she seemed distracted, and Brona was not reassured.

And so they flew to London, and John Delaware met her at the airport. She was shy and awkward with him, and he was kindly, chivalrous, amusing, just as she had remembered him, just the way he was when they walked in Trinity.

'I never wrote to thank you for the book on Trinity,' she said. 'I loved it, though, and I'm always looking at it.'

'I want you to get there,' he said. 'I quite like the idea of my daughter studying at Trinity.'

And there it was. It had been said. He had brought it out into the open as an accepted fact with those two words – 'my daughter'.

His apartment was off Sloane Square, and he had had the spare bedroom recently redecorated. It transpired it had been done just for her. It was quaintly renovated, in an old-fashioned way, but fitted in with the decor of the rest of the apartment. The paintings in the hall and drawing room were mostly portraits in heavy gold frames, but what stood out for her most was the picture of a bomber with the crew standing beside it, and a silver cigarette box on a table behind the chesterfield.

'I remember you said that you used to be married,' she said to him over dinner that night.

'That's right,' he replied. 'I was married to June for eight years, and then we went our separate ways. I have two sons,' he added. 'Your half-brothers. I think you'll like them.'

She was amazed. This was an angle she could not have foreseen.

Two brothers, she thought, and there I was thinking I had two sisters.

'Did you know I was your daughter?' she asked him.

'Not until I saw the letter . . . I read it in the ambulance. And then in the hospital, do you remember, you looked up at me, and then I was absolutely sure that you were mine,' he said.

She remembered that then. It was a moment in time which she could now see clearly – looking up at him and thinking, They are my eyes. And then the moment had slipped somewhere deep into her subconscious and she had forgotten it in the shock of everything which was happening.

'I don't know what to call you,' she said.

'You can call me anything you like. Whatever you're comfortable with, whatever you want.'

'What do your sons call you?' she asked.

His sons, Henry and Rupert, were nineteen and seventeen years old, and they called him 'Dad'.

'I don't think I can call you Dad,' Becky said. 'You see, that's what I always called . . . call . . . you know . . .'

And now she had found yet one more person for whom she had no name. She could not refer to Baby's disappearance, or to her mother's death, she had no name for the man who had brought her up, and no name for her natural father.

He fetched the cigarette box and she was fascinated to see the wooden inlay with compartments within, in which various types of cigarettes were neatly displayed.

'How many different sorts do you have in there?' she asked.

'Oh, just a few. Your aunt Nancy wouldn't approve of me offering you one,' he said as he passed it to her.

She smiled.

'No, she wouldn't,' she replied, as she declined the offer.

'You could call me John,' he said, as he took one of the untipped cigarettes from the box.

'That's beautiful,' she said, looking at the box.

'Regimental present,' he replied, showing her the engraved signatures of many of his comrades.

She slept surprisingly well that night, thinking of the taste of the port she had had after dinner, and of the photograph albums she had pored through. She listened to his tales of both war and postwar, and a clearer image of him was forthcoming – a man who had used what he had learned to successfully launch himself in the aviation world when the war had ended.

'You can see this as your second home,' he had said to her.

My third home, she thought to herself, as my second is Mr Jones' flat in Sutherland Square.

But she kept that to herself.

She wondered if her feelings for Mr Jones were like the ones her mother must once have had for this man. It was difficult to imagine her mother feeling such passion. She would have liked to have asked, but knew that she didn't really want to know the answers, as she was afraid of them.

But in the morning, they breakfasted in a nearby hotel, and while they walked, she with her arm linked through his, she asked him tentatively, 'Did you love my mother?'

'Oh yes,' he said. 'I loved her.'

Back in Dublin she wrote in her diary:

He did love my mother, but had got himself caught in a situation he couldn't get out of. He said that I was born of love and passion, and that not every child in the world could say that about themselves. That he regretted not having been there for me, but that he would be here now, whenever I need him. Coming home was difficult – facing Dad, who is so remote. He seemed pleased to see me, but you can't really talk to him, whereas you can talk to John.

Brona did not come to the airport to meet her, and was not at home when she got there. Later, when Brona returned from Rhona's, she kept looking at Becky as if to see if there was any change. Becky had no idea how to behave towards her. It was all so difficult.

I didn't really want to come back home, she wrote. *But John said that I must, that I have my schooling to finish here, and that I have a life here. Also there is Mr Jones. But I didn't tell John about Mr Jones.*

After Brona came home and did a bit of furniture kicking and slamming doors, Becky, after grimacing at each action, eventually realised that she was going to have to say something.

'Hey, Brona,' she said.

'Yup.'

'Look, if you're cross about something . . . well, be cross. I don't care. But I don't want to be a boarder again, so keep it away from Dad.'

She heard herself saying 'Dad'. And she knew that Brona had heard it too, and had taken it in.

Brona didn't say anything else, but she did seem to brighten a little, and for the first time since Becky had got back Brona looked her in the eye.

Later in the day Brona sought Becky out.

'Sorry,' she said.

'Sorry? Whatever for?' Becky asked.

'For being so grumpy when you got back.'

'It's okay,' Becky said. 'It's not easy. For either of us. But I don't think it should change things between us. I mean, we had such a great holiday, and we enjoyed each other's company, and you and me . . . well, we're the only two people in the whole world who know what the other has gone through.'

'I just couldn't bear the fact that you aren't my real sister,' Brona said.

'I think I am,' Becky answered her.

Brona brightened and smiled at her.

'It was awful,' she said. 'Awful, when Dad told me. At first I thought – no, I *knew*, I was absolutely sure that there was a mistake. I mean, how could you not have been my real sister?' Brona asked. 'You'd been there all my life.'

'I know,' Becky said.

'I cried that night. I cried like I hadn't cried since Mummy died. It was like the last straw. There was no one left. And then later I started to realise that you were still my sister. That that hadn't changed. Aunty Nancy said that too. She said that if you'd been adopted and had been there since I was born, that you would be my sister. And that this was the same. That once I got over the hurdle of dealing with the truth, I would see that you were a constant in my life and that nothing had changed.'

Becky smiled.

'In some ways Aunty Nancy is very sound, isn't she?' she said.

'As sound as we've managed to come across anyway,' Brona said.

They both smiled – a wry, sad smile.

'We weren't very lucky, were we?' Brona commented.

'Luckier than most,' Becky replied. 'Born in the second half of the twentieth century in Western Europe – in a time and place where there are anaesthetics.'

'Is that your bottom line?' Brona asked.

'Pain relief? Oh yes. I'm not too keen on pain,' Becky responded.

'What was it like, that day you opened the bathroom door?' Brona wondered aloud.

'That day? You mean the day God died?'

They touched each other's fingers and neither said anything.

Mr Jones came back from England, and it was with trepidation that Becky went to meet him. She was afraid that because so many things had changed, maybe he would have too. She dressed carefully in a cotton maxi skirt with tiny polka dots on it, and a white cotton T-shirt which showed off her tan, with her dark hair, longer now, loose on her shoulders. They met in Sutherland Square at four o'clock on the afternoon they had arranged before they had separated earlier in the summer. She arrived early and forced herself to walk around the Square so that she wouldn't be sitting there waiting for him. On her return journey she cut across the grass and appeared from between the bushes, to find him on their bench. He was lolling with his legs outstretched, and her heart did a leap and a flutter with excitement. He was tanned, and his hair seemed blonder, and his short shirtsleeves revealed the golden hairs on his forearms. He seemed to her the picture of relaxation, and she wondered how she would appear to him.

'You look wonderful,' he said to her. 'All brown and healthy – and more grown up.'

He stepped back from her to take another look.

'Yes, you look older,' he said. 'More confident, is that what it is?'

She didn't really know how to answer. She did feel different, but she was unsure if the difference was confidence or just a different kind of certainty – because some of the questions had been answered.

'Can we go to your place?' she asked hopefully.

'My very thoughts,' he said. 'Come on.'

He put his arm around her shoulders.

'I think you've grown as well,' he said with a smile.

'I won't have to tilt my head so high for kisses,' she responded.

'Oh,' he said. 'Are kisses high on the agenda?'

They were.

When she sat on his knee, and he lifted her skirt to look at her legs, her platforms were revealed and her new height explained.

'John bought them for me,' she said. 'In London.'

'I got your letter,' Mr Jones said. 'When I got back yesterday. Are things easier now that you've got at least one answer?'

Becky told him about London, about John Delaware and about her return to Dublin.

'Coming home was difficult,' she said. 'I wanted . . . I don't know what I wanted. I think I wanted to share it all with someone. That's when I wrote to you. Brona is different. Everything is different.'

'And your father?'

'Dad? He took me out to dinner the night I got home. He's not a great talker – not any more, anyway. I asked him if he had known . . . if he'd known all along – since I was born.'

'And?'

'He said no.'

*   *   *

Becky and John Dunville had dinner on the way home from the airport that evening she got back from London. It had been her first time flying alone, the first of many as it would turn out, and she had spent the time staring from the tiny window wondering what she and 'Dad' would talk about.

At dinner she asked him if he had known.

'No,' he said.

She wondered if she could hear sadness in his voice or if she were imagining it.

'But,' she was hesitant, 'but you always treated me differently to the others.'

'I don't think I did,' he said. 'In what way?'

'You were harder on me,' she said, looking up at him from the menu.

'No. I hope not. I didn't mean to be.'

'It always felt like I couldn't do enough, get enough right – even my reports. You were tough on me even though they were good.'

She had been going to say, 'better than Baby's', but she changed it at the last moment.

'You were the brightest,' he said. 'Therefore we expected more.'

But I was hard on myself, she thought. You didn't need to be.

But she didn't say it aloud.

How can you express these things? she wondered. If he says he wasn't tougher on me, how can I say or prove that he was?

'He was tougher on me,' Becky said to Mr Jones. 'So I don't know that he is necessarily telling the truth . . . about not knowing that I wasn't his daughter, I mean.'

'Sometimes parents do treat their children differently,' Mr Jones said thoughtfully. 'They may not mean to, or indeed it may be like he said, that he wanted you to fulfil your potential. Or maybe you imagine he was tougher on you.'

Becky thought about that. 'No,' she said, 'he always wanted the best from me. I think that was it. But it did hurt, his attitude to me, I mean.'

Mr Jones stroked her hair.

'Tell me more,' he said.

'He also said,' she confided, 'that a baby is like a bulb.'

'A bulb? A light bulb?'

'No, not a light bulb. Like a tulip bulb, or something. And when you get it, you have to nurture it so that it will reach its potential. He said that you don't know many of its features, but you must tend it carefully as you would a bulb. And if you do it properly it will grow to its full height and blossom as it was meant to.'

Mr Jones watched her as she talked. She could feel his eyes on her as she tried to explain what she was trying to get at.

'John said the same thing. John, my real father, I mean. But Dad says that although I carry John's genes, I am still me. Just like Brona, or Baby. Each of us a bulb, which ended up in his and Mum's care, and that they did their best.'

Becky paused. She thought of her dad's face as he had said these things. It was reassuring on the one hand, because it gave her roots, and her roots were Dunville roots, just as if she had been adopted by her parents, they had nurtured her and she was theirs for ever. But these thoughts were only beginning to formulate. It would be a long time before she would see them clearly.

'Did he mention Baby?' Mr Jones asked.

'Yes, he did. It was in that context – of being given a bulb. It's the first time he's mentioned her since . . . well, since Mum . . . you know.'

'What else did he say?' Mr Jones asked.

'Not a lot. There was sadness in his voice. But then there would be, wouldn't there? It's not a very cheery topic. John – Delaware, I mean – he said to me that I must be kind to myself, but that I must see that others have lost an awful lot as well. Like Dad, for example – he's lost as much as me, but in a different way: his wife, and two daughters.'

'And so, whose daughter do you feel like?' Mr Jones asked, as he stroked her hair.

Becky smiled.

'I don't know,' she said. 'I haven't worked it out yet.'

'You must keep talking,' said Mr Jones. 'You're doing so well.'

'*Fill the kettle,*
Clear the decks,
I want to hear you now,' whispered Becky.

Chapter Eighteen

Sometimes at night Brona still came into bed with Becky. 'I'm scared,' she would say, and Becky would move over, and they slept side by side.

Sometimes Becky thought of slipping out of the house late at night so that she could spend more time with Mr Jones, but when she thought of that she would recall Baby – Baby slipping out of the house to visit Hugo – and so she didn't do it. There were nights when Brona was sleeping soundly in her own bed and Becky considered going downstairs and out through the breakfast-room window. She wondered if she did that, might she find out what had happened to Baby, because she could see the similarity in their behaviour now.

Baby had a double life, she thought, and so do I, yet I'm not really like her at all. Slipping out would be easy, but if Brona woke and found her gone, it was not her father's fury that she feared, but the idea that she might cause them further distress. They've suffered enough, she thought. None of us deserve or need any more pain.

As she went through her last two years in school, she found she no longer cared that she had no special friend among her peers. Although now more lost in many ways, she did seem to have found some sort of stability in her very unstable world.

John Delaware came monthly to Dublin, where he was welcomed in the Dunville home on Lansdowne Road.

On the first of those occasions, he came by to collect her, and Becky's father invited him in.

Afterwards, in the hotel, when Becky and he were having dinner, she said to him, 'I didn't know what that would be like – you and Dad meeting – if it would be awkward or what . . .'

He patted her hand in a paternal way.

'Your dad and I were always friends,' he said. 'That may be difficult to understand, considering the relationship between Elizabeth and myself, but it is the case. And after Elizabeth died, both John and I

266

read her letter, and so much was explained – there was no way we could not talk. Your dad is a very civilised man – clearly he was devastated by what he and you girls were going through, but your interests were high on his priority list. During that term that you and Brona boarded, he and I had dinner regularly – often in your home. Mrs O'Doody had all these pheasants in the freezer – we worked our way through them over a period of eight or ten weeks, we drank good wine, and we talked.'

'About me?'

'Yes, about you. No one could work out if you had read the letter – you referred to it that day, but afterwards you said nothing. You seemed to have forgotten it, and because you had so much to deal with, we all thought the time was not right.'

'Who are "we all"?' she asked.

'Your dad, Nancy, James and myself.'

Becky thought about that. It seemed strange to think that during that long, cold winter of being a boarder in St Martin's, there were people sitting down and discussing her. She didn't mind that so much because she could see and feel that they genuinely had her best interests at heart. What she did find hard to understand was why no one had spoken to her. It made her think of Mr Jones and the song she had written about talking. 'You've got to talk' were his words.

'If everyone had talked more, then none of this would have happened,' she said aloud.

'Explain what you mean,' John Delaware said gently to her.

'I don't know,' she said vaguely. 'It's sort of to do with all the things that are unsaid in families, and all the pretence that goes on.'

Term restarted, and back they went. Becky, seeing Simon Carter, the under-gardener, was amazed that she had ever harboured feelings for him. He no longer seemed to mean anything to her. He was simply the boy in the garden. She wondered then had she fancied him because he was simply the only boy in her world, and she thought with relief about her relationship with Mr Jones. It offered her security, and gave her strength in the loneliness of her life. The term progressed with little or nothing surprising.

'What's up?' Rhona Brophy asked Brona, who was lying on the floor while she, Rhona, lay on the bed, hanging over the side, looking at her.

'I hate the idea of Christmas,' Brona said. She had grown since the summer, and was now a good four inches taller than Becky.

'What's wrong with Christmas?' Rhona asked her.

'Dunno,' Brona replied.

'Remember last Christmas and the chocolate decorations?' Rhona said, and then clamped a hand to her mouth. 'God, I'm sorry, Bro, I wasn't thinking.'

Brona shrugged. She knew that Rhona had not meant it, and also that once Rhona had realised, she was really sorry. She did not know which was better. At first people had made allowances, they seemed to know and to remember that these terrible things had happened to the Dunvilles, but then later they seemed to forget, as if they did not realise that the events of the previous January did not just disappear. Brona was aware of it in school. It was as if what had happened was over for other people, and that was that.

'I'm afraid that Becky is going to want to go to London for Christmas.' Brona finally got the words out, blurting them out at the Brophys' dinner table that evening, totally out of context, as Rhona's father had just finished describing a try he had seen at a rugby match that afternoon.

Mr Brophy put a hand on her shoulder. 'If you're afraid of that, then just tell her,' he said.

'I can't,' Brona mumbled, her face red with embarrassment, as she had not meant to say anything. It was as if she had suddenly realised what it was that was worrying her, and out it came. It was the first time she had managed to express a complete thought aloud.

'Yes you can,' Mr Brophy said. 'You may be surprised – it may well be that she doesn't know where she should be, and you telling her that may help you both.'

As Christmas loomed closer, Brona kept hovering around Becky, coming into her room where she was studying, throwing herself on the bed and staring at her.

Eventually Becky said, 'Look, what's up? What's on your mind?'

'I don't want you to go to England for Christmas.' Brona finally got the words out.

Becky stared at her.

'You won't go to England?' Brona pleaded with Becky. 'You'll stay here with me, won't you?'

Aunty Nancy and Uncle James had invited them over for the day, just as John Delaware had invited Becky to London.

'Please don't go,' Brona said when Becky was silent.

'I won't go,' Becky eventually said. 'I'll stay with you and Dad and we'll go to the Fitzgeralds' for dinner.'

'It'll be all right now, won't it?' Brona asked her.

'How do you mean?'

'We'll be all right – that's what I mean,' Brona said. 'We're safe now, aren't we?'

Becky didn't answer at first. She thought of how Brona had started to defer to her and to ask her opinion of everything after that last Christmas. As if her confidence was damaged, Becky thought to herself. And why wouldn't it have been? Of course it was damaged. She was only fourteen.

'Yes,' she said aloud. 'We're safe now.'

Eventually they had found words to position various events in their lives. *The Last Christmas* meant the end of childhood as they had known it. *The Disappearance* was Baby climbing out of the breakfast-room window and never being seen again. *Mummy, you know . . .* referred to their mother's death. *My first visit to London* was the first meeting between Becky and John Delaware after she had found out that he was her father. And *The Coming of the Delawares* described the arrival in Dublin of John and his two sons for the New Year of 1972.

'You are related to me, you know,' Brona said tentatively to Henry and Rupert Delaware in the drawing room in their house on Lansdowne Road.

Both boys grinned at her.

'That's what I was saying to Henry on our way here,' Rupert said. They both had dark hair and brown eyes, like their father and like Becky.

'Yes,' Brona said. 'If Becky is my half-sister, and you're her half-brothers, then you are my quarter-brothers.'

Becky smiled at John, who gave her a wink. She had been apprehensive about this meeting, unsure if Brona would feel left out, but clearly Brona had her own thoughts on that. She wondered if John Delaware had primed his sons.

'You're very lucky, you know,' Brona continued. 'Becky's okay as a sister.'

269

'Greater praise knows no man.' Her father addressed the table.

James, Nancy and Eleanor Fitzgerald were there too. Eleanor, who once had thought that she and Becky resembled each other, could see clearly who it was Becky really resembled. Both Henry and Rupert had the same fine bones and the same sallow skin.

They went on day trips, sightseeing tours, the cinema and the theatre. And Brona went with them.

'Thank you for including me,' she said to Becky after the Delawares went back to England.

'You'll always be included,' Becky said. 'We're family.'

She was aware of the anomaly, of the fact that for months she had felt as the outsider in the Dunville household, and that it was now she who was reassuring Brona about the Delawares.

And so Becky got through her last two years in school, 'participating well in class', as Mother Immaculata wrote regularly on her reports, spending time with Mr Jones in his basement flat, where the sun shone in on her in their bed, and keeping the home in Lansdowne Road running smoothly, with the help of both Mrs O'Doody and Brona.

'*I once was lost, but now am found,*' the song went, and Becky went on playing the piano, trying to find the right chords for the ballads she had written for Mr Jones.

'We're safe now,' Brona had said. 'Nothing worse can happen to us, sure it can't?'

And Becky reassured her over and over, just as she reassured herself.

When the next tragedy in her life arrived, it came from the one quarter she could not have foreseen.

It was June 1973, and she had finally done her Leaving Certificate. Brona, a year behind her in school, seemed to have settled down, and the fears Becky had had for her diminished. As soon as she had finished her last exam, Becky collected her things from the school and left. She had formed no friendships in those final years. Studying and 'visiting' Mr Jones was what kept her going. She knew that she had done well, and now it was over. She had not seen Mr Jones since the previous weekend, when they made love on his bed with the windows open and the sunlight streaming in on them.

Becky was eighteen and a half. Old to be doing her Leaving Certificate, but John Dunville had very strong views about the length of time his children should be in school, and so he had started them late and kept them there, those who did not disappear, until they were eighteen.

Trinity beckoned, and, Becky imagined, long afternoons and evenings on Mr Jones' bed in Sutherland Square, interspersed with the library, lectures and a newly found freedom. Eleanor was studying History at Cambridge, and while Becky had toyed with the idea of History or Architecture, it was John Delaware's silver cigarette box and her fascination with objets d'art and art in general which directed her towards Fine Arts. Her university application had been accepted, dependent upon her examination results, and she could see her future opening up.

With her pencil case in her hand, she headed down Sutherland Street. She was almost running. Her heart was light and there was a smile on her face. For once she did not look back to see if anyone could see her, because her graduation from school gave her liberty. Pausing at the railings, she looked down into the basement. The way the sun was hitting the glass meant that she could not see through the windowpanes. Over the previous two years she had always approached with caution because he had told her to. There had never been anyone else inside the apartment other than he, and she had made sure she was never seen entering. Swinging open the gate, she headed down the tiny stone steps and took her key from her pencil case. She rang the bell as she let herself in.

Mr Jones was in the sitting room. There was something different. She could feel it instantly. He embraced her as usual and then he led her to the table.

'How did it go?' he asked, referring to her last exam.

'It went fine,' she said. 'What's happening?'

It was like that day in Herbert Park long ago when she had felt panic rising in her as he explained he was leaving St Martin's. Only this time, it appeared that he was leaving Ireland.

'But why?' she asked, imagining herself looking for a place in a British university. Her mind was racing ahead, as she knew that John would be disappointed about her not going to Trinity, but she comforted herself with the thought that he would be pleased if she were closer to hand, because despite his apartment in Dublin, he was only occasionally over. She hoped she was not too late to get a place this coming year in England.

'We're done,' Mr Jones explained gently. 'You now need to grow up among your peers, and Trinity will offer you that. You don't want to be tied to an old fogey like me.'

'What are you talking about?' Becky asked. 'I don't understand at all.'

'I'm leaving,' he said. 'I've got work back in the UK, and you're off to Trinity.'

She cajoled, she pleaded and then the fear really started to rise in her.

'I can't bear to lose you,' she protested.

Over and over she asked him why.

And he kept saying that it was time, the right time, time for her to move on.

'But I don't want to move on,' she said. 'It's great that school is over. I've got through that, but only because of us, of you and me, of you helping me, supporting me, carrying me. You carried me right through the last two and a half years. How could you end it now?'

'Everything is transient,' he said. 'It is time for us to move on.'

'But what about what we feel for each other?' she asked him. 'Is that nothing?'

But he kept saying things about rites of passage, about her youth, about how she needed relationships with people her own age.

'But I don't want relationships with people my own age,' she said. 'It's you I want to be with. I've never managed to relate to or form friendships with girls who are my peers.'

'You will now,' he said. 'In a new environment, where you start afresh, with the confidence you now have.'

Alone in bed that night, she thought about the term 'rites of passage', and wondered if that was indeed what it was. It had not seemed like that to her. For her it was love and security, warmth and passion in a world where she had felt totally abandoned.

I never understood why he wanted to be with me anyway, she thought as, grief-stricken, she curled in a ball and wiped the endless stream of tears from her face. She wondered at his callousness, because that was what this new sense of abandonment seemed to her. He had never been callous to her before, she had never seen him in that light. It was devastating. There was no one to tell because no one knew what she had been doing for the past two and a half years, and the sense of isolation was intense. When she realised that it really was over, that he really meant it, that he was really going and that he clearly had no plans to return, or to have her with him, she had asked him how he had seen his relationship with her.

'See me like your Guardian Angel,' he said.

'But Guardian Angels don't abandon their protégées,' she said.

'I've put it badly,' he said. 'I think girls only need Guardian Angels until they are eighteen.'

'I don't get it,' she said.

'I have always had your best interests at heart,' he said. 'You do believe that, don't you?'

She nodded.

'Then you have to trust me now. That hasn't changed. This is right for you.'

And like that it was over. She had learned through the earlier desertions that there are some tides, flowing too fast in one direction, which you cannot swim against. Some courses in life are unalterable.

Even as she said goodbye to him, a bit of her kept thinking he would change his mind, that he would write and summon her, that their relationship was stronger than the mere rites of passage to which he had referred. But there was no letter, and there was no phone call.

The contact ended completely.

At first there was the shock and the sadness, and later she was angry that he couldn't see what it was like for her to be abandoned – yet again.

She spent part of that summer in London with the Delawares, but on the streets her eyes always roved, hoping to spot that one familiar face, even though she had no idea what part of England he had gone to.

At least he is out there alive and working, she thought. It's not like Baby's disappearance, where we always hope and yet are always without hope.'

But she did still hope – for months she hoped there would be a sign from him, something that would reassure her that she still meant something to him. She picked up the pieces and went to university, empty and alone. She and Brona then moved in different worlds. Brona was still at school, and when not in school she liked to be at the Brophys' or at home, while Becky spent her time in Trinity, and flew to London for holidays.

'You're leaving me behind,' Brona said. She was standing in her school uniform in the kitchen, while Becky dried the dishes.

'I'm not,' Becky said. 'It's just that university holidays are longer than school ones.'

'But I don't want to be here by myself. You're always going over there, and I get left behind.'

'Oh, Bro, you're not by yourself. Dad is here. And Mrs O'Doody most of the time, and . . .'

'But . . .' Brona tried to find the words.

'Anyway,' Becky said with a smile, 'look what I have for you.' She scrabbled in her bag and pulled out a small folder.

Taking it, Brona opened it and pulled out return tickets to London. 'For me?' she said.

'Yes, for you. You finish school in two weeks' time, and then you join me. Henry is in Austria, but John says that Rupert will be around – you like him, don't you?'

Becky and Brona's paths diverged but they stayed close and gave each other what support they could. Sometimes Becky thought of telling Brona what had happened to her, of confiding in her and asking her for help. But she always held back. Brona was younger, she had her own vulnerability, and for her to find out now that Becky had been having a relationship with Mr Jones all through the agony of the previous years might wound her excessively. And Becky loved her too much to cause her any more pain.

Seeing the smile on Brona's face on being given the tickets was as good as Becky could hope for. The best she could do was to hold the bond between them in whatever way she could. She had promised Mr Jones to help her sister just as he had helped her.

And then he abandoned me, she thought, her sadness acute as her love for him washed over her again. But I won't do that to Brona.

Chapter Nineteen

They moved through the years, Becky and Brona, using the structures within which they felt some security to travel forwards. They holidayed with the Fitzgeralds and the Delawares, touching each other's fingertips as they once had done in Bewleys on Grafton Street on a cold and terrifying Tuesday in January 1971. They grew from teenage girls to women. Brona married and had two children. Becky expanded her mind but never settled down. She moved between various auction houses, immersed in the timelessness of beautiful objects which, if properly cared for, would endure for ever. She re-found the poetry which had been so much a part of her childhood.

> *Time doth transfix the flourish set on youth*
> *And delves the parallels in beauty's brow . . .*

She knew that human beings aged, withered and died, but silver cigarette boxes carried their own history. They could not hurt you. You could talk about objets d'art dispassionately or with passion. You could catalogue and describe any item, and trace its journey across the world as it was bought and sold. Paintings which she went to see, classical works which hung in one gallery or another, could be taken to other exhibitions, and then returned. They were traceable, trackable, observable, and their beauty in her eyes was unchanging.

Time passed, and then the year came when Becky and Brona decided to take a holiday together.

Queueing outside the Uffizi Gallery in Florence, Becky checked her list of what she particularly wanted to see, while Brona watched her. Becky's list included the numbers of the rooms where the various paintings were on display. She had been before many times but she wanted to show Brona particular pictures.

'Why did we never go away together before, just the two of us, I mean?' Brona asked.

'You wouldn't,' Becky said. 'I did suggest it before, but you wouldn't.'

'The kids . . .' Brona said. 'I think it was because of the kids.'

'And this time?' asked Becky. 'What makes it different this time?'

'Don't you know?' Brona asked.

'I'm not sure,' Becky answered. 'Never having had any children – I'm not really sure.'

'It's because they are older than Baby was – I got them through to adulthood,' Brona said. 'It was Rupert who pointed it out to me. All those fears – all through teenagehood – never being sure what they were doing – like Baby . . . you know.'

And Becky did know. She understood that. She also knew that her decision not to have children was because she would have been too afraid . . . afraid of things she could not name, the things that were out in the dark on foggy nights, outside left-open windows.

'You were lucky with Rupert,' Becky said.

'Yes, I know. He understands everything.'

Well, he would, Becky thought to herself. After all, I told him everything.

'Have you really never met anyone you'd like to marry?' Brona asked suddenly.

'Not really,' Becky said.

They both thought about the various male friends Becky had produced from time to time. Short-lived relationships. That was how she liked it.

'My work,' Becky said. 'That's always absorbed me.'

'That's just an excuse,' Brona said.

'I know.'

They were silent for a few minutes as the queue moved along.

'I've just realised why you married Rupert,' Becky said to her sister. 'It was to connect us, wasn't it?'

'I fell in love with him,' Brona said. She paused for a while. 'No, you're probably right. It's something I don't really think about. I wanted a happy family, and me marrying your half-brother . . . it brought us all together. And I do love him. I loved him right from the beginning. And we're very happy.'

'So I became your sister-in-law as well as your half-sister.'

'Well,' Brona laughed. 'I needed to be sure that I'd be related to you, one way or another. You seemed so complete, and I felt like a shadow.'

'You did very well,' Becky reassured her. 'You really did.'

'Did I?' Brona asked. 'Did I? I know now that I got married as fast as I could because I wanted to put distance between myself and the end of our childhood. And I suppose I lost out on some things by doing that.'

'But you gained other things,' Becky said. 'You really did. Look what you have – a husband who adores you, two healthy children, not to mention a great bunch of in-laws,' she added with a laugh.

'I, on the other hand,' Becky continued, 'once harboured notions of finding Hugo Mombay Humphries. I thought that my being with him would in some way recreate the past.'

'Really?' Brona was surprised. 'I never knew you felt like that. You seemed so in control, so focused and determined when everything was collapsing.'

'Therein lies a tale,' Becky said, thinking of Mr Jones. She toyed with telling Brona, but for some reason, despite the confidences they were exchanging, it didn't seem to be the right time.

'A tale?'

'Oh, nothing really,' Becky replied. 'It's more to do with me not coping, and floundering and trying to find a foothold.'

'You gave a good impression,' Brona said. 'I admired you no end. And later, when I was a bit older and looked at it from your angle, then I really, really admired you. We lost so much, didn't we?'

Becky murmured yes, as she felt herself sinking into the past.

Lost so much? she thought. God, you've no idea. In some ways we lived in silence. To the outside world we were this perfectly contented happy family – a mother, a father and three little girls. And the truth? I suppose we were no different to most families. We just lived and accepted out lot – what choice did we have? But Mum and Dad thought they had a handle on us, on our behaviour and our actions. Really it was a conspiracy of silence. You think you talk and share, and yet who really does – me and Mr Jones, Baby and her sub-life, Mum and John Delaware, and everyone living a life on the surface, while underneath truth and reality bubbles away – until the day that it blows up . . .

'Now,' she said, as they entered the building, 'we're going to start with the Botticellis, and then I want to show you a work by Filippo Lippi – so that you can compare the faces of the angels.'

Brona half smiled. Becky's dedication amused her on one level, although she admired it on another.

At the *Primavera*, Brona glanced at Becky. 'Do the Three Graces remind you of anyone?'

Becky shook her head. 'No, not really. Why?'

'Not you and me and Baby?'

Becky looked again, and said with interest, 'Why, which of them is you? And which is me? No, I don't relate to them at all.'

'I was sort of joking, I think,' Brona replied. 'All the angels we have seen, all the beautiful faces . . . Actually, I think I like Cupid most, with his bow and arrow and mischief on his mind. But the Graces made me think of us. I don't know why.'

'I don't know either,' Becky said, almost with a snort. 'You and me maybe. But with Baby we never reached any kind of harmony.'

Her eye wandered to the right side of the picture. Now there, she thought, that is what brings me back to this time and again. She looked at Zephyr, God of the Winds, and how he forced his way into the picture in pursuit of the nymph Chloris, while just beyond her, moving purposefully into the foreground, Flora scattered the flowers of Spring. Zephyr's hands reached the beautiful nymph and Becky felt, as she always did, that in another moment Chloris would be plucked from the picture, and removed for ever.

She tried to read the look on Chloris' face. Was it fear? she wondered. Had she enticed the god, and so brought about her own fate?

'I like Flora,' Brona said. 'She is so dedicated to her work.'

'In a moment I'll show you the statue it is thought she is modelled on,' Becky said. 'It's called the *Hora of Autumn*. You'll be amazed at the similarity in the stance and the general depiction.'

'You know so much,' Brona said. 'I envy you that. All that you've learned . . .'

'No reason why you couldn't go to college now – with the kids grown up and all. It would do you good,' Becky said, uttering a thought which she kept returning to.

'I don't know,' Brona said vaguely. 'I'm needed at home . . .'

Becky did not pursue it. She hoped that maybe she might have planted the seeds of an idea in her sister's mind, but she could not be sure.

*   *   *

That afternoon, back at the hotel, lying by the pool, Brona turned to her sister on the sunbed beside her. 'Do you remember those decorations . . . the foil-wrapped ones . . . that last Christmas? Do you remember they were filled with nougat?'

Becky, lying on her back, soaking up the heat, cast her mind back down the years, to try to find that moment and to hold it.

'No, when? When do you mean? That Christmas day?'

'No,' Brona replied. 'No, it must have been about a week before Christmas. We each had friends over for dinner . . . you had Gabi von Whatnot. Remember?'

'I remember Gabriela almost bursting a skirt of mine,' Becky replied with a shiver. 'That must have been then. I only had her over once for dinner. And yes, it was that last Christmas . . . during the holidays. Must have been a Saturday. Remember how we had to dress up?'

Brona smiled.

'God, the embarrassment of having to tell one's friends about the Dunville dinners, and Mrs O'Doody, and no trousers please, we're ladies.'

They both laughed.

'And the gong. Do you remember the gong?' Brona went on. 'I wonder what happened to it. Do you know?'

'No.' Becky shifted on to her side. 'I have no idea. I could tell you exactly what was in each of those rooms, and where each item was positioned, but I have no idea what happened to any of them.'

'Dad took some of them when he moved out, and we sold the rest,' Brona said. 'I think you must have been in London at the time. It was Rupert's suggestion. He said that if we were going to live in our old home after our marriage we should revamp it completely to make it ours.'

'I remember you asking me if I wanted anything, but I suppose I just didn't.'

'And now, are you sorry you didn't take anything?'

'No. I didn't need anything. I think I was glad, though, that you stayed in the house.'

They looked at each other. Both knew exactly what the other was thinking: that Brona had stayed in the house just in case Baby ever came back.

Both were silent for a moment. A lizard crawled on the bark of a tree behind Becky's bed. She watched its movements, noted its surefootedness, wondered how it coped in the heat, knew that it would not survive in a different climate.

'How strange,' she said slowly, referring back to the contents of the house. 'All those things – they just disappeared, along with so many memories. It's funny. I remember the furniture and the people, and we must have conversed, endlessly I suppose, and all those words are gone – they've disappeared into time.'

'Mr Jones – do you remember Mr Jones?' Brona asked her. 'You must remember him. He came in after Christmas – that last Christmas . . .'

'I do remember him,' Becky replied. 'I remember him very well.'

'He told our class something to do with some physicist trying to make a word-memory machine. And he said that if this guy succeeded in constructing this, then millions of historical questions would be answered.'

'I don't follow,' Becky said. 'What did the machine do?'

'It wasn't ever made. I think it was more an idea than anything. He said that answers to questions usually come in words, but the truest words are the ones first spoken – whereas other words are like rumours . . .'

'Like Chinese whispers?' Becky asked. 'They grow and get distorted?'

'Yes, exactly,' Brona continued. 'Anyway, Mr Jones said that if this machine were constructed and it collected all the words ever spoken, and you could tap in questions to it, you could find out things – things that had puzzled you all your life.'

'You mean like the nougat thing you were talking about?' Becky asked.

'No.' Brona shook her head. 'The nougat was never a puzzle to me. That wasn't what I meant.'

'I know,' Becky said, lying back on her bed, and closing her eyes. There was a smile on her lips. She did remember the nougat, very clearly.

'Would you have changed things if you could?' Brona asked, switching the conversation once more.

'How do you mean?'

'I mean, would you do anything differently?'

And Becky, looking back down the years, suddenly remembered the smell of cabbage in the refectory, and a girl with a large bottom, whose name she couldn't remember, leaning across the table to lift a jug of water, and someone asking her something in a kind way, and she had realised that other people cared, and her cousin Eleanor with her gentle eyes and polished brown hair looking up startled from whatever she was reading under the table.

'Do differently?' she asked. 'You mean, if we could put the clock back? But you can't change things. Isn't it all preordained in some way? I mean, we got up in the morning and went to bed at night, and in between we did the things we were supposed to do. Well . . . you and I did. I think Baby was a bit different.'

'But we didn't do what we were supposed to do,' Brona said. 'I mean, there were rules and we were supposed to adhere to them. And to a large extent I suppose we did adhere to them, because they were reasonable guidelines for getting through the day from morning until bedtime. But I didn't do exactly what I was supposed to. I cut corners, skirted the things I didn't like. Didn't you?'

'I don't think I did,' Becky said. 'I was the model pupil until Baby . . . until that week . . . until that Monday . . .'

They did the memory thing almost every day. They did the sights in Florence again, just as they had once done with the Fitzgeralds, but now with the knowledge of adulthood. In the afternoon they lay by the pool while the Italians had their siestas. They swam and ate and soaked up the afternoon sun, their books beside them, but seldom were the pages turned. As they drifted in the heat, a thought would come to one, and then she would share it with the other. The water in the pool lapped gently against the sides, just as memories flowed and lapped and overlapped.

'Do you remember walking down Grafton Street that day – it must have been the Tuesday. We'd been to get your hair dyed back. Do you remember?'

'Oh yes, I do,' Brona smiled. 'I do. You bought me Mary cakes in Bewleys. You let me have two. I don't think I've had one since then. I wonder do they still make them? All that chocolate. And you were so nice. I remember thinking that you were the only safe person . . . no, I mean . . . thinking that everything was rushing past and there was nothing to hold on to – except for you.'

'I remember that day so clearly,' Becky said. 'You spoke about feeling surreal and it had been what I was thinking. I remember it must have been very cold because people were wearing gloves and scarves and I couldn't really feel anything at all. It was as if we were going through the motions, not knowing why – just hoping, I suppose.'

'Yes,' replied Brona. 'Hoping . . .'

'We learned to adapt, didn't we?' Becky continued.

She looked at the lizard as he moved across the bark.

'Would he survive in our environment?' she wondered. 'Would he adapt? I suppose he would. That's how we survive. We adapt, otherwise we go under.'

And Brona, lying on her sunbed, with her sun umbrella covering her head and most of her upper torso, nodded her agreement.

That evening on the bus to Fiesole to see the opera, sitting side by side, Brona turned to Becky.

'We sat together on the bus going home – that day we went to town, to get my hair done,' Brona said. 'I remember that. I think it was the first time we'd willingly done that.'

'Didn't we sit together going into town?' Becky asked.

'I don't know. I don't remember. We probably did because we were feeling so scared. But I don't remember. I just remember that safe feeling sitting by the window and your arm pressed against mine coming out of town. I asked you what you thought they were all doing in school.'

'What did I say?' Becky asked.

'You said some of the nuns were probably losing their vocation because of Mr Jones. And I laughed and laughed. I thought it was the funniest thing I'd ever heard.'

'It was such a relief to hear you laughing – once you'd explained what you were laughing at,' Becky said with a smile. 'At first I was bewildered. I'd no idea what you were finding so funny.'

'And then I felt guilty because Baby was missing.'

'Yes, I remember. And the thought of Mummy and Dad at home, worried out of their minds.'

'Yes, that just intensified the feeling of guilt.'

'Did they buy you extra things too?' Becky asked, suddenly thinking of the clothes she had seen in Anne Marie's house, and remembering the feelings of jealousy she once had had towards Baby.

'Who? How do you mean?' Brona said.

'Baby had all these garments over in Anne Marie O'Mahony's house – expensive things – and I wondered if they gave you extra things like that too?'

Brona looked at her in surprise.

'Of course they didn't buy me extra things. I know we both feel that they favoured Baby, but they were fairly fair that way. Okay, you got cast-offs from Baby, and I got them from you – but overall they were even-handed. What on earth do you mean, that Baby had clothes in Anne Marie's?'

Becky frowned and turned to look at Brona.

'There were all these clothes in Anne Marie's wardrobe which belonged to Baby ... I don't know. I haven't thought about this in years. Anne Marie asked me if I wanted to take them home, and I thought it was better not to. At the time, I think I was just puzzled and I thought it would upset Mummy and Daddy if I appeared with them. Later I told Anne Marie to wear them herself or to get rid of them or something. I don't really remember.'

'But where on earth did Baby get them from?' Brona asked.

'I don't know,' Becky said. 'I don't have a clue.'

'What kind of things?' Brona queried as she considered this.

'There was a small fur coat, some skirts and tops and some kind of little black number, I think, fancy underwear ...' Becky said. 'In today's terms certainly a couple of thousand pounds' worth ... back then I vaguely remember thinking more than a couple of hundred. But I wouldn't really have known the cost of clothing. I just felt that they were expensive things.'

'Why didn't you tell anyone?' Brona asked. 'God, I wonder was it relevant? I mean ... where she got the stuff, what she paid for it with, and what she did with it. I mean, where on earth would she wear such things?'

Becky sighed.

'She used it for picking up men in pubs and nightclubs with Anne Marie. That's what I gathered anyway. But how she paid for the stuff I have no idea.'

'Could she have been selling that stuff she was growing in her room?'

'No, I gather that was strictly for home consumption,' Becky replied.

'Why didn't you tell me about the clothes before now?' Brona persisted.

'I don't know. No, that's not true. You were only fourteen – I thought you'd be shocked to find out what Baby did at night.'

'But Dad – did you tell him?'

'No, I didn't tell anyone. You see, I thought that if he had given her the money for them, then what was the point in telling him that I knew. I'd just sound jealous or something. And if he didn't know about them, then what was the point in adding to his worries. I mean, what could he do? He already knew that Baby had another life going on. He already knew that she was up to something – a whole other life was being uncovered. I just thought it was better to say nothing. And then Mummy, you know . . .'

They were silent for a while, Brona digesting these facts about Baby, Becky thinking about the look on Baby's face when she had spoken to Father Monaghan.

'Baby was tough,' she said.

'Determined.'

Selfish, Becky thought.

'Dad was too easy on her,' Becky said.

Arriving in Fiesole, they headed for a bar for coffee before going to the amphitheatre where they would watch the opera. The subject of their father came up again, and Brona said, 'God, I hated boarding.'

'I suppose it was the best he could do. Afterwards, after Mummy, you know . . . the boarding bit, I mean. He was grieving too, and he couldn't get outside his own pain . . . I suppose.'

'You're probably right,' Brona said. 'He was always quite aloof, wasn't he? I suppose it's no surprise that he just became more so.'

'Not a man in touch with his own emotions,' Becky replied. 'But then, how many of us are?'

'But can you imagine what that must have been like for him – getting in decorators for the bathroom, and the carpet . . . can you imagine?'

'Oh, Aunty Nancy did that. She told me some time later.'

Neither spoke for a while as they thought about how Nancy and James had carried them through that time.

Becky thought of how Nancy had helped her personally – all the unanswered questions, all the fear and pain – and how Nancy had dealt with the horror of the bathroom, and the blood-red bath. She shuddered and pushed the memory aside.

'I suppose we better go in and get our seats,' Brona said. 'You okay?'

Becky nodded, and getting up they joined the crowds going across the road.

'When we were children,' Brona said, 'I could never have imagined that you and I one day would want to do this.'

'Do what?'

'Holiday – together. In a place like this. Culture. Time together. That kind of thing.'

And Becky smiled. She could not have agreed more.

'And they say your childhood is the best time in your life,' she said.

Brona laughed. 'Depends on the childhood,' she said, slipping her arm through Becky's.

'Your kids,' Becky said. 'I think you gave them the perfect childhood.'

That's easy to say now, Brona thought. At the time it was a struggle. All that worry, all one's fears. Never knowing what they might really be thinking, really be doing. Getting up at night when they were babies to check they were still breathing. And later, getting up at night to check that the windows were locked, and that they were safely inside.

'Thanks, Becky.'

'For what?'

'For saying that. I did my best. Rupert and I – we did our best.'

And Becky nodded, knowing that her parents had done their best too.

They found their seats, at the end of a row, and settled down under the night sky as the opera unfolded. Puccini's *Turandot* held them both captivated, and the tenor's voice rising up into the night sky, singing '*Non, piangere, Liù*', brought tears to Becky's eyes which she tried to blink away.

At the end of the second act, Becky said, 'Bro, we've time for a drink. Interested?' Brona agreed, and they left the theatre talking about the riddles which Turandot had asked.

'The one I like the most is "What is born each night and dies at dawn?"' Brona said.

'I don't think either you or I would have got the answer to that,' Becky said. 'I don't think that hope would have been on my list of possibilities.'

'Oh, I would have known,' Brona replied. 'In the early days after Baby disappeared, before Mummy, you know . . . I went to bed each night with hope.'

'Did you?' Becky asked, surprised.

Brona thought a moment and then said, 'Actually, no, I don't think I did, but when I got into bed with you I definitely felt hope then. I used to sleep quite heavily, and when I woke I'd be waiting for you to find out ... for you to check, for you to see if ...'

They went back to the bar, where they sat and drank a glass of white wine.

'Bro,' Becky said, 'would you mind if I don't go back for a bit ...' She didn't finish the thought, but Brona nodded. She suddenly and instinctively knew that Becky did not want to see the stabbing in the next act, when Liù would take the dagger and kill herself.

'You go back,' Becky said. 'I'll either join you in a bit, or just sit here. Sure you don't mind?'

'Finish my wine when you've had yours,' Brona said. 'Join me if you feel like it, otherwise just sit here. I'll find you when it's over.'

Standing up and straightening her skirt, Brona leaned over and kissed Becky on the cheek, then headed off across the square.

Becky watched her and was reminded of Baby.

I probably wouldn't recognise her now, she thought, as Brona, with her shoulder-length blonde-streaked hair pinned up, walked on long legs away from her.

Becky looked up at the top of the umbrella above her. She noticed how all the spokes came together and that that was how the umbrella stayed up.

Break a spoke, she thought, and the whole caboodle comes tumbling down. She looked back across the square, where so many people, both Italians and tourists, were heading back in the direction of the theatre.

Baby could be there, she thought. One of those women could be she, elegantly dressed, living her own life, completely disconnected from us. She tried to find Brona among the crowd, but she had already disappeared.

'Excuse me.' A male voice intruded on her observations. 'Becky Dunville?'

Becky looked up. She recognised the face, although it had been many years.

'Mr O'Connor,' she said in surprise. 'It is you, isn't it?'

'Conor,' he said. 'Conor O'Connor. It's good to see you. I noticed you and your sister earlier.'

'And you recognised us? After all this time?'

'It was my first case,' he said. 'I don't think I will ever forget any of you.'

Becky gestured to the chair beside her.

'Do join me,' she said.

She was busy taking him in. It dawned on her now that the detective couldn't have been that old back then, but because she was only fifteen when it started she had never tried to put an age on him.

He was an adult, she thought to herself. But he could only be in his fifties now.

He was heavier, and there was grey in his hair, but his face was unmistakably the same – handsome, kind, with smiling eyes.

He sat beside her.

'Can I get you anything?' she asked. 'Would you like a beer or something?'

He shook his head.

'No, not now, thank you. I don't want to intrude.'

They went through the niceties – how long are you here? When are you going back? Have you enjoyed it?

It transpired that he had arrived the week before Becky and Brona, and was due to leave in two days' time, whereas they still had another week.

'Are you with someone?' Becky asked.

'I'm with a group of friends,' he replied. 'My marriage broke up a while ago, and . . . well, you know. Are you and Brona married?'

'Brona is – she married one of my half-brothers. I don't know if you remember . . .' These were difficult things to broach.

'I remember,' said Conor O'Connor. 'There is nothing to do with that case and its sad consequences which I will ever forget.'

Becky nodded.

'Brona and Rupert have two children – a boy and a girl. They are in their twenties now.'

'A good age, I would imagine,' he said.

'Older than Baby was,' Becky agreed.

There were things not being said, and yet she had the feeling that he understood.

'Did you have children?' she asked him.

'No,' he replied. 'No.'

He couldn't tell her that he hadn't had children because he was so shocked by what had happened to the Dunvilles, that he couldn't bear the idea of waking one morning and finding one gone and never knowing why or how or where.

Becky sipped her wine and, nodding across the road, said, 'Brona's gone back in for the last act. Shouldn't you be going too?'

'I've seen it before,' he said. 'Last week in fact. I think I'd prefer to sit and talk with you. Why aren't you going in?' he asked as an afterthought.

'Death by dagger,' Becky said wryly, with a slight shrug of her shoulders, and a grimace on her face. 'It makes me think of my mother's throat.'

'Well, if you really aren't going back, may I get a drink and join you after all?' He signalled for the waiter and ordered wine.

'So, how are you?' Conor O'Connor asked. 'How has life treated you?'

'I'm all right,' Becky said, responding to this air of companionability which was suddenly created at the table. 'I've had a good life. It has been full in its own way. I didn't get married, didn't have children. I love my niece and nephew – Brona's children – and spend an amount of time with them. Though they're quite grown up now, we have a good relationship.

'Dad died, you know,' she continued. 'He had a stroke a couple of years ago. A bad one. It was better that way – he'd always been so busy, so active. It's been difficult, but Brona and I both know that it was better.'

Her voice was a mixture of both sadness and pragmatism.

'I'm sorry,' Conor said. 'I was away at the time, and was told about it when I got back. I meant to write to you, but it was difficult – difficult to imagine what it was like for you.'

Becky nodded. 'And John – my biological father, John Delaware – he's been wonderful,' she continued. 'He has a place in Dublin as well as his home in London, so I see a lot of him.'

'Yes,' Conor said. 'I remember him. I met him.'

They were touching on the past, on a time and a place which seemed another country, and yet, to Becky's surprise, that past had clearly haunted him too.

There was the odd pause as they tried to evaluate the situation, each wondering how much could be said while on a chance meeting on a summer holiday.

'Would you and Brona join me for dinner tomorrow night?' Conor asked.

'That would be nice,' she said.

They talked a bit about his holiday, and then he said, 'I should go back in for the end. I've always loved the drama of Puccini, and want to melt when Princess Turandot says that the stranger's name is Love. Are you sure you don't want to come too?'

Becky shook her head. She wanted to sit and think, and so she said, 'No thank you. I'm sure.'

'I'll see you tomorrow, then. I'll pick you up at eight.'

Becky sat there looking at the night sky. The stars flickered in the darkness, and she finished her wine while she waited for Brona to return. She thought of Princess Turandot, and the way Conor O'Connor had said he liked Puccini, and she smiled, realising that he had surprised her. The surprise was not just his appearing out of the night and standing beside her at the table, but was also to do with how comfortable he was with himself, and how at ease she had felt, and how interesting the conversation had become. She also realised that she was looking forward to seeing him again.

Brona overdosed on sun the next day, and took an early night, while Becky dressed up for dinner with the detective.

They met in the hotel foyer and went by taxi into the town. She took his arm when they got out of the car and they walked the rest of the way to steps which descended from street level to a restaurant where he had already reserved a table. They sat outside at the back, where they were in view of the piazza with its life and activity, and the constant coming and going of tourists. Tiny white bulbs around the open wooden structure of the restaurant lit up the darkening sky, and candles in little glass bowls flickered on the tables.

'It's nice here,' Becky said appreciatively. 'We must have passed it and not known it was hidden away.'

'It's a pity Brona is missing this. Will you bring her here?' Conor asked her.

'Yes,' Becky affirmed. 'Definitely.'

The food was wonderful, the conversation warm and at times intense.

They covered all the people who were connected with 'the case', as Conor referred to Baby's disappearance.

'Hugo Mombay Humphries was arrested,' he told her. 'Somewhere odd – like Mozambique. I don't quite remember the details. Smuggling contraband.'

'Aunty Nancy is in a nursing home,' Becky told him. 'And my cousin Eleanor married a German – a trapeze artist.'

'A trapeze artist? How unusual,' Conor said.

'Well, he's not really a trapeze artist, but that's what Brona calls him. In fact he is a diplomat. Brona says he walks a fine line between outrageous rudeness and oily diplomacy. You've gathered Brona is not that fond of him, but Eleanor and he are happy, and that's what counts. They're out in Central America at the moment, but due for a transfer next year. Eleanor does a bit of lecturing, and a lot of research, and says she doesn't mind where they are moved to next. She is still the same. Nice. Kind. An intellectual. You may remember.'

'And your uncle?'

'Uncle James is well. He's aged a lot now, as you can imagine, but he's brilliant fun. Brona and I love to go out with him, which we get to do quite often.'

And on they went, down through the list, placing and positioning all the old characters. Becky was surprised at the detail with which Conor remembered each of them.

'Do you remember the Brophys?' she asked. 'Rhona Brophy was a friend of Brona's. Her best friend. Still is, in fact.'

'Yes,' he said. 'I do. I met them at the funeral.'

'Rhona married, had three children. She's incredibly good fun. She was fun as a child too. I think I was jealous of Brona for having such a good friend, and I suppose I was jealous of Baby for having Anne Marie. Do you remember her?'

'I do indeed,' he said. 'Tall girl. Slightly shifty, I think.'

'She wasn't much support when everything fell apart,' Becky said thoughtfully. 'Unlike the Brophys, who were.'

'I think she was rather irresponsible,' Conor said.

The word made Becky think of Lieutenant Calley.

'I wonder what happened to Lieutenant Calley?' she asked.

'Calley – the massacre at My Lai? That Calley?' he asked, surprised at her train of thought.

'Yes. I've thought about him on and off over the years. But at one point I was obsessed with him and his behaviour.'

Conor looked at her with interest. 'Why? What was the interest? And what is the connection?'

'I'm not sure,' she said slowly. 'We got a television – sometime after Mummy, you know . . . and I think his trial was on. Anyway, I read somewhere that he said he would always be proud if My Lai showed the world what war was really like.'

'And?'

'Well, not really an and, I suppose,' Becky admitted. 'It was more to do with responsibility. Somebody said something to me about people being responsible for their own actions, and I wondered. He was found guilty, do you remember? I think he was sentenced to life. I just wondered what happened to him.'

'He *was* sentenced to life, with hard labour,' Conor confirmed. 'But he only served something like a year and a half, and then, in nineteen seventy-five or thereabouts, he was released. He works in a jeweller's somewhere now. Georgia, I think.'

'Thank you,' Becky said.

'For what?' He was genuinely puzzled.

'I suppose for giving me an end to that particular story.'

He looked at her carefully. 'Closure?' he asked. 'Is that what you mean?'

'Yes. I think so.'

'I've been there,' he told her then. 'To My Lai. A couple of years ago. There's a museum in the village and you can see the names of the five hundred plus people who died.'

She looked at him in amazement. 'Why did you go there? Why on earth would you go there?'

'It's an odd coincidence,' he said. 'But I too was fascinated by Calley. He was only twenty-one, he had been given a gun and power . . . I can't make any judgement on him, because I wasn't there. I wasn't the one with the gun, or the facility to make life-and-death decisions. But I was interested – shocked, I suppose.'

'We only lost two people,' Becky said. 'That village lost hundreds . . .'

She didn't finish the sentence. She wasn't trying to compare. Grief was grief. Loss was loss. The most you could do was learn to accommodate and try to adapt. I suppose, she thought, that the difference is that they knew what happened to their people, and therefore knew what it was they had to learn to accommodate.

'I wanted to ask you something yesterday,' he said tentatively, feeling that they were close enough to pursue what had been puzzling him. 'And forgive me if I'm intruding – well, I'm know I'm intruding . . .'

'Ask,' Becky said. She was curious at his sudden hesitancy. 'Go ahead, please.'

'Well, you know when you said that about the stabbing in *Turandot*? I wondered what you meant about your mother's throat.'

There was a long silence as she looked at him. Eventually she got the words together.

'I just meant about my mother slitting her throat in the bath,' she said. 'I just suddenly didn't want to see the death in the opera.'

Conor's face changed. He looked totally shocked. He reached across the table and took her hands. 'Becky,' he said. 'My God, Becky . . .'

She sat there staring at his large hands holding her small ones.

'Becky, look at me,' he said.

She looked up into his face, saw the kindness and concern there that she had seen as a child.

'Becky, your mother didn't cut her throat. My God, you poor thing. She didn't cut her throat,' he repeated. His voice portrayed the horror of the words. 'Becky, darling, she didn't cut her throat.'

She sat and stared at him.

'But I saw . . .' she tried. 'I saw . . . you know, her head, the blood . . .'

'Becky, I know it makes no difference because either way she is dead. But she didn't cut her throat. She cut her wrists.'

He got her a brandy and made her drink it.

'I know it makes no difference in one way,' she said. 'But in another way it does. For some reason death by wrist-slashing doesn't seem so shocking, and yet of course it is. I'm sorry, I thought I was going to faint.'

She was finding it difficult to put the words together.

'It's all right,' he said gently to her. 'It really is. It's a shock for you on several levels – not least because for thirty years you've thought she died like that. And then there is the factor that some types of suicide are more acceptable in our culture . . . in our psyche . . . I don't mean acceptable . . . I think I mean we can accept them in some way. Well, on some level . . .'

It brought them closer. This sharing of information, this process of her being informed or enlightened drew her towards him, and other inhibitions were let go. As the brandy settled her, they talked on about what had happened.

'And you never found out who the second letter was from?' she asked.

'The O letter,' he said, pensively. 'No. We never got to the bottom of that.'

'Why did you call it the O letter?' she asked as she sipped her red wine.

'Well, the other one we called the H letter, and that one was the O one,' he replied.

'Surely you'd have called it the C letter?' Becky said, slightly bemused.

Conor looked at her, puzzled.

'I don't follow,' he said. 'The H letter was from Hugo Mombay Humphries. We always assumed the O letter was from someone beginning with the letter O.'

'But it was a C,' Becky said.

'What was a C?' asked Conor O'Connor.

Becky looked at him in bewilderment.

'The second letter was signed with the letter C,' she said.

'No, you're mistaken. It was an O,' he said.

'Well,' she said with a small laugh, 'I'm not going to fall out with you over dinner – especially when you're paying – but Conor, it was a C.'

He reflected on this for a few minutes.

'Well,' he said eventually, 'we're not going to be able to resolve this here. One of us is wrong. We'll check when we get back to Dublin.'

Becky agreed. But she was puzzled and in some way a little peeved – after all, he seemed to remember all the other details so accurately, she couldn't understand why he would have got that one wrong. She felt that something as significant as that letter he should have recalled. She was so sure that she was correct, and yet she could see that he was equally sure.

But this one, she thought, he has got this one wrong.

'Oh,' she said. 'I've just remembered a conversation Brona and I had yesterday – or maybe the day before. Shall I tell you?'

And then she filled him in on the clothing which Anne Marie had been keeping for Baby in her house.

'Brona said it might be important. You see, Dad and Mum were very careful with money – and these items were quite expensive. At least, that's how I remember them.'

'Anne Marie never said anything when she was being interviewed,' he said thoughtfully.

'I don't think she saw them as being relevant. She appeared to really believe that our parents had given Baby the money for them.'

293

'That's interesting,' he said. 'And you never mentioned it to anyone?'

'No,' Becky replied. 'I only found out that last weekend, and Mum
and Dad were so upset, I thought that it would upset them even
further – and then on the Monday, Mummy, you know . . . And I
forgot about it. It was about Easter, I think, when Anne Marie asked
me about them again, what to do with them. And I said to sell them
or to keep them, that I didn't care.'

'I see,' Conor said. His voice was still thoughtful.

'Relevant?'

'Maybe.'

They finished dinner and returned to her hotel, where they had a last
drink in the bar.

'Pity I didn't see you earlier,' Conor said to her. 'This has been far
and away the nicest evening of my holiday. Perhaps when you get
back to Dublin, you'd like to go out again?'

'Yes, I would,' she smiled. 'I've enjoyed it too, even though we did
talk a lot about the past. And you won't forget to look up that letter?'
she reminded him.

'Trust me, it's the first thing on my list when I get home. Expect
to hear from me,' he said, kissing her good night.

'He's lovely,' she said to Brona.

'He must be ancient,' Brona said.

'No, honestly, he's not. Maybe ten or twelve years older than me –
not much more than that anyway. He's the image of Sean Connery.'

'Going for older men now, are we?' Brona teased.

'I always liked older men,' Becky said.

She was thinking of Mr Jones, of blond hair and grey-flecked
eyes, and the maturity to bypass what she had encountered in
university – boys who asked her out, kissed and groped and didn't
understand the excitement of the relationship she had formed with
the 'older man'.

It had bothered her for years. She'd worried about it, intelligent
enough to know that what she had found was, in some sense, unreal,
but that it had been terribly real for her at the time. She knew that
he had carried her through and out of the nightmare, even though he
had abandoned her at a particular point.

And she had searched, over and over again, to find that same feeling

– the security, the safety, the comfort. Sometimes it seemed to be there, but it always slipped away.

'Remember the two letters?' Becky asked Brona. 'The ones you found and passed to me?'

Brona did remember.

'I felt so awful – they'd been sitting in my pocket for two days. We hadn't gone to school . . . remember? We went to town and I got my hair fixed for Mother Immaculata.'

'Did you really not look at them before you gave them to me?' Becky asked her.

'No.' Brona shook her head. 'I didn't. I gave them to you as soon as I found them. I was terrified.'

'And were you never puzzled about what was in them or who they were from?' Becky asked her sister.

'I don't know.' Brona was a little unsure. 'I remember that day getting in from school and someone . . . it might have been Mr O'Connor . . . asked me again if Baby had a boyfriend or boyfriends.'

'And you never saw the letters?'

'No. I assumed they were love letters the way everyone was going on about them,' Brona replied. 'Why, what was in them?'

'It's a little odd,' Becky said. 'One of them was a positively indecent letter from someone who signed himself with the letter H who turned out to be Hugo. It's the other one where the problem lies – and yet it was quite innocuous at the time.'

Becky told her about how she was convinced it was from someone signing himself with the letter C, but that Conor O'Connor thought it was an O.

'But they never found out who it was from anyway, did they?' Brona asked.

'No . . . no, they didn't. It's just that I'm sure I'm right, and so is he.'

'Well, it can be checked, can't it?' Brona said reasonably. 'I mean – they wouldn't have thrown out the file or anything like that?'

'No, I gather there is still a file. It's strange. I remember asking Uncle James about them – the letters, I mean – and he told me not to worry, that it was all in hand. And I knew that because of the contents, the adults weren't talking to us about them or showing them to us . . . They saw us just as children, all of us, even after Baby's deception. Or perhaps because of it. They had no idea.'

Chapter Twenty

Home from Florence, relaxed and reassured, Becky and Brona hugged each other in the airport, and Brona went out to meet her family. Becky hovered at the luggage carousel, wanting time alone before she took a taxi to her apartment. She listened to the messages on her voice mail as soon as she got in. The one she was waiting for was there. Conor O'Connor's voice, low but clear, said, 'Contact me when you get back. We need to talk.' He had left a number.

She phoned him immediately.

'I've retrieved the file,' he said. 'I think it would be best if we meet.'

'When?' she asked.

'Can you make it tomorrow?'

She agreed without hesitation. She knew that something was definitely up. It was in his voice. Unpacking and sorting clothes for the washing machine, and putting away her case, she kept going over in her mind how he had sounded, and what the implications might be.

She felt she wouldn't be able to sleep that night, but it was already evening by the time she had done her bit of shopping for food, got petrol, and had the car washed. She poured herself a glass of wine as she contemplated which of the other messages she should respond to. She also wanted to phone Brona to tell her that Conor had already got back to her, but then she felt maybe she should wait until she'd actually seen him.

After all, it might be to say that I am wrong. That I got it wrong. And anyway, Brona will be busy with the family tonight, she reasoned. It can wait until tomorrow.

Brona, home with Rupert, lay in his arms in bed.

'You look brown and healthy, and you feel so warm,' he said.

'I'm glad to be home,' she said.

'Did you miss me?'

296

She squeezed her arms tightly around him.

'What do you think?' she asked.

'I think that maybe that's a yes,' he said.

Becky sat down with a pen and listened to the messages again, taking in ones which she had bypassed the first time around. A long-distance one from Eleanor calling to say 'hello, and how are things', and one from Uncle James asking Brona and herself out for lunch on Sunday. Another one was from John Delaware asking if she was coming over to London the following week.

That may have to wait, she thought. Again, I'll have to get back to him tomorrow – after the meeting.

She was restless and over-energetic. One moment she was sitting sipping her wine, the next she was out in the kitchen switching the washing machine from wash to tumble-dry. She kept wondering how Brona was doing, and if Brona were wondering was there any news.

It can wait, she thought again. Until tomorrow.

And then tomorrow came. At ten o'clock she entered the foyer of the building where Conor O'Connor had said they would meet. He appeared from an elevator, and having greeted each other with a hug, he ushered her back into the waiting lift and up they went.

She found her heart was pounding, as she knew from his face that he had found something.

He brought her to an office where a large file was lying on the desk, and asked her to sit.

'I'm going to talk you through this,' he said, as he lifted a sheet of paper from the file. It looked old now, not the reasonably fresh sheet of paper she had seen all those years ago, but as he handed it to her she had no doubt that it was the same one. Her mind slipped back to that day in St Martin's when Brona had handed her the two envelopes. The letter simply said:

Dear Barbara,

I gave you my number – phone me. I'm thinking about what we did. Let's do it again.

Love

O

It was the same letter in all but one detail – the letter O.

She read it again.

'Conor,' she said. 'I know it was a C. I swear it was a C.'

He nodded.

'And you're right,' he said. 'At least we think you're right. I've had it checked. The same pen was used to close the C. You can't see it with the naked eye, but the test is conclusive, in that either the person who wrote the O always wrote their O's by forming a C and then filling it in, in which case you are simply mistaken. Or that it was a C and was later closed.'

Becky shivered. She was scared now; deep inside she knew what had happened, but it was terrifying. It was like looking into a kaleidoscope and seeing all the tiny pieces falling together, and the shape they were forming was horrible.

She looked up at him.

'Is there anything else?' she asked. She could hear her voice, hear how normal it sounded, but it reflected in no way what was going on in her mind as the last pieces fell into place.

'The notebook,' he replied.

He took it from the file and passed it across to her.

'I never saw this before,' she said. 'Is it all right to hold it? I mean . . . fingerprints . . .'

'Don't worry about that,' he said. 'Take a look in it and tell me what you think.'

Becky opened the notebook and took in the figures on the various pages. Sometimes there were initials beside them, sometimes dates, sometimes question marks. In all but one case the question marks had been crossed out. Down the right-hand side of each page were a variety of symbols, mainly ticks and crosses.

Her eyes moved up and down the pages.

A typical page read like this:

JL	10	8	11	?√
PC	20	15	11	?X
DV	10	22	11	?√

'Sums of money?' she asked.

'Yes,' he said. 'I think so. I think that now. In the past it had no meaning. But now, does anything make sense to you in it?'

He reached out and took the book from her, and opened the second last page.

298

Becky looked again, working down the notations.
The last line read:

CR   10   19   12   √

'Nineteen, twelve,' she said. 'That could be December the nineteenth, I suppose. I think that one might make sense,' she added thoughtfully.

'Tell me about it,' said Conor O'Connor.

'We had a party on the Sunday before Christmas – before the last Christmas, I mean. It might have been the nineteenth.'

'I can check. Go on.'

'Well, Baby got money off Mr Robinson – Charlie Robinson – that day. He was attached to the Australian Embassy. He owed me for babysitting. Long story. He'd slobbered all over me, and Baby got my money off him – a pound, she got me. And then she mentioned the kiss that he'd given me, and she got an extra tenner off him. That was a lot of money back then. When she told me, I remember thinking that it was like blackmail. And of course, she kept the money for herself.'

'Yes. I see,' said Conor thoughtfully. 'That fits.'

'These add up,' Becky said, flicking through the notebook again. 'Quite a lot of money here.'

'She was quite methodical,' Conor said. 'It's a long time ago now, and it will be impossible to work out who these initials belong to. And in fact, in many cases there are no initials. Just a date and a figure. And in some cases a figure and a question mark. Now, turn the page – I want you to look at what is on the next page.'

Becky turned it over, and looking at it, she nodded.

'This is very difficult for me to handle,' she said.

She swallowed uneasily. It made her feel sick just to think about it.

'We're going to have to go through everything,' said Conor O'Connor. 'And then I think you're going to have to make a statement.'

Becky nodded. She looked again at the last entry. There was no date. In the main column there was the figure '20' and then the two initials.

'Do you think,' she asked hesitantly, 'do you suppose that she was looking for twenty pounds from . . . and . . .'

She couldn't finish the sentence.

'Look at it this way,' Conor said to her. 'On previous lines where there is a question mark, in every case the question mark has a symbol entered after it, or else it has been crossed out. It's possible that when she entered the symbol, it meant that she'd been paid, and then she entered the date. In some cases where there is a question mark and no symbol, the complete line has been crossed out, as if she had abandoned the possibility of getting money from that quarter. In this case the money was outstanding, so there is no date, and the question mark hasn't been deleted. So let's suppose that she was looking for the twenty pounds, and whoever she was trying to blackmail wasn't having any of it.'

'Yes,' replied Becky. 'I see. So what now?'

'Now you tell me what happened to that letter. How you got it. What you did with it. Everything.'

'Brona came to me that morning,' Becky said slowly. 'We had just had a special Assembly, because you were coming in to talk to Baby's friends.'

'Go on,' said Conor O'Connor.

'During Assembly I remembered about the window being left open downstairs, and that I had shut it on the Sunday night late. And I came out of the hall and I was really shocked at the memory because it meant that Baby had definitely been planning on returning, so either something had happened to her, or I had locked her out and she couldn't get back in. Then Brona came up to me. And she was really scared too. She'd found the two letters in her pocket – she'd removed them from Baby's room to read at a later date, and then simply forgotten that she had them.'

'Had she read them?'

'No. She said not. And I believed her. I'm sure she hadn't. Knowing Brona, she'd have mentioned the contents if she had, and when we talked about it on holidays, she said again that she hadn't.'

'Okay. Go on.'

'Well, I took them to the cloakroom, I think, and I read them. I noticed they were from two different people. One was H and the other C.'

'And then what did you do?'

'I wanted to get them to you, and I knew that Mother Immaculata would be sitting in on any interviews and I didn't want her to know about the contents of the letters. And if I asked to see you, she would have asked why ... and then she would have demanded to see the letters, and I couldn't let anyone read them because of what the other one said. The Hugo one. You know.'

'I know. I understand,' said Conor O'Connor.

'So I gave them to Mr Jones to give to you. He said he would.'

'That's just how I remember it,' said Conor O'Connor. 'He gave them to me from you, sometime that day.'

Becky said nothing.

'Do you know what his first name is?' asked the detective.

Becky nodded, and she looked down at the page and the letters CJ. Her hands were shaking.

'It's Christopher,' she said quietly. 'Oh Conor, this is so awful. You don't know . . .'

'Tell me,' he said.

She sat silently for a few moments. Grief and fear washed through her again. She struggled to find the words.

'After Mum died, I had a . . . a relationship with Mr Jones. It lasted over two years, until I went to Trinity. I've always been so grateful to him. He saw me through it, kept my feet on the ground, kept me focused, listened to me during all of that dreadful ghastly time . . .'

Becky was fighting back tears at this point.

Conor got up and came and put an arm around her.

'I am sorry,' he said. 'I can see that this makes it worse for you.'

He got her coffee and she drank it in silence in his office. He went out again briefly, and then returned having given her time to compose herself.

'Well,' he said, when he eventually came back and sat down, 'I've put it all in motion. A warrant will be issued later today for his arrest.'

'What? Oh, I see. Oh.' She didn't know what to say.

'He's living in England and he's going to be picked up some time today or tomorrow. Good co-operation . . . it'll all work out now.'

'But can this be proven?' Becky asked.

'Oh, yes. We've every confidence.'

A few days later, Becky and Brona were sitting in Brona's drawing room in the old Dunville house on Lansdowne Road when Conor O'Connor arrived. They greeted each other. Rupert came in and joined them. Every so often Becky and Brona touched fingertips, just like they had the first time, long ago one Tuesday afternoon in Bewleys over Mary cakes and coffee, and had done since down through the years.

'Shall I tell you what happened?' asked Conor O'Connor of the expectant women.

'He's confessed?' asked Brona.

'Yes. We have more or less the whole story, and what we don't have we can piece together. We've spoken to Anne Marie, and while she doesn't remember what day it was, she was able to fill in some of the details. I need to go back to just before the end of that Christmas term.'

About three weeks prior to that fateful night when Baby Dunville let herself out of the breakfast-room window, Baby and Anne Marie were sitting in a pub on Duke Street, and Anne Marie got fed up and said she was going home. She'd been nursing a cold all week and wanted to go to bed.

'Oh, go on then,' said Baby Dunville, flicking a little ash off her miniskirt. 'Just mind you leave the basement window open for me.' Baby was a dab hand at having windows at the ready.

'Sure you don't mind?' asked Anne Marie. 'My abandoning you, I mean.'

It wasn't a night that would stand out for Anne Marie; all that she would remember about it later was that she was shivering by the time she got home, and she gratefully slipped into her bed. She had left Baby the odd time before, but in every other case she had left her with a man. In this one instance, she left her alone. Anne Marie had no sooner left when Baby picked up a tall, fair-haired young man in his mid twenties with flecks in his grey eyes.

'May I buy you a drink?' asked Christopher Jones.

'Yes,' said Baby Dunville. 'Mine is a Guinness.'

'Are you from Dublin?' he asked.

She said she was, and then she asked him where he was from.

'I'm from Dublin too, but I've been living in England. I'm over here now, organising a job and a flat.'

He had a car, and he offered to drive her home. On the way to Anne Marie's house and the open basement window, they took a short detour to Sandymount Strand, where Baby Dunville practised her sucking technique, and Christopher Jones ran his fingers through her long blonde hair, and groaned and groaned before he finally sighed. Conor O'Connor left out some of these details while telling the story to the surviving Dunville sisters.

Then Christopher Jones brought Baby back to Anne Marie's house, and she said, 'That was yummy.'

He said, 'Look. I'd like to see you again. May I call you?'

'Oh no,' said Baby Dunville. 'Give me your number and I'll call you. It's a bit awkward – getting calls at home, I mean.'

He wrote it on a piece of paper for her.

'Is this your house?' he asked, nodding at the O'Mahonys'.

'No,' said Baby coolly. 'I'm staying over with friends tonight. I live just down on Lansdowne Road.'

They kissed briefly, and grinning at him, she got out of the car and headed for the O'Mahonys' basement window.

A few days passed, and when he didn't hear from her, Christopher Jones looked her up in the telephone directory. There was only one Dunville family on Lansdowne Road listed. So he wrote her the letter which Brona found in January and passed to Becky, who passed it back to him, and he changed the C to an O.

On the last day of that Christmas term, Baby went to her locker during class to get a book she had forgotten.

In the hallway she bumped into Mother Immaculata with Christopher Jones, who had just come in for a short interview for the job his relative had already tied up for him.

Baby Dunville took one look at the nun and the man she had played with on Sandymount Strand. She wondered what on earth was going on.

Christopher Jones took one look at Baby in her school uniform and his eyes nearly fell out of his head.

'Honestly,' he said to the detective who interviewed him in custody. 'Honestly, I swear to God, I had thought she was in her twenties.'

Baby had smiled coolly and approached the pair.

Mother Immaculata swung around on her heels, sensing her presence, 'Ah, Barbara Dunville,' she said. 'What are you doing out of class?'

'Just fetching a book, Mother,' said Baby with a little smile. She looked at Christopher Jones, and she opened her big blue eyes very wide.

'This,' said Mother Immaculata to Christopher Jones, 'is Barbara Dunville. Mr Jones,' she addressed Barbara, 'will be teaching you singing.'

'Yes, Mother,' said Baby. 'It's very nice to meet you, Mr Jones,' and she stuck out her hand.

Exceptionally nice, thought Baby Dunville to herself. I'd love some new clothes for Christmas.

'I am looking forward to singing classes, Mr Jones,' said Baby, with her limpid blue eyes.

She phoned him that evening when she got in from school.

'Twenty pounds,' she said to him.

'Whatever for?' he asked.

'Consider it a down payment,' she replied.

'A down payment on what?' he said.

'Well,' she replied. 'One has one's reputation to think of. Doesn't one?'

'What do you mean?' His voice sounded a little tighter now.

'Well,' she said, 'there you are teaching me singing, and imagine if it came out what you got me to do to you.'

Her voice was like a cat's purr. It was smooth and soft, but very determined and quite unrelenting.

'Look,' said Mr Jones, 'I had no idea that you were a schoolgirl. It never occurred to me. And just think how it will look if it comes out that you tried to blackmail me.'

'Blackmail you?' said Baby evenly. 'What an unpleasant word. But maybe you aren't pushed about your career. Maybe you don't need a job in St Martin's.'

'You are joking,' he said. He felt furious. 'I've worked hard to get to where I am. And I actually would rather like to keep the job in St Martin's. It'll supplement what I'm getting from the orchestra, and it keeps my options open.'

'I don't think Mother Immaculata will see it that way,' said Baby Dunville. 'You should think about it for a few days. You have until term restarts.'

Baby hung up.

'I didn't know what to do,' Christopher Jones said during the interview while he was in custody. 'I thought of not taking the job in St Martin's, but I needed it, and part-time teaching jobs like that were not easy to come by. I had just got a flat. This English friend was leasing it, and we shared the rent. Everything was nicely set up. I had been looking forward to January – everything was going right until this happened. I knew that if I paid her once, she would just keep after me. Then I discovered that Hugo – my flatmate – was going out with her. He'd referred to a girlfriend called Baby. Imagine my surprise when

I discovered that Baby was Barbara Dunville. He showed me a photo of her. We were in London over Christmas when I discovered that. Then I thought of a way to stop the blackmail. I reckoned that all I needed to do was to tell her that I'd tell Hugo.

'I spent Christmas in London clearing out the last of my things from my place there. I met Hugo a couple of times and I knew that he was due to meet Barbara on the Sunday night. My problem was how to make contact with her. I came back to Dublin on the Saturday, settled into the flat, and spent most of Sunday worrying about what to do. I tried phoning the house, but someone else answered and I couldn't ask for her or give my name, as no one must know that we knew each other. And Monday was approaching.

'The fog came in on Sunday night, and it occurred to me that Hugo mightn't get in. He was coming by ferry. I rang the port, and sure enough the ferry was caught outside the harbour. I drove up to Lansdowne Road, and waited near the Dunvilles'. I was just about to give up when Barbara came out. She just materialised out of the fog and started walking down towards the railway line. I gave her a small start and then I drove after her.'

The car pulled in beside the kerb, and the window opened.

'Can I give you a lift?' Christopher Jones asked Baby Dunville.

'Oh, good, yes,' she replied. 'I can hardly see a thing. Have you got my money?' she asked as she got into the passenger's seat.

'Let's talk about that for a little,' he said to her, as they set off down the road.

'I have never seen anyone so angry. It was as if she couldn't handle being thwarted,' he said at the interview. 'As far as I was concerned the matter was closed. She couldn't blackmail me, because I had a hold over her. Foolish of me, I must admit. When I first met her she reminded me of something beautifully feline – one moment like a kitten, purring and soft ... difficult to explain, and the next like a cat, lithe, supple ... In the car she turned from that cat into an animal with serious claws. She was furious. She said that she wanted the money and that if I pulled another stunt like this, she would accuse me of rape. She said that she didn't care if I told Hugo – that she'd already realised we were flatmates because of the phone number. I told her to grow up – then she started to scream at me and hammer me with her hands, yelling "Rape, rape!" I nearly crashed the car. It was all I could do to stop it, and I fought back. I didn't mean to kill her. I really didn't. We were fighting – she trying to hurt me, I trying to stop her. I got her hands off my face, and I tried to shake her . . . I did shake her and she whacked her head off the window – very hard. Suddenly she slumped down in her seat. For a couple of seconds I thought that maybe she had just had the fight knocked out of her, and then I realised that there was something wrong. She was dead.

'I hadn't meant to kill her. That wasn't my plan,' repeated Christopher Jones. 'I wanted to talk to her, to explain that I hadn't done anything wrong – that it was she who had picked me up, that she had to take responsibility for the things she had done, and that to blackmail me was out of the question.

'She simply wouldn't listen, couldn't see what I was saying. It was terrible. My whole life was in front of me. I had got my degree, got two jobs in Dublin – I was just starting out. The only thing that I had done wrong was to buy a girl a drink in a pub . . . She said that she would destroy me if I didn't pay up.'

'And what did you do with the body?'

'I drove up the Dublin Mountains – beyond the Featherbeds. There was no fog up there, but it was dark. I wrapped her in plastic sheeting I had in the car.'

'Plastic sheeting? You'd gone prepared?'

'No. It was stuff I used to protect the car when I was buying coal or turf for the fire. I wrapped her in it, and I dumped her up there. Up in the Featherbeds.'

'She has never turned up.'

'I know. I assumed she'd be found quite soon. But it snowed during that week. I don't know what happened to her. I kept thinking she'd be found.'

'Could you find where you put her?'

'I don't know. I went up that spring – I can't tell you what it was like. I went up to look in the hope that maybe I could make her remains obvious in some way. I needed her found. Because of what had happened, that family was destroyed. I kept thinking that if Baby were found then at least they could put her to rest and pick up the pieces. I am not a heartless man. I had listened to Rebecca over a period of months at that point, watched her in school. I couldn't atone for what had happened.'

'So did you find where you had put the body?'

'No. When I got there, I didn't really look for it. I thought I was

306

going up to search, but when I got there, I realised that maybe that wasn't why I had gone up there at all. I think I went up because I wanted to make peace with her – or something like that. I know – that doesn't make sense. But I think I went up just to say goodbye. I don't know.'

'And could you find now where you put her?'

'Again, I don't know. I know that the night I brought her up there, I took the mileage on the car on the way back – the miles from between where I left her and the start of the forest. You know when you are going up there, you drive through a forest and then you come out into the open on to the Military Road. Well, I know how many miles it was from the forest to where I put her. But that's a long time ago now and all I know for certain is that she is up there. When I went back I was too scared to look properly.'

'So Baby is up there in the Featherbeds – we may find her now,' Conor O'Connor said.

Becky and Brona sat side by side.

'So we must wait a little longer,' Becky said.

'Just a little.'

'What are we supposed to feel?' Brona asked.

No one answered.

'Won't it all be different up there now?' Becky asked. 'The landmarks, the forest, all of that?'

'Yes,' said Conor O'Connor. 'We're getting aerial maps and Ordnance Survey maps from nineteen seventy-one and seventy-two,' he added.

Both sisters nodded.

Rupert went and got them coffee, and they sat there as the story sank in.

'There's something I don't understand,' Brona said slowly. 'It's to do with Mum.'

'Go on.'

'If Mr Jones killed Baby on the Sunday night – oh, I don't know.'

'I know what you're wondering,' Becky said. 'It's occurred to me too. Mum was sure that Baby was alive all that week – and it wasn't until the Friday night that she said that Baby had died.'

'I don't think it means anything,' Conor said. 'I was aware of that, and I did ask Christopher Jones was there any chance that Baby wasn't dead when he put her in the Featherbeds. But the reality is that it was freezing up in the mountains. You'll remember how cold and foggy it was down in Dublin – well, it would have been way colder up there.'

'But if Baby were alive . . .' Brona said.

Becky could hear the pain in Brona's voice, and knew it reflected what she was feeling.

'Christopher Jones is absolutely sure that she was dead. But let me reassure you anyway,' Conor said. 'No one could have survived one night, let alone five or six, up there in the mountains.'

'Even wrapped in plastic?'

'No,' Conor said firmly. 'Absolutely not. Baby died instantly – I promise you.'

'And the plastic would have suffocated her anyway,' Becky said, trying to add to the reassurance.

Brona started to cry quietly, and Rupert came and put his arms around her.

'What did you feel?' Becky asked Conor later. 'When you interviewed him, I mean. It was you who interviewed him, wasn't it?'

'Yes, it was. You may not like what I felt,' he said. 'But he did feel a sense of responsibility, and I actually felt compassion for him. I think that is the right word. He was haunted by what he had done. He had lived with guilt and shame. He was never able to settle anywhere.'

'Do you literally mean haunted? I mean, haunted by her ghost?' Becky asked.

'No. Haunted by something he had done – a crime he had committed, haunted by its consequences. And I think he really cared for you.'

'I don't know what to feel,' Becky said sadly. 'He destroyed us. My mother took her own life – our family fell apart. He did that. And yet he helped me pick up the pieces. And Baby was . . . bad? Can I use that word? I don't want to say that she was evil, but . . .'

'She was bad news,' Conor helped her. 'And it was a bad day for Christopher Jones when he bumped into her.'

'And he was Hugo's flatmate?' said Becky in disbelief. 'How come no one knew that?'

'It just never came up. There was no reason at any point to be suspicious of Christopher Jones,' said Conor O'Connor. 'Hugo had only just got the flat that November, but he spent a fair bit of time in his parents' house. And he actually gave us his parents' address when we interviewed him. Christopher only moved in properly that January.'

'Goodness,' Becky exclaimed. 'That day we had lunch in The Hibernian before Mum ... you know ... Christopher was sitting in reception – he was waiting for someone. I suppose it could have been the Mombay Humphries.'

'It probably was. And then if he saw you, he would have left. He couldn't afford to be seen with them, in case someone started putting things together.'

'But wasn't he taking a terrible risk in changing the C to an O on the letter?' Becky asked.

'Yes, he was. But it never came up. You were the only one who had read the letter. I probably asked you if you had any idea who had written it – and as it happened, neither of us mentioned whether it was a C or an O. He was going to brazen it out, say that you had read it wrong. After all, he had changed it with the same pen. It could be said that you were too upset to have taken it in properly.'

'But Brona – what if she had read it? She would have confirmed that it was a C.'

'Apparently he checked with you who else had seen it, and you told him no one.'

Becky acknowledged this. It was all perfectly possible, and he had covered himself quite carefully.

'But his friendship with me?' she asked. 'What about that? Wasn't that taking a risk too?'

'I felt so sorry for her – for both of them, Rebecca and Brona. They were nice girls,' he said to the detective during the interrogation. 'I really liked Rebecca. That's why I left St Martin's during that year. I wanted to make it up to her. I wanted to help her. She was virtually destroyed by what had happened – and I felt it was my fault. I felt such guilt. I didn't want her to be a drop-out, and I could see that coming. And if I stayed on teaching in St Martin's I couldn't really help her. It seemed to me that I could do more for her if I were on the outside.'

'But to have an affair with her? She was little more than a child.'

'She was lovely. She had a fine mind, she was a great reader, and because she was a complete loner she was isolated. She had no support system whatsoever. I didn't mean to have an affair with her. It started as me simply trying to give her support, help . . . a sense of direction.'

'You gave her that all right.'

'What should I have done? I really liked her. After encountering her older sister I didn't want anything more to do with so-called sophisticated young ladies. I was really burnt. In fact I reckoned I might never have anything more to do with women again – and then Rebecca was there, and she needed me. She was so – vulnerable . . . I think that's the right word. She was fragile and uncared for in a strange way. And I felt it was my fault that her mother had killed herself, and then that awful thing about her father not being her father. You have no idea of the guilt I felt.'

'What now?' asked Brona.

'We'll just get on with our lives,' Becky answered her.

They were back in the old Dunville drawing room, sitting opposite each other, comforting each other.

'If they find Baby,' Becky continued, 'then we'll bury her with Mum and Dad. Conor seems to think they may find her. It's a long time ago, but Mr Jones is assisting in every way he can.'

'It's strange – how it's all over. All those years of wondering. We didn't waste our lives, did we?'

Becky shook her head.

'No, not waste. I think we were damaged – seriously damaged by what happened, but no, we didn't waste them.'

'But we lost so much,' Brona said. 'I can only see it now, now that we know that it was an outside force which did this.'

'If we'd been in an earthquake we could have lost more,' Becky said. 'And that,' she continued, 'would have been an outside force – but Baby was at least partially responsible for what happened.'

'But Dad – think of Dad – he lost Mum,' Brona said. 'And he died not knowing what had happened to Baby.'

'Forces took over, and that's what happens. But he picked up the pieces – at least as best as he could,' Becky tried to reassure her. 'He had a full life. He picked up the pieces, which is what you have to do after a tragedy.'

But of course it was not that simple. Becky was consumed with the notion of Mr Jones having had the affair with her because he was sorry for her.

310

It was with Conor O'Connor that Becky let it all out. She told him of Brona's anger towards Mr Jones, of Brona's sorrow. And eventually she got to her own situation.

'Our lives were ruined,' she said, contradicting what she had earlier said in reassurance to Brona.

'Redirected,' said Conor to her.

'But my relationship with Mr Jones,' she said. 'That would never have happened but for him and Baby. I've never formed a proper relationship since.'

'Maybe you just never met the right man,' Conor said to her, his fingertips stretched across the table to touch hers lightly.

Brona sat with Rupert at their kitchen table, biting back the tears and beating one fist on the tabletop.

'Tell me,' he said. 'Just tell me.'

'I wasted ... I tried ... I spent my whole life waiting for her to return,' she said angrily.

'No you didn't,' he said. 'You most certainly didn't. You married and had a family. You loved and were loved. And you still have the rest of your life to look forward to.'

'I don't know if I know how to live without just waiting,' she said.

'I think it's time that maybe you went to university,' he said tentatively.

She looked up in surprise.

'Becky suggested that too, while we were away,' she said.

'Well then ...'

On the Sunday, Uncle James took Becky and Brona to lunch in his favourite hotel, where he was well looked after. They joined him at his regular table, and he hugged them both with undisguised pleasure.

Their conversation covered everything from their recent holiday in Sicily, through Eleanor and the trapeze artist, to, of course, Baby Dunville, still resting in the Featherbeds.

'We used to go there as children,' Brona said. 'Remember, Becky?'

'I do. I always loved going up there – being in the car, the tinned salmon sandwiches and homemade fruit cake.'

'And the expanse of the hills ...'

'And the utter peace ...'

It suddenly seemed not such a bad place for Baby to have lain all those years. To Becky and Brona, the Featherbeds sounded like a soft and safe place.

'It will all be all right,' said Uncles James. 'Everything will come good.'

'You've such faith, Uncle James,' Becky said.

He patted her hand.

'Sure, that's all we've got,' he said.

'That and laughter,' said Brona.

They ate and laughed and talked, and Becky constantly looked at him and thought, Yes, he is an example to us all. Even though I don't have faith, I can follow his example.

He led them through the restaurant to the table at the door where he went to settle his bill. There was no one at the desk, so he seated himself on a chair, and smiling at the girls, he waited for someone to come.

Two elderly ladies left their table and they too came to the desk to pay.

He said hello to them, and they said they wanted to settle up, thinking that he was the man to do that with.

Uncle James smiled his mischievous smile. 'It's on the house today, ladies,' he said.

Brona and Becky turned away to hide their laughter.

'Thank you, thank you,' said the two old ladies, and out the door they went.

'Spread a little happiness,' said Uncle James.

'Oh, Uncle James.' Becky was giggling so hard that she nearly knocked him off the chair as she went to hug him.

'That was so funny,' Brona said.

In the car park he held both their hands in his.

'There may be a difficult time ahead,' he said to them. 'But always remember you can find things to laugh at. It will help carry you through. And I'm here for you.'

On Monday afternoon, Conor O'Connor phoned Becky. She knew at once that something had happened. It was in his voice.

'I was going to ask you for dinner tonight,' he said.

'But?' she helped him out.

'But Baby was found about twenty minutes ago.'

Becky said nothing for a moment.

'We could still do dinner,' she suggested.

'The media will be around,' he pointed out carefully.

'Would you like to come here? I'll do something – pasta maybe.' She felt her voice sounded dead, but she needed . . . she wanted him there. She could not be alone.

'I'll be over in an hour. I suggest you phone Brona and tell her, and then tell her not to answer the phone or the door. The media are going to be on your trail as soon as this is released.'

'Do you have to release it today?'

'No. But it may get out.'

Becky talked to Brona. Their conversation was terse.

'They found her.'

'When?'

'About half an hour ago.'

'Are they sure?'

'Conor says yes, but that the dental records will be used.'

'Do you feel it is Baby?'

'Yes . . . yes, I do.'

Silence.

'You okay?'

'Yes. You?'

'Yes.'

Silence.

'Do you want to come over here?'

'Thank you, no. Conor is coming here for something to eat. He said don't answer the door or the phone. The media may get hold of this today.'

'Okay.'

'You alone?'

'No, Rupert and the kids are here.'

'Will you phone Uncle James? I'll phone John – I know he'll come over from London.'

'Good. Talk tomorrow.'

'Talk tomorrow.'

Epilogue

Wednesday, 17 October, 2001
The headlines in the paper a week later were to do with the North of Ireland, but also on the front page there was a photo, and a snippet which read: *Baby Dunville laid to rest at last. See inside for details.*